For [illegible]

with many

thanks for the

best division

I ever had!

[signature]

June 2010

ISBN 978-90-04-18683-5

Full text of the lecture published in May 2010 in the *Recueil des cours*, Vol. 340 (2009).

Cover illustration : © Wassily Kandinsky, *Farbstudie-Quadrate mit Konzentrischen Ringen,* 1913, c/o Pictoright Amsterdam, 2009.

HAGUE ACADEMY OF INTERNATIONAL LAW

*A collection of law lectures
in pocketbook form*

AIL-POCKET

2010
MARTINUS NIJHOFF PUBLISHERS
Leiden/Boston

Unifying and Harmonizing
Substantive Law
and the Role of Conflict of Laws

Unifying and Harmonizing Substantive Law and the Role of Conflict of Laws

KATHARINA BOELE-WOELKI

PREFACE

In 1978, I attended the Private International Law summer course of the Hague Academy of International Law. Since then many things have changed. The old Academy building has been replaced by a beautiful glass house with all its sophisticated equipment. In my time as a Hague Academy student we sat on wooden chairs writing on our knees. We had no internet, nobody used a computer and PowerPoint was still to be invented. Convenient services like plinklet, now provided by the Peace Palace library, were simply not available. More significantly, since then the law of private relationships with cross-border implications has changed considerably. At the end of the 1970s the Vienna Sales Convention of 1980 was in the course of being negotiated. At the same time, and in the years thereafter, negotiations proceeded apace on several Conventions of the Hague Conference on Private International Law which later turned out to be highly successful. At that time they were hardly to be seen on the horizon. Nobody imagined back then, as far as the European Union is concerned, that the European legislator would make laws in the field of cross-border relationships through Regulations which in some areas would bind almost 27 Member States. No one had a clue that not only in Europe but also worldwide, many academic initiatives to harmonize substantive private law would be undertaken, covering even family law. Many of these initiatives take as an example American law-making techniques, such as Restatements ; some of them even go far beyond the Restatement of the law. Compared to some 30 years ago we are currently experiencing exciting times which raise questions as to how the plethora of instruments relate to each other.

*Undeniably, increasing globalization and the conse-
quent internationalization of the law poses new questions and challenges. It is beyond doubt that in a few
years from now — let us say within the next 20 to 25
years — participants in the summer courses on private
international law of today will be lecturing on private
international law topics at the Hague Academy of
International Law tomorrow. My prediction is that by
then the developments and trends which I present in
this book concerning the interaction between instruments for the unification and harmonization of substantive law on the one hand and rules of conflict of
laws on the other will become more visible and substantive than they are today. This prediction will fall to
be assessed critically by the following generation and
without doubt they will share their views with new generations who are interested in the magnificent world
of international private law.*

Katharina Boele-Woelki,
Utrecht, December 2009.

CONTENTS

CHAPTER I

SETTLING THE PRELIMINARIES

*1. The Law to Be Applied in Private Law
Relationships with Cross-border Elements*

1. Generally, private law relationships with foreign
elements, such as differing nationalities of the parties
or their habitual residence/place of business in different countries, are subject to national substantive law.
The "conflict" as to which possible substantive law of
the legal systems involved is to be applied falls to be
decided by the respective rules of private international
law determining the law applicable. These rules use a
connecting factor such as the common nationality or
place of habitual residence of the person, say, who is
performing the most characteristic contractual obligation in order to "connect" the private relationship with
a specific set of legal rules under the relevant national
law. The choice of the connecting factor is based on
the consideration that, on the one hand, the factor must
be relevant to the specific relationship and, on the
other, that a national system is to be applied which is
found to have, conceptually, the closest connection
with that relationship. In family law we used to use
nationality which to an increasing extent has been
replaced by the habitual residence of one or more of
the parties.

2. In the law of obligations these connecting factors
make no sense. Instead, the principle of the place of
business of the party, who is performing the most characteristic obligation of the contract, is decisive or — to
provide another example of a claim based on delictual
or tortious liability — in the main the place where the

damage occurred connects the relationship with the specific law of delict or tort applicable in that place. This is the approach generally applied in conflict of law. A "conflict" between legal systems is to be decided in which several, or at least two, are involved of which the respective national laws could be applied. Under specific circumstances national legal policy may, and frequently does, require the application of rules of national law. This is the case when overriding mandatory rules are to be taken into account [1]. In most cases, however, national legal policy will offer rules of national law to be applied and may not care, for instance, whether the nationals of the country concerned obtained their divorce in another country where probably a different, and less restrictive, divorce law has been applied or whether a contract is governed by a law with which none of the parties has a connection and which has only been chosen as the most neutral law.

3. However not all legal systems and the societies which they serve are prepared to accept everything. When the recognition of a specific status which has been obtained abroad (divorce, marriage, adoption), or the enforcement of a foreign judgment, is sought the legal system where this is to take place applies its recognition and enforcement rules. At this stage certain safety mechanisms come into play, the most important of which is the prevention of violation of national public policy. This falls within the area of the third part of private international law : recognition and enforcement. The first part addresses the issue of the international jurisdictional competence of courts and tribunals

---

[1] A. V. M., Struycken, "Co-ordination and Co-operation in Respectful Disagreement, General Course on Private International Law", *Recueil des cours*, Vol. 311 (2004) 33-44.

and the second part deals with the issue of the law applicable. The first and third parts contain rules which are generally characterized as international procedural law, whereas the issue of applicable law is commonly characterized as the "conflict of law" or, to use the German terminology, "Kollisionsrecht" [2].

4. The schematic overview below indicates these different parts. The answers to the three questions are provided by the respective legal sources, whereby a specific hierarchy is to be respected, at least within the Member States of the European Union [3]. In jurisdictions outside the European Union the row which indicates EU Regulations is not relevant. Only the legal sources which address the specific private international law issue are to be consulted. Obviously, the answer to the question whether a court has jurisdictional competence cannot be found in a Convention which contains only rules of applicable law. It is therefore essential to know exactly what question is posed and the kind of rules which the legal source (a Regulation or a Convention) contains. In particular, those who are not familiar with the methods and techniques of private international law often find it difficult to find their way through the jungle of private international law rules. The schematic overview on the next page might be of assistance in this endeavour.

In respect of the three different questions it depends on the nature of the cross-border relationship (e.g.,

---

[2] According to German law all three parts of private international law are indicated as *Internationales Privat- und Verfahrensrecht*.

[3] Generally European law demands that it takes priority, however there are situations where the respective Regulations give precedence to Conventions. As an example in this regard see the Brussels II *bis* Regulation (Art. 60, Sect. 2) and its relationship with the Hague Convention of 1980. See further Chapter VI.

Table 1. The Three Questions to Be Answered
by Rules of Private International Law and the Hierarchy
of Legal Sources (including the EU Perspective)

Cross-border relationship	*Which court decides ?*	*Which law applies ?*	*Can the foreign decision/the status obtained abroad be recognized and enforced ?*
Legal sources	*International procedural law*	*Conflict of laws*	*International procedural law*
EU Regulations			
Conventions (in general subordinated to EU law)			
National statutes and case law			

contract, delict and tort or family relationship) which instrument is to be consulted by the competent forum.

2. *Further Distinctions in Respect of the Applicable Law in Cross-border Relationships*

5. Conflict of law rules [4] determine the applicability of national substantive law. This is the classical approach. The most relevant issue, which plays a central role in this lecture, concerns the question whether a private law relationship can only be governed by national substantive law. Posing the question as to whether private international relationships may only be governed by national substantive law logically leads to the following question : to what extent, in what circumstances and subject to which criteria is it possible for a cross-border relationship to be governed by non-national law ? Should rules of private international law

---

[4] See on the use of this term and its demarcation from "private international law", and "rules of applicable law" Chapter II, Sections 1 and 4.

enable non-State norms to be designated as the applicable law ? When referring to non-national law we tend to indicate, automatically — as the only option — rules of uniform substantive law adopted in an international Convention. However, recently, within the framework of the new European rules of the law applicable to contracts which are unified in the Rome I Regulation, the applicability of non-State norms derived from sources other than uniform law has been extensively discussed [5]. It has been rightly submitted that the question whether non-State norms can be the applicable law moves from the periphery to the centre of consideration once we view conflict of law through the lens of globalization since States and non-State communities both create norms, which pose a challenge to conflict of law rules since, traditionally, these designate only State norms as the law applicable [6]. More particularly it has been suggested that the Euro-

---

[5] See the contributions by F. Zoll, *Rome I Regulation and Common Frame of Reference, Verona Conference 19-20 March 2009 (The Rome I Regulation)* and by Tell, O., *Choosing as Applicable Law the Principles and Rules of the Substantive Law of Contract Recognised Internationally or in the Community*, Bari Conference 23-24 March 2009 (The New European Contract Law : From the Rome Convention to the "Rome I" Regulation).

[6] R. Michaels, "The Re-State-ment of Non-State Law : The State, Choice of Law, and the Challenge from Global Pluralism", 51 *Wayne Law Review* (2005) 1209-1259 (1210). The same author considers the focus on the applicability of the UNIDROIT Principles of International Commercial Contracts as the law chosen by the parties in isolation to be erroneous, see R. Michaels, "Umdenken für die UNIDROIT-Prinzipien, Vom Rechtswahlstatut zum Allgemeinen Teil des transnationalen Vertragsrechts", *Rabels Zeitschrift für internationales und ausländisches Privatrecht* (2009) 866-888 (869-874). See in particular D. Oser, *The Unidroit Principles of International Commercial Contracts : A Governing Law ?* (2008).

pean legislator should start thinking in terms of the coherence of the European legal system and clarify his position towards private law making, particularly in the field of contract law [7]. Opinions differ and the debate is still ongoing.

6. If it is permissible to apply non-national law it becomes essential to determine the nature and sources of that law. Besides the application of uniform substantive law (such as the Convention on Contracts for the International Sale of Goods — CISG) is it feasible, desirable and possible also to apply the rules of instruments which are aimed at harmonizing substantive law ? In particular, in the field of international commercial law, Model Laws, Principles and Restatements, which to a certain extent have been specifically designed for international relations, such as the UNIDROIT Principles of International Commercial Contracts of 1994, have increasingly gained importance [8]. What are the essential characteristics of these instruments ? Do they constitute "law" which can be applied in cross-border relationships ? In the following chapters these questions will be taken further.

7. It seems clear that the possibility of applying non-national substantive law constitutes the starting point for our purposes. The question which will be examined is as to whether and, if so, to what extent non-national law may be applied in private law relationships with cross-border aspects in contrast to the application of national substantive law. In considering this question the following distinctions are of importance :

---

[7] C. Kessedjian, "Party Autonomy and Characteristic Performance in the Rome Convention and the Rome I Proposal", in J. Basedow, H. Baum, and Y. Nishitani (eds.), *Japanese and European Private International Law in Comparative Perspective* (2008) 105-125 (117).

[8] E. Loquin, "Les règles matérielles internationales", *Recueil des cours*, Vol. 322 (2006) 9-241.

Whether :

1. the decision as to the applicability of unifying or harmonizing substantive law is made by a court *or* an arbitral tribunal ;
2. the unifying or harmonizing substantive law regulates either contract and delict/tort law *or* family law relationships ; and
3. the application of unifying or harmonizing substantive law depends on a choice by the parties *or* it can also be applied in the absence of any choice.

The combination of these different perspectives informs different factual patterns which are illustrated in the schematic overview below.

Table 2. The Determination of the Applicable Law
in Respect of Private Law Relationships
with Cross-border Elements

	Contracts and delicts/torts		*Family relations*	
	Choice of law by the parties	*Absence of any choice*	*Choice of law by the parties*	*Absence of any choice*
Litigation	The *court* decides according to its conflict of law rules whether the choice is decisive	The *court* decides according to its conflict of law rules which law is to be applied	The *court* decides according to its conflict of law rules whether the choice is decisive	The *court* decides according to its conflict of law rules which law is to be applied
Arbitration	The *arbitral tribunal* decides whether the choice is decisive	The *arbitral tribunal* determines the applicable law		

8. In respect of private law relationships, a major distinction arises from the method of dispute resolution which the parties have chosen. In commercial relationships two possibilities are available, either litigation or arbitration. The latter depends on an agreement of the parties to submit their dispute to an arbitral tribunal

which can either be an institution (institutional arbitration) or a private tribunal. In the case of litigation the court decides according to its own rules (the rules of the court seised = *lex fori*) whether it has jurisdiction and which law is to be applied. In the case of arbitration the rules of the place where the arbitration takes place do not necessarily determine which law is to be applied. The arbitral tribunal is generally free either to apply the appropriate private international law rules (such as the rules of the Rome I Regulation) to determine the applicable law or to apply the applicable law directly without reference to any private international law rules regarding the law applicable unless the parties have designated the applicable law. It will be demonstrated that this distinction is essential when exploring the possibility of applying non-national law. The non-availability of arbitration dispute resolution for family law relationships with cross-border elements justifies making a distinction between contract and delict/tort relationships, on the one hand, and family law relationships on the other. In the case of a dispute arising out of the latter category of relationships the parties, generally, can only go to court. Since the use of international mediation in family matters is increasing — it has not yet reached the level of international commercial arbitration however — attention will also be paid to alternative dispute resolution mechanisms [9].

9. Furthermore, in the context of the investigation into the possible application of non-State law the following distinction between two different situations is important.

Did the parties agree upon the law to be applied ? This can be described as the *subjective* conflict of laws approach. If the parties have determined the applicable

---

[9] See Chapter VIII, Section 5.

law the competent authority [10] deciding the dispute
reviews different aspects : firstly, whether the parties
are allowed to determine the applicable law since in
not all private law relationships is party autonomy
admitted. Secondly, only a precise and clear choice of
law can be considered to be valid. Thirdly, and this
relates to one of the main issues examined in this book,
namely, the question as to which competent authority
has been designated. Is a close connection, between the
selected national substantive law and the dispute,
required or may the parties choose any substantive law
and what are the consequences of designating non-
national law as the law governing the relationship ? It
all boils down to the question as to how far the parties'
freedom extends in determining their own relationship.

Should the parties have failed to stipulate the applicable law to govern their dispute, for whatever reason
— be it because of inattention, bad legal advice or
because they simply could not agree — the competent
authority will decide which law is applicable. This is
the *objective* conflict of law approach. Generally, the
rules of applicable law, to which effect should be given
in the forum of the court or tribunal where the dispute
is to be decided, are to be consulted. They determine
the law to be applied whereas in the case of an international arbitration arbitrators are not bound by the applicable law rules of the place of arbitration. Is the applicable law to be determined by either a court or an
arbitral tribunal restricted to national substantive law ?
It is worthwhile considering the possibilities which
exist in this respect, whereby again the distinction in
the approaches to the determination of the law applicable applied in litigation and arbitration is of fundamental significance.

---

[10] Which can be a court, an administrative body or an
arbitral tribunal.

3. Fields of Law to Be Analysed and Compared

10. The focus of the issues examined in this book lies on contractual, non-contractual (delict/tort) and family relationships. Admittedly, this is a large area to cover and therefore only the most important instruments and developments can be discussed. Restrictions are necessary. No attention will be paid to international corporate law [11], international property law, international intellectual property law (including internet law [12]) and international private maritime [13] and transport law.

The concentration on contractual and family relationships arises from this author's research experience. Starting her academic career in the field of international family law, she worked and published for many years on international contract law. In particular the

---

[11] Proposal for a Regulation on the Statute for a European private company of 25 June 2008, COM (2008) 396 final. See G. Bachmann, "Die Societas Europaea und das europäische Privatrecht", *Zeitschrift für Europäisches Privatrecht* (2008) 32-58. D. F. M. M. Zaman, C. A. Schwarz, M. L. Lennarts, H. De Kluiver, and A. F. M. Dorresteijn (eds.), *The European Private Company (SPE)* (2009).

[12] L. R. Helfer, G. B. Dinwoodie, "Designing Non-national Systems : The Case of the Uniform Domain Name Dispute Resolution Policy", *Stanford/Yale Junior Faculty Forum* (2001) 141-273.

[13] W. Tetley, "Uniformity of International Private Maritime Law — The Pros, Cons and Alternatives to International Conventions — How to Adopt an International Convention", 24 *Tulane Maritime Law Journal* (2000) 775-856 (www.mcgill.ca/maritimelaw/maritime-admiralty/uniformitymarlaw). A new legal regime governing the rights and obligations of shippers, carriers and consignees under a contract for door-to-door carriage that includes an international sea leg has been established through the United Nations Convention on Contracts for the International Carriage of Goods Wholly or Partly by Sea of 11 December 2008 (Rotterdam Rules).

question which this author posed almost 15 years ago, namely whether the Principles of Contract Law can be applied in international contracts [14], is still under discussion. Some 10 years ago she refocused her research on family law relations not only with cross-border implications but more intensively on the comparison of substantive family law systems in Europe [15]. Having established the Commission on European Family Law [16] in 2001, the activities of which are aimed at contributing to the harmonization of family law in Europe [17], a great deal of the experience gained in the field of international contract law was, and still is, of precious value in the work of the Commission. Experience obtained in this latter field of law can always be of inspiration in other areas. At the beginning it is all about the feasibility, desirability and possibilities of comparative research-based drafting of principles or models. Later issues concerning the presentation and applicability of the final result gain more importance. As a result, similarities and differences can be discerned ; they can be compared and, most essentially,

[14] K. Boele-Woelki, "Principles and Private International Law — The UNIDROIT Principles of International Commercial Contracts and the Principles of European Contract Law : How to Apply Them to International Contracts", I *Uniform Law Review* (1996) 652-678, and K. Boele-Woelki, "Terms of Co-Existence : The UN Sales Convention and the UNIDROIT Principles of International Commercial Contracts", in P. Volken and P. Sarcevic, *CISG Revisited, Dubrovnik Lectures 1998* (2001) 203-240.

[15] K. Boele-Woelki, "What Comparative Family Law Should Entail", *Utrecht Law Review* (2008) 1-24. Also published in K. Boele-Woelki (ed.), *Debates in Family Law around the Globe at the Dawn of the 21st Century*, European Family Law Series No. 23 (2009) 3-35.

[16] www.ceflonline.net.

[17] K. Boele-Woelki, "The Principles of European Family Law : Its Aims and Prospects", *Utrecht Law Review* (2005) 160-168.

evaluated. Consequently, a great deal of the material in this book consists of comparisons of the various approaches.

4. *The Main Issues to Be Addressed*

11. The topic addressed in this lecture focuses on the interaction between the unification and harmonization of substantive law on the one side and conflict of law rules on the other. In particular it addresses the issue of the applicability of a law other than national substantive law in private law relationships with cross-border elements. This "other" law encompasses uniform law, on the one hand, and non-national law such as Restatements, Model Laws and Principles on the other [18].

Part I ("The Objects") provides an overview of the relevant instruments : the unifying (Chapter III) and harmonizing (Chapter IV) substantive law and private international law instruments (Chapter VI). Chapter V offers some considerations about the choice to be made, in other words which instrument can and should be selected in pursuing the objective of unifying or harmonizing substantive law.

Part II ("The Interaction") contains the core issue examined in this lecture. The scope of application of unifying and harmonizing substantive law instruments is investigated in Chapter VII, whereby specific attention is paid to the discussion on the applicability of a

---

[18] L. Gannagé, "Le contrat sans loi en droit international privé", in K. Boele-Woelki and S. Van Erp (eds.), *General Reports of the XVIIth Congress of the International Academy of Comparative Law — Rapports généraux, XVIIᵉ Congrès international de droit comparé* (2007) 275-308. Also published in 11.3 *Electronic Journal of Comparative Law* (2007) (www.ejcl.org/113/abs11310. html).

European substantive private law instrument (Common Frame of Reference) in cross-border situations. Chapter VIII analyses the solutions provided by conflict of law rules in the various fields as regards the applicability of a law other than national law [19]. Final observations are contained in Chapter IX.

To start with, clear working definitions of the terms "unification of, unified and unifying substantive law", "harmonization of, harmonized and harmonizing substantive law", "conflict of law" and, obviously, "interaction" are needed as well as examples which illustrate the differences between the various instruments. The issue of terminology is addressed in Chapter II. This makes it possible to outline properly the problem of the interaction between the one and the other.

Initially, this author had intended to address only the interaction between uniform substantive law and conflict of law [20], It is clear, however, that, when dealing

---

[19] Michaelis, *op cit.*, footnote 6, 1210 :

"The question is not new, of course, although it is seldom discussed systematically. . . . Textbooks in the United States and in the United Kingdom usually define conflict of laws as the field dealing with situations that have contacts with more than one state. Choice of law is the choice of which state's law applies ; non-state law is not discussed. In Europe, particularly in Germany, some debate the applicability of a specific body of non-state norms, the new *lex mercatoria* ; but usually no general discussion of non-state norms ensues. Individual proposals rarely lead to general discussions. Choice of law as a discipline has largely defined itself as choice between laws of states. As a discipline, it considers issues regarding the applicability of non-state normative orders as peripheral at best."

[20] C. P. Pamboukis, "Droit international privé holistique : droit uniforme et droit international privé", *Recueil des cours*, Vol. 330 (2007). For the state of the art of the rela-

with uniform substantive law, the new instruments which are aimed at harmonizing substantive law cannot be disregarded if the applicability of a law other than national law is to be investigated since they pose the most challenging questions in this respect.

---

tion between the unification of substantive law and conflict of laws of almost 45 years ago see A. Malintoppi, "Les rapports entre droit uniforme et droit international privé", *Recueil des cours*, Vol. 116 (1965) 1-87.

CHAPTER II

TERMINOLOGY

12. Terminology is the study of terms and their usage. In order to classify the various instruments into several categories it is necessary to know which categories can be distinguished and their main features should be explained and also which terms are to be used in a specific context ? It is submitted that the current legal literature focusing on international substantive rules is not consistent in its use of terminology.

In this chapter an attempt is made to label systematically the concepts which we create and use within the arena of international law which deals with cross-border private relationships.

1. Private International Law and International Private Law

13. One might argue that "private international law" and "international private law" are synonyms. Indeed, in the French and German language both terms can only be translated by *droit international privé* and *Internationales Privatrecht* respectively. However, in the English language it is possible to make a distinction which is essential for our topic. To this author's understanding the term "private international law" can be applied only to the rules which address jurisdiction, applicable law and recognition and enforcement. In contrast, "international private law" has a broader meaning. It also covers comparative research-based law-making for private law relationships which encompasses substantive law rules. The instruments drafted and adopted under the auspices of international organi-

zations, such as UNIDROIT and UNCITRAL, for instance, fall under this broad definition. The CISG, which generally requires that the buyer and the seller have their principal place of business in different States, does not contain private international law rules but substantive law for international sales contracts, or, to put it differently and consequently more exactly, international private law. Therefore, in order to cover all international private law-making and rules the term "international private law" should be employed.

2. *Substantive Law*

14. Substantive law is the law which governs rights and obligations of those who are subject to it. It is the body of statutory or written law which creates, defines and regulates these rights, whereas procedural law sets the rules and methods to ensure that legal rights are fulfilled. Occasionally, substantive law is indicated as domestic law or material law.

3. *The Difference between Unification and Harmonization*

15. The concepts of harmonization and unification are more than just instantaneous activities. It is regrettable that in the field of international private law, the terms "unification" and "harmonization" of the law are often used incorrectly [21].

---

[21] A striking example can be found in the Proposal for a Council Regulation amending Regulation (EC) No. 2201/2003 as regards jurisdiction and introducing rules concerning applicable law in matrimonial matters (17.7.2006), COM (2006) 399 final, in which the drafters of the explanatory memorandum constantly refer to "harmonised conflict-of-law rules in matters of divorce" whereas undoubtedly the "unification" of these rules is what is meant.

The statement, for instance, that "the unification of private law through soft law is a promising alternative concept" [22] is an example of the use of misleading terminology.

A recent evaluation of the use of language through a review of relevant literature provides two insights : firstly, it reveals a vague usage of the expressions "unification" and "harmonization" of laws. Secondly, the expression "harmonization" serves to disguise the process of "uniformization", a reference to which is avoided due to its political relevance. In this respect it has been suggested that "harmonization" is a euphemism and means "uniformization" and this is the meaning which has been attached to it in a study on the UNIDROIT Principles in International Legal Doctrine and Practice [23].

Whatever may be required by certain sensitivities and political considerations, this author disagrees with the interchangeable use of the terms "unification" and "harmonization" [24] since the two terms indicate different developments, objectives and results [25]. Their meaning and potential differ.

---

[22] G.-P. Calliess, "The Making of Transnational Contract Law", *Indiana Journal of Global Legal Studies* (2007) 469-483 (475). See also Oser, *op. cit.*, footnote 6, 13 who speaks of "unification by non-legislative means".

[23] M. Heidemann, *Methodology of Uniform Contract Law, The UNIDROIT Principles in International Legal Doctrine and Practice*, Springer (2007) 6.

[24] See, however, C. Kessedjian, "Codification du droit commercial international et droit international privé", *Recueil des cours*, Vol. 300 (2002), 79-293 (108-110) who acknowledges that both terms do not have the same meaning but prefers to use the term unification for several reasons.

[25] Incorrectly used also by this author. See Boele-Woelki, *op. cit.*, footnote 14, 652.

3.1. Unification, unified and unifying law

16. The international unification of law is conceived of as the process of providing identical rules for different countries so that the same solution applies everywhere, in Argentina and Germany, in the United Kingdom and Russia, if a difficulty concerning a given relationship happens to arise [26]. In all areas of law the unification of the law has taken place. For our purposes the unification of substantive private law and the unification of private international law are relevant. The unification of substantive private law is predominantly achieved by international Conventions. The same applies to matters of private international law. The adoption of these instruments by international organizations does not *per se* create unified or uniform law. The Conventions merely tend to unify the law. Therefore the adopted Convention rules of international organizations should be characterized as *unifying* instruments since the unification of the law through Conventions requires legislative action by individual States. Only after the ratification of the unifying instrument has the unification of the law been achieved.

Within the European Union another instrument is used for the unification of private international law, namely the Regulation. In accordance with the Treaty on the Functioning of the European Union (TFEU) a Regulation shall be binding in its entirety and directly applicable in the Member States on the date of its entry into force as determined in the Regulation.

Admittedly, differences can arise even in the case of uniform rules. Preferably, in the optimum situation, States which are bound by uniform law would have granted to a supranational court the authority to take

---

[26] R. David, "The Methods of Unification", *American Journal of Comparative Law* (1968) 13-27 (13-14).

the final decisions in cases of different interpretations and applications of the unified rules. In the majority of cases, however, except as regards the European Union, such a supranational court does not exist and adjudicators are only reminded that, in the interpretation of uniform law, consideration is to be given to its international character and to the need to promote uniformity in its application. A main feature of the process of the unification of the law is the top-down approach which is aimed at creating binding law.

3.2. *Harmonization, harmonized and harmonizing law*

17. In contrast, the "harmonization" of the law is less far-reaching [27]. Similar rules indicate that the laws of the legal systems in a specific area are in harmony with each other. The differences are reduced to a minimum and are less pronounced. Different instruments are used to achieve the harmonization of law : Model Laws, Restatements and Principles or Rules. Within the regional context of the European Union, Directives are also used whereby, as far as their harmonizing effects are concerned, distinctions are made between minimum harmonization and full harmonization. Actually, the latter is not much different from unification. The process of harmonization can also be stimulated and achieved by court decisions and legislative

---

[27] M.-T. Meulders-Klein, "Towards a European Civil Code on Family Laws ? Ends and Means", in K. Boele-Woelki (ed.), *Perspectives for the Unification and Harmonisation of Family Law in Europe*, European Family Law Series No. 4 (2003) 105-117 (106) :

" 'Harmonisation' implies a concern to reconcile the preoccupations and the interests of the various systems so as to avoid conflicts and clashes whereas 'unification', on the contrary, means the voluntary or imposed uniformisation of different systems."

measures by national legislators which result in the
approximation of the laws of different jurisdictions
(harmonized law). This specific development is not
further explored here. Instead, the focus is placed on
instruments which are aimed at harmonizing substantive law. Harmonization activities by international
organizations or self-appointed commissions are aimed
at elaborating non-binding rules which could provide
models for voluntary — bottom-up — harmonization.
These frames of reference are primarily addressed to
national, regional or international legislatures in their
potential quest to reform a specific area of law.
Therefore the various instruments which are drafted so
as to contribute to the harmonization of substantive law
should be indicated as *harmonizing* instruments in
order to express their objectives.

4. Conflict of Law

18. In the various legal systems different terms are
used to indicate : (1) the rules which determine the law
which is applicable to a particular legal relationship —
rules of applicable law ; (2) the rules which determine
the jurisdictional competence of courts and tribunals
— *jurisdiction rules* ; and (3) the rules and procedures
for the recognition and enforcement across borders
of judicial decisions or matters of status — *rules of
recognition and enforcement*. The portmanteau or
generic term used to refer to and describe these elements of cross-border relationships between systems of
law is variously, depending on the legal system concerned, *private international law* or *conflict of law*.
This latter term has another, narrower, meaning which
is more suited to our purposes in this work, and that is
equivalent to the meaning of *applicable law* ; it follows
that in this work the term *conflict of law* is only used in
this, narrower, sense and the investigation of this ele-

ment in the theme of the lecture is restricted to those rules which serve to designate the law applicable to any particular type of cross-border legal relationship. Where the law designated as applicable is that chosen by the parties *rules of conflict of law* can comprehend the *rules on choice of law* whereas within the American context *conflict of law rules* are also indicated as *choice of law rules*.

5. *Interaction*

19. Interaction has different tailored meanings in various sciences. Interaction occurs as two or more objects have an effect upon one another. The question as to whether a law other than national law may be applied in cross-border relationships depends on the legal interaction between unifying and harmonizing substantive law on the one side, and conflict of law on the other. What does the first set of rules offer and how does the latter respond ? Does the one need the other ? Are the systems in(ter)dependent ? It should be kept in mind that the idea of a two-way effect is essential in the concept of interaction. A different question is whether substantive law instruments have any influence on the content of conflict of law rules. This effect is not investigated here.

PART I

THE OBJECTS

20. Traditionally international organizations have focused their activities on unifying and harmonizing substantive law [28]. UNIDROIT, along with UNCITRAL, has developed a wide range of international Conventions and Model Laws. UNCITRAL, for instance, was responsible for the Convention on Contracts for the International Sale of Goods (CISG). The sister organization UNIDROIT has recently adopted the Model Law on Leasing [29] and has produced the highly praised Principles of International Commercial Contracts. Within the European context the Principles of European Contract Law, Tort Law and Family Law, which have been drafted by academic groups, are gaining increasing attention. Moreover, based primarily on the Principles of European Contract Law, a European substantive law instrument for the law of obligations is envisaged. Depending on its scope of application it might be applicable in cross-border relationships. In effect this is the very point of this project. Whether such an instrument should apply in cross-border relations within the European Union, at least electively if

---

[28] Compared with the harmonization of substantive law, the harmonization of transnational civil procedure is at a much more preliminary stage. But see the Principles and Rules of Transnational Civil Procedure jointly developed by the American Law Institute (ALI) and UNIDROIT. See in particular S. McAuley, "Achieving the Harmonization of Transnational Civil Procedure : Will the ALI/UNIDROIT Principles Succeed ?", *American Review of International Arbitration* (2004) 231-252 (233).

[29] Adopted on 13 November 2008.

not prescriptively, will be investigated in Chapter VII, Section 5.

21. The following two chapters focus on unifying (Chapter III) and harmonizing (Chapter IV) substantive law instruments whereby particular attention will be paid to the respective law-making bodies. Most of them adopt instruments which pursue both objectives and, in turn, some of their instruments serve both purposes. It is therefore difficult to draw the borderline. In addition, some instruments prepared by academic groups in Europe are aimed at achieving the status of binding instruments and, to this end, they might be adopted by the European legislator. However the current, and not the envisaged, status of the (Draft) EU Common Frame of Reference, for instance, has been decisive for its categorization as a harmonizing substantive law instrument. Despite the fact that organizations are producing both kinds of instrument and the fact that an instrument might, eventually, change its legal nature, an attempt has been made to classify the organizations and their respective instruments as having the aim of (1) unifying and (2) harmonizing substantive law. In view of their interaction with conflict of law rules the distinction between the one and the other will be of the essence. After the overview of organizations, instruments and areas of law the justification and motivation as to the furthering of the unification and harmonization of substantive law will be considered.

22. A final introductory remark should be made in respect of the actors to whom the great variety of instruments are addressed, such as national legislatures, courts and natural or legal persons within a private law relationship. In Part II, where the interaction between the different instruments containing substantive law, on the one hand, and instruments regulating private international law on the other hand, will be

analysed, the various addressees and their respective perspectives and interests will be further examined. They play the major role.

It is generally known that in order to develop their unifying effect multilateral Conventions need to be ratified by *national legislatures*. Also, whether Directives, Model Laws, Restatements, Uniform Laws and Principles are incorporated or enacted into national substantive law depends upon national legislatures.

Regarding European Directives the freedom of legislatures of the Member States is, however, limited to the (procedural) way in which the Directive's provisions are to be implemented, before a certain date, into national law by statute or ministerial decree. The Member States are, however, obliged to achieve all (substantive) results prescribed by the Directive. In cases where the Directive contains very detailed rules, the Member States are left with hardly any real discretion — the "copy and paste" exercise. In the latter case, one could say that EU Directives have rather a *unifying* than a *harmonizing* effect on the substantive law of the Member States. Where the Directive merely sets *minimum* norms (to be recognized from the use of phrases like "no more than", "at least", and the like) the Member States are free to adopt more stringent rules than as prescribed by the Directive. Especially Directives in the fields of environmental protection and labour law provide for such *minimum harmonization*. In the field of consumer protection also, the relevant Directives often set only a minimum standard and the Member States are allowed to go beyond the minimal protection prescribed by the EU Directive [30]. Recently,

---

[30] H. Rösler, "Europeanisation of Private Law through Directives — Determining Factors and Modalities of Implementation", *European Journal of Law Reform* (2009) 305-322.

however, the European Commission has changed its policy and is now defending the use of *full* (or : *total*) harmonization in this area, meaning that Member States are not able to deviate from the Directive at all, not even in order to offer, say, the consumer *better* protection. The term "minimum harmonization", hence, does *not* mean that the Member States would only have to implement the "core rules" of a Directive but not necessarily the "less important"/"additional" provisions of the Directive — who would be able to make that distinction anyway ? *Below* the substantive norms of a Directive there is never any freedom for Member States ; it is only *above* these norms that Member States enjoy discretion and then, sometimes, only in case of minimum harmonization and never in the case of full harmonization.

Courts, on the other hand, are free to take over solutions which they find in international or regional instruments whether they are aimed originally only at the unification of the law or are drafted specifically as a source of inspiration. This approach is however, subject to specific circumstances, for instance, in the case of a lacuna in the applicable national law. To what extent courts may dispose of this freedom depends perceptibly on the jurisdiction to which the judges belong. A common law court is, probably, more inclined than a civil law court to seek inspiration from a-national sources if the applicable law does not provide for a justifiable solution. However, this is just a commonplace supposition which is based upon the general distinction between these two systems. Empirical research into the background to this statement has — to this author's knowledge — not yet been undertaken.

Finally, *parties* to an international contract, for instance, are free to exclude the applicability of an international Convention or to determine that their contractual relationship should be governed by, for instance, the UNIDROIT Principles for International Commercial Contracts or the Principles of European Contract Law. The legal consequences of their reference to or incorporation of these set of rules into their contract is, however, a point for discussion.

CHAPTER III

UNIFYING SUBSTANTIVE LAW

23. In this chapter the various unifying substantive law instruments are introduced. The general characteristics of the different instruments will be explained and some specific examples of several unifying substantive law instruments will be provided. These examples will also be used when the interaction with rules of conflict of law come to be explored further.

The table below refers to different thematic aspects which will be examined further in this chapter.

Firstly, which organizations are drafting and adopting unifying substantive law instruments (1st column), secondly, which kinds of instrument are used to unify substantive law (2nd column) and thirdly, in which fields of law have the different organizations been active so far (3rd-5th columns).

Table 3. Unifying Substantive Law :
Organizations, Instruments and Areas of Law

Organizations	Instruments	Contracts	Delicts/torts	Family relations
International organizations	Conventions	yes	yes	yes
European Union	Regulations	no	no	no
	Directives	yes	yes	no
Organization for the Harmonization of African Business Laws	Uniform Acts	yes	no	no
US National Conference of Commissioners on Uniform State Laws	Uniform Acts	yes	yes	yes

1. Organizations

24. In the following paragraphs concise descriptions of significant organizations working in the field of the unification of substantive law are provided. This information is, to an extent, equally relevant to the following chapter on harmonizing substantive law instruments. For obvious reasons, the overview is restricted to important organizations which have produced significant instruments relevant to the law of contracts, delicts/torts and family relations. A start is made with international organizations which work at the global level before focusing on the regional organizations in Europe and then the United States of America. The introductions are brief since these organizations provide, on their respective websites, excellent information about their projects, working methods, achievements and application in legal practice.

1.1. International organizations

25. The leading organizations at the international level which draft and adopt instruments aimed at unifying and harmonizing substantive law are the International Institute for the Unification of Private Law (UNIDROIT) and the United Nations Commission for International Trade Law (UNCITRAL). Both organizations work predominantly in the same area, that being international commercial law.

1.1.1. UNIDROIT

26. The purposes of UNIDROIT [31], situated in Rome and established in 1926 [32], are to examine ways of harmonizing and co-ordinating the private law of States and of groups of States, and to prepare gradually

---

[31] www.unidroit.org.
[32] Re-established in 1940.

for the adoption by the various States of uniform rules of private law [33]. States acceding to the UNIDROIT Statute acquire membership. Currently 63 States are Member States. They are drawn from the five continents and represent a variety of different legal, economic and political systems. UNIDROIT has adopted nine Conventions and two protocols covering mainly international business and financial law [34]. The first two Conventions on Uniform Sales Law constituted the building blocks for the CISG adopted in 1980 by the sister organization UNCITRAL. Furthermore UNIDROIT has adopted two Model Laws on Franchise Disclosure (2002) and on Leasing (2008) and drafted two sets of Principles for International Commercial Contracts (1994 amended in 2004) [35] and for Transnational Civil Procedure (2004), the latter in co-operation with the American Law Institute (ALI). International case law and a bibliography on the CISG and the Contract Principles are available at UNIDROIT's database, UNILEX [36]. In addition, the UNILAW database regarding uniform law Conventions and other instruments has been established. Work started on the 1956 Convention on the Contract for the International Carriage of Goods by Road (CMR). This latter database is still under construction.

1.1.2. UNCITRAL

27. UNCITRAL [37] was established by the General Assembly of the United Nations in 1966. It has its seat

---

[33] Article 1 of the Statute.

[34] The Convention providing a Uniform Law on the Form of an International Will of 1973 constitutes an exception.

[35] Currently a new Working Group is preparing a third edition of the UNIDROIT Principles.

[36] www.unilex.info.

[37] www.uncitral.org.

in Vienna. In establishing the Commission, the General Assembly recognized that disparities in national laws governing international trade created obstacles to the flow of trade, and it regarded the Commission as the vehicle by which the United Nations could play a more active role in reducing or removing these obstacles. The Commission is composed of 60 Member States elected by the General Assembly. Membership is structured so as to be representative of the world's various geographic regions and its principal economic and legal systems [38]. The Commission has established six working groups to carry out the substantive preparatory work on topics within the Commission's work programme. These topics cover procurement, international arbitration and conciliation, transport law, electronic commerce, insolvency law and security interests.

In order to promote international awareness of the Conventions and Model Laws drafted by the Commission, and to facilitate uniform interpretation and application of those texts, UNCITRAL has established a system for collecting and disseminating information on court decisions and arbitral awards relating to the CISG and several Model Laws [39] which have emanated from the work of the Commission. This Case Law on

---

[38] Members of the Commission are elected for terms of six years, the terms of half the members expiring every three years. In addition to Member States, all States which are not members of the Commission, as well as interested international organizations, may attend sessions of the Commission and of its working groups as observers. Observers are permitted to participate in discussions at sessions of the Commission and its working groups to the same extent as members.

[39] The Model Arbitration Law on International Commercial Arbitration (1985), the Hamburg Rules (1978), the Model Law on Electronic Commerce (1996) and the Model Law on Cross-border Insolvency (1997).

UNCITRAL Texts (CLOUT) database is updated regularly and easily accessible.

1.2. European organizations

28. In Europe, there is no one single organization which has been established by an international agreement of States in order to enhance the unification and harmonization of substantive private law. The Council of Europe and the European Union, however, have produced several instruments which are aimed at meeting these objectives. Whereas the Council of Europe in general makes use of Conventions and Recommendations to Member States [40], the European Union has its own legislative power derived from the Treaties on European Union (TEU) and on the Functioning of the European Union (TFEU).

1.2.1. The Council of Europe

29. The pioneer among pan-European organizations is the Council of Europe [41] with its seat in Strasbourg. It has 47 Member States. It was established in 1949 in order to achieve a greater unity between the Member States for the purpose of safeguarding and realizing the ideals and principles which are their common heritage and facilitating their economic and social progress. The Council pursues this objective by agreements and common actions in economic, social, cultural, scientific, legal and administrative matters [42]. In all these areas more than 200 Conventions, protocols and agreements have been adopted. These are not statutory acts of the

---

[40] Adopted by its Committee of Ministers and Parliamentary Assembly.

[41] www.coe.int.

[42] Article 1, paragraph *(b)*, Statute of the Council of Europe.

Council but need to be ratified by the Member States in order to become effective. Non-Member States of the Council of Europe and the European Community may, by accession, also become parties to the Conventions.

Only 11 Council of Europe Conventions are aimed at unifying substantive law of which the most important, in terms of the number of ratifications or accessions, are in the field of child law [43]. The most significant instrument of the Council of Europe, however, is the Convention for the Protection of Human Rights and Fundamental Freedoms of 1950 which is effective in all the Member States.

1.2.2. *The European Union*

30. The European Union, consisting now of 27 Member States, was established in 1993, through the Treaty of the European Union, upon the foundations of the pre-existing European Economic Community. On 1 December 2009, the Treaty of Lisbon [44], which was designed to restructure the European Union by amending the Treaty on European Union and the Treaty establishing the European Community [45], entered into force for all Member States. The Treaty on European

---

[43] Conventions on the Adoption of Children (1967, amended in 2008), on the Legal Status of Children born out of Wedlock (1975), on the Exercise of Children's Rights (1996) and on Contact concerning Children (2003). In 2002 the Council of Europe drafted a White Paper on Principles concerning the Establishment and Legal Consequences of Parentage.

[44] Signed on 13 December 2007, *Official Journal* 2007/C 306/01.

[45] See J. Dutheil de la Rochère, "The Lisbon Compromise : A Synthesis between Community Method and Union Acquis", *Fordham International Law Journal* (2008) 1143-1160 (1144).

Union kept the same name and the Treaty establishing the European Community (TEU) became the Treaty on the Functioning of the European Union (TFEU). Both Treaties have founded the *Union* which replaced and succeeded the European Community. According to Article 249 TEU, which was effective until 30 November 2009, the European Parliament acting jointly with the Council, the Council and the Commission had the competence to make Regulations and issue Directives, take Decisions, make Recommendations or deliver Opinions. Article 288 TFEU contains similar wording [46].

The European Union has five different legal acts at its disposal : the *Regulation* has general application ; it is binding in its entirety and directly applicable in all Member States whereas the *Directive* must be implemented by the Member States to which it is addressed. They are at liberty to determine the form and method of bringing their national law into accordance with the content of the Directive. Also *decisions* shall be binding in their entirety. In contrast, *Recommendations* and *Opinions* have no — and cannot acquire any — binding force.

31. It is beyond doubt that the European Union has competence regarding the unification of the rules for *private international law* relationships. For this reason, special European contract, delict/tort and family law for cross-border situations is now a reality. The legal basis for this development was to be found in Article 65 of the EC Treaty, as revised by the Amsterdam Treaty [47]. Since 1 December 2009, Article 81 TFEU

---

[46] It reads : "To exercise the Union's competences, the institutions shall adopt regulations, directives, decisions, recommendations and opinions."

[47] M. Tenreiro *et al.*, "Unification of Private International Law in Family Law Matters within the European Union", in K. Boele-Woelki (ed.), *Perspectives for the*

provides the competence for the European legislature to adopt measures of private international law.

32. In respect of substantive law a distinction is to be made between contract and delict/tort on the one hand and family matters on the other. Regarding the law of obligations the European Union can take legislative measures to unify and harmonize substantive private law in the form of Regulations, Directives or Recommendations. The legal basis for a European instrument containing substantive law can also be Article 352 TFEU [48] (formerly Article 308 TEC).

In respect of substantive family and succession law, it is generally accepted that the European Union had *no* competence under the EC Treaty to unify or harmonize these areas [49]. The Lisbon Treaty has not brought about

---

Unification and Harmonisation of Family Law in Europe (2003) 185-193, and M. Jänterä-Jareborg, "Unification of International Family Law in Europe — A Critical Perspective", in K. Boele-Woelki (ed.), *Perspectives for the Unification and Harmonisation of Family Law in Europe* (2003) 194-216.

[48] Which reads :

"If action by the Union should prove necessary, within the framework of the policies defined in the Treaties, to attain one of the objectives set out in the Treaties, and the Treaties have not provided the necessary powers, the Council, acting unanimously on a proposal from the Commission and after obtaining the consent of the European Parliament, shall adopt the appropriate measures. Where the measures in question are adopted by the Council in accordance with a special legislative procedure, it shall also act unanimously on a proposal from the Commission and after obtaining the consent of the European Parliament."

[49] W. Pintens, "Europeanisation of Family Law", in K. Boele-Woelki (ed.), *Perspectives for the Unification and Harmonisation of Family Law in Europe,* European Family Law Series No. 4 (2003), 3-33 (22), with many references, and Jänterä-Jareborg, *op. cit.,* footnote 47, 195.

any changes in this respect. Like Article 65 of the EC Treaty, Article 81 of the TFEU speaks of measures in the field of judicial co-operation in civil matters "having cross-border implications". Due to the fact that no time indication is provided regarding the required cross-border implications, the following view can be taken. Each relationship which is only connected to one national jurisdiction can — hypothetically — become a cross-border relationship. In order to guarantee the free movement of persons in Europe the EU Commission should take appropriate steps to avoid a loss of legal position, which, for instance, can arise with a change of residence if the connecting factor is not immutable, but where the applicable law is based on the habitual residence in question. According to this broad interpretation of Article 81 TFEU (formerly 65 TEC) the European Union could even take measures in order to harmonize or unify substantive family law in Europe.

Hence, the question whether the European Union has competence to unify the substantive private law of the Member States depends on the measure to be taken and the issue to be regulated. In all cases European legal acts must meet the requirement of proportionality and compatibility with the principle of subsidiarity. Moreover, they must further the enhancement of the single market which is aimed at bringing down barriers and simplifying existing rules for individuals, consumers and businesses alike.

1.3. African and American organizations

33. Both within Africa and the United States of America two organizations draft and adopt instruments which aspire principally to achieve the unification of substantive law. They are worth mentioning in this context.

1.3.1. The Organization for the Harmonization of African Business Laws

34. The Organization for the Harmonization of African Business Laws (Organisation pour l'Harmonisation en Afrique du Droit des Affaires) (hereinafter "OHADA" by its French acronym) was established in 1993 by a Treaty between 16 African countries [50]. This African collaboration aims to implement a modern legal framework in the area of business laws in order to promote investment and develop economic growth. Although this organization indicates in its name that its aim is the harmonization of the law, its activities essentially are aimed at the unification of the law. The OHADA Treaty calls for the elaboration of Uniform Acts to be directly applicable in Member States, notwithstanding any provision of domestic law [51]. The OHADA is an interesting and ambitious organization. It has set up a remarkable infrastructure with a single court and a growing number of Uniform Acts predominately in the field of contract law.

1.3.2. The US National Conference of Commissioners on Uniform State Laws

35. The National Conference of Commissioners on Uniform State Laws (NCCUSL) [52] has worked for the uniformity of the laws of the United States of America since 1892. The conference is comprised of state commissions on uniform laws from each state of the union.

---

[50] 14 of the 16 countries belong to the French-speaking area.

[51] S. Mancuso, "Trends on the Harmonization of Contract Law in Africa", *Annual Survey of International & Comparative Law*, Golden Gate University School of Law (2007) 157-178 (165).

[52] www.nccusl.org.

The more than 300 uniform law commissioners must be members of a state bar (that is licensed attorneys) [53]. The NCCUSL draft and propose specific statutes — Uniform Acts — or Model Acts in areas of the law where uniformity between the states is desirable [54]. Since its establishment the NCCUSL has proposed hundreds of Uniform Acts and Model Acts on numerous subjects and in various fields of law. The Uniform Commercial Code, which was drafted in co-operation with the American Law Institute, remains the signature product of the NCCUSL and has been universally enacted. Also, in the field of family law, several issues have been addressed through the NCCUSL's uniform law-making, such as child custody and child and family support [55]. The Uniform and Model Acts cannot become binding law unless they are adopted by states [56];

---

[53] Article 2 of the Constitution, Bylaws, and Rules of Procedure.

[54] Uniform Law Commission, Reference Book (2008-2009), 8 :

"With the development of interstate transportation and electronic transactions, the states have become increasingly interdependent socially and economically so that a single transaction may cross many state lines and involve citizens in many states. Citizens of one state constantly travel to other states or move their residence. A confusion or difference of laws among the several states may present, in some fields, a deterrent to the free flow of goods, credit, services, and persons among the states ; restrain full economic and social development ; disrupt personal planning ; and generate pressures for federal intervention to compel uniformity. The ULC seeks to alleviate these problems in areas of law traditionally left to the states, thus preserving the federal system."

[55] See on the Uniform Acts in the field of family law : Boele-Woelki, *op. cit.*, footnote 15, 10, 22.

[56] A formal denunciation, which in the case of Conventions is required according to international law if a

however they may modify and adjust the instruments according to their specific needs. In many states, however, the content of the enacted Uniform Law has not been changed or, if so, only slightly. State legislatures are urged to adopt Uniform Acts exactly as written in order to promote uniformity in the law among the states whereas Model Acts are designed to serve as guideline legislation, which states can borrow from or adapt to suit their individual needs and conditions. They are designated as such if it is unlikely that a Uniform Act will be uniformly adopted, but the drafters have an expectation that individual states are likely to adopt, or modify and adopt, parts of the act. The Uniform Acts have generally a unifying effect whereas Model Acts are intended, primarily, to contribute to the harmonization of the law.

2. Instruments

36. Genuine international substantive law, that is to say sets of rules which exist on a supranational or regional level and which are detached from a national context, can become effective through various instruments which contain "hard" law.

Some of the instruments become binding without specific legislative acts of legislatures whilst others require that instruments of ratification or accession pass through standard legislative procedures, such as in the form of a bill.

2.1. Conventions

37. At the multilateral level international Conventions are the most effective means of unifying substan-

---

contracting state wants to terminate its binding effects, is not possible as far as Uniform Acts of the NCCUSL are concerned.

tive law. Under international law a Convention is binding on States and other entities with treaty-making
capacity which choose to become a party through ratification or accession to a specific instrument. Conventions have the advantage of encouraging compliance
amongst those countries which have agreed to become
contracting States. The unifying effect depends on ratification of or accession to the Convention by individual States, the disadvantage being that a potential sig-
natory may be hesitant or even unwilling to become a
party to a particular Convention because of the requirements which the Convention places on the sovereign
State. Moreover, Conventions only permit departures
from their provisions if reservations to that end have
been agreed upon. It has been observed that many
existing international Conventions, for instance, while
forming part of what might be considered international
commercial law, remain largely ineffective because of
their sparse application in the day-to-day functioning
of domestic legal systems [57].

38. However, even if States are bound by a Convention containing uniform law, the rules may be
applied differently by the national courts [58]. It should
be borne in mind that no supranational court has been
established in respect of any of the Conventions containing uniform substantive law. Generally, just as in
the CISG, national courts are reminded to regard as
paramount the international character of each Convention and thus the need to promote uniformity in its
application. Efforts to achieve uniform interpretation,
as far as the uniform interpretation of sales law is concerned, are supported by two private initiatives : the
Autonomous Network of CISG Websites, which is a
global jurisconsultorium on uniform law for jurists and

---

[57] McAuley, *op. cit.*, footnote 28, 233.
[58] Struycken, *op. cit.*, footnote 1, 104-110.

arbitrators of all jurisdictions [59], and the International Sales Convention Advisory Council (CISG-AC) [60], which was established in 2001 to support understanding of the CISG and the promotion of, and assistance in, its uniform interpretation [61]. In practical terms, the CISG-AC issues opinions relating to the interpretation and application of the Convention on request [62] or on its own initiative. Since its establishment the CISG-AC has delivered nine opinions on various issues.

2.2. *Regulations*

39. To date, no European Regulation concerning substantive private law has been adopted. This might change in the future. According to the positions taken at, and reports adopted by, the Council of Justice and

---

[59] See the Charter of the Autonomous Network of CISG Websites : www.cisg.law.pace.edu/cisg/charter.html. The consortium of CISG websites began with Faculties of Law of the United States, Germany and France. The consortium has expanded to include websites in Australia, Austria, Belgium, Brazil, Canada, Denmark, Finland, Germany, Greece, Israel, Japan, Mexico, Netherlands, Spain and Latin America, Switzerland and Thailand with regional sites for Africa and the Arab States of the Middle East.

[60] www.cisgac.com.

[61] The CISG-AC is a private initiative in the sense that its members do not represent countries or legal cultures, but they are scholars who look beyond the "cooking pot" for ideas and for a more profound understanding of issues relating to CISG. Accordingly, the group is afforded the luxury of being critical of judicial or arbitral decision and of addressing issues not dealt with previously by adjudicating bodies.

[62] To be submitted, for instance, by international organizations, professional associations and adjudication bodies. The CISG opinions are available in the English language ; some are also available in Arabic, Chinese, French, German, Japanese, Russian, Slovak and Spanish.

Home Affairs Ministers of the European Union of April and November 2008 [63], it has been announced that a Common Frame of Reference for European Contract Law will be drafted. Apparently, the discussions about this also focus on the choice of the most suitable instrument for such a project and whether or not it should be binding. The Council, the European Parliament and the Commission will be involved in setting up this instrument which — to take the least pretentious objective — will be a non-binding instrument to be used by legislators at Community level. In the long run, and depending on its content, usefulness and acceptance, the Common Frame of Reference might be transformed into a Regulation [64]. However, a decision to that end has not yet been taken. Moreover, in June 2009 the Committee on Civil Law Matters considered it too early to decide on the form in which the Common Frame of Reference should be presented [65]. Anyhow, it will be less extensive than the Draft Common Frame of Reference which has been drafted by the Study Group on a European Civil Code [66]. As to its structure, it will consist of definitions, common fundamental principles and model rules ; as to its scope, it will deal with the general law of contracts, also including consumer contracts as in the proposed Directive on consumer rights of 8 October 2008 [67], and possibly

---

[63] Press Release 16325/08, www.consilium.europa.eu/ueDocs/cms_Data/docs/pressData/en/jha/104584.pdf, 30.

[64] According to Article 288 TFEU a regulation shall have general application. It shall be binding in its entirety and directly applicable in all Member States.

[65] Justice and Home Affairs Council Meeting, 5 June 2009, at which Guidelines on the setting up of a Common Frame of Reference for European contract law were approved.

[66] See Chapter IV, Section 1.1.1.

[67] COM (2008) 614/3.

special contracts falling within the consumer *acquis* might be included at a later stage. In view of the diversity of legal traditions, alternative solutions on certain subjects could be presented [68].

2.3. Directives

40. A Directive is a legislative act of the European Union which requires Member States in transposing it to achieve a particular result. According to Article 288 TFEU a Directive shall be binding, as to the result to be achieved, upon each Member State to which it is addressed, but shall leave to the national authorities the choice of form and methods. Generally, Directives are characterized as harmonizing instruments. The major features of the Directives' legal nature are that they must be implemented into the law of the Member States [69] within a restricted period of time [70], but the national legislatures are free to either restrict the incorporation of European law into their national law to the Directive's mandatory rules (core rules) or go above this minimum and implement in whole or in part all

---

[68] O. Remien, "Zweck, Inhalt, Anwendungsbereich und Rechtswirkung des Gemeinsamen Referenzrahmens : Eine erste Analyse des Standpunktes des Justizministerrates vom 18.4.2008", *Gemeinschaftsprivatrecht* (2008) 124-128.

[69] The transposition of these Directives into the laws of the Member States is documented and analysed by H. Schulte-Nölke, C. Twigg-Flesner and M. Ebers, *EC Consumer Law Compendium — The Consumer Acquis and Its Transposition in the Member States* (2008). See for the online version : http ://ec.europa.eu/consumers/rights/docs/consumer_law_compendium_comparative_analysis_en_final.pdf.

[70] If a Member State has failed to implement a Directive within the transposition period, citizens can enforce their rights against the State before national courts. See Rösler, *op. cit.*, footnote 30, 305-322.

rules of the Directive. Quintessentially, this means that a Member State cannot dispose of an unpopular private law Directive by simply ignoring it, as it could do regarding a Convention even if this Member State has been overruled due to a majority vote in the European Council and Parliament. After transposition of a Directive into the national laws of the Member States, the law is not totally unified but, in respect of several aspects, only approximated.

41. From its very beginning the strategy of the European Community has been to promote economic integration through legal harmonization [71]. Against this background several Directives on the law of obligations — mainly in the field of consumer law — have been issued [72], such as the Directive on Unfair Terms in Consumer Contracts, Self-employed Agents, Doorstep Sales, Consumer Credit, Package Tours, Time-share, Product Liability, to name but a few [73]. The legal basis of Directives is Article 288 TFEU (formerly Article 249 EC Treaty). However, the fragmentary and partly uncoordinated communitarization of contract law through Directives has been criticized and further steps are being undertaken. The draft proposal for a Directive on Consumer Rights [74], for instance, which leads to a reform of four existing consumer Directives, indi-

---

[71] A. M. López Rodríguez, *Lex Mercatoria and Harmonization of Contract Law in the EU* (2003) 5.

[72] Rösler, *op. cit.*, footnote 30, 305-322.

[73] See Communication from the Commission to the Council and the European Parliament on European Contract Law, Brussels, 11.07.2001 COM (2001) 398 final, Annex I, Important Community Acquis in the Area of Private Law.

[74] COM (2008) 614 final. Critically assessed by J. M. Smits, "Full Harmonization of Consumer Law ? A Critique of the Draft Directive on Consumer Rights", *Tidskrift utgiven av Juridiska föreningen i Finland* (2009) 573-581.

cates the intention to move away from minimum to full harmonization, which is actually equal to unification. It has been suggested that Member States may not maintain or introduce, in their national law, provisions diverging from those laid down in this Directive, including more or less stringent provisions to ensure a different level of consumer protection [75]. This proposal has received a lot of criticism. From a private international law point of view the Committee of the Regions on Consumer Rights expressed serious doubts about full harmonization on the grounds that, since the Commission has so far failed to give cogent reasons for switching to full harmonization in this area, it does not appear to be strictly necessary, seems inconsistent with the basic tenets of subsidiarity, and implies that the Member States may have to sacrifice particular consumer protection provisions, even where these have proved effective in the country concerned. Moreover consumer difficulties have mostly been caused by the uncertainties and complexities of law enforcement in cross-border trade (language barriers, legal fees, courts costs and the like) which are not removed by the proposed Directive [76].

So far substantive family and succession law has never been regulated by European Directives. This area is considered to fall within the exclusive legislative competence of each individual Member State.

2.4. Uniform Acts

42. As to their legal effects Uniform Acts have two different meanings. A distinction is to be made

---

[75] Article 4 of the Draft Proposal.

[76] Official Journal J, C 200/76. This view is supported by H. W. Micklitz and N. Reich, "Cronica de una muerte anunciada : The Commission Proposal for a Directive of Consumer Rights", *Common Market Law Review* (2009) 471-519.

between the OHADA Uniform Acts and the NCCUSL Uniform Acts. The OHADA Treaty calls for the elaboration of Uniform Acts to be directly applicable in the Member States, notwithstanding any provision of domestic law [77].

In 1997, the Uniform Act Relating to General Commercial Law was adopted [78], followed in 2004 by the Uniform on Contract Law [79]. These Uniform Acts do not need to be ratified by the African Member States. Once adopted these Acts are automatically enacted in OHADA Member States and replace domestic law. Without further intervention or decisions to be taken by the Member States the unification of the law takes place [80]. In contrast, the Uniform Acts of the NCCUSL do not necessarily always achieve their objectives of unifying substantive law in all US States.

First and foremost, Uniform Acts lack the power of enforceability. They undoubtedly embody a high level of flexibility in their application because they only contain a recommendation that they be enacted into the law of the states of the United States of America. States are not only free to choose either to adopt or to reject the exact content of the Uniform Act but its content may also be modified according to the interests of the individual State. This flexibility allows tailor-made law for each individual State.

---

[77] Mancuso, *op. cit.*, footnote 51, 165.

[78] www.jurisint.org/ohada/text/text.02.en.html.

[79] N. Hagge, *Das einheitliche Kaufrecht der OHADA* (2004).

[80] However, several commentators have stressed the passive attitude of the legal actors involved in the implementation of the uniform texts. See L. G. Castellani, "International Trade Law Reform in Africa", *Yearbook of Private International Law* (2008) 547-563 (552) with further references.

3. Does the Unification of Substantive Law Belong to the Past ?

43. From the overview of Conventions drawn up under the auspices of UNCITRAL and UNIDROIT [81] it can be deduced that the number of Conventions which are aimed at unifying substantive law is substantial. To date, in the field of commercial law and finance law, 17 Conventions have been adopted. They cover banking, credit, finance, general aspects of contract law, sales law, agency, carriage of goods and the law of delict/tort. The majority of the substantive law Conventions — ten in total — were adopted between 1980 and 2000, four Conventions were adopted before 1980 (dating back to 1956) and three Conventions after the year 2000. Two of these Conventions are of recent date. UNCITRAL prepared the Convention on Contracts for the International Carriage of Goods Wholly or Partly by Sea, which was adopted by the General Assembly of the United Nations on 11 December 2008, whereas the Convention adopted on 9 October 2009 under the auspices of UNIDROIT tends to unify the substantive rules regarding intermediated securities. The argument that the unification of substantive law through Conventions clearly belongs to the past cannot be sustained. The process is still ongoing. However, a certain trend is visible. The number of Conventions adopted in the various periods indicates that the attempt to unify substantive law through multilateral agreements reached its peak in the last 20 years of the previous century. Before that period, which dates back until 1954, only four Conventions were adopted

---

[81] See Information Document No. 1 of March 2009 for the attention of the Council of March/April 2009 on General Affairs and Policy of the Hague Conference on Private International Law.

whereas, so far, the twenty-first century has already produced three Conventions. However, to this author's knowledge, new Convention projects are not envisaged.

44. Several explanations for the present record on the unification of substantive law through Conventions can be postulated. Firstly, a lot of areas have been covered by Conventions. Secondly, the Conventions differ in terms of importance and content. Thirdly, the success of the uniformization process evidently depends on the number of ratifications by States. Fourthly, the time has come to amend and replace older Conventions by modern Conventions which is a complicated process. Fifthly, for more than 25 years UNCITRAL and UNIDROIT have also put a lot of effort into the harmonization of substantive law through Model Laws, legislative guides and Principles.

45. At the regional levels diverse developments are noticeable. At the outset it is evident that within the European Union the unification of substantive law does not have a past, but it might have a future. In particular, the Uniform Acts of the OHADA on the one side and European regulations on the other side, the latter of which have the potential, and might eventually be used, to unify the law of obligations within the European Union, have similar effects. Once these instruments are adopted, they become binding in the Member States without ratification. Within the African context the unification of commercial law has the future, whereas it is uncertain whether a comparable path will be followed by the European legislator. It has a legal instrument at its disposal, however to date the political will to use it is lacking. In contrast, within the framework of the United States of America the innumerable Uniform Acts of the NCCUSL still enjoy wide appreciation, since they cannot be imposed on the federal States.

CHAPTER IV

HARMONIZING SUBSTANTIVE LAW

46. This chapter introduces the various instruments which fall under the category "harmonizing substantive law instruments". Explanations of the general characteristics of various instruments as well as specific examples of several harmonizing substantive law instruments will be provided. These examples will also be used when the interaction with conflict of law rules comes to be explored further.

Which instruments are harmonizing substantive law instruments ? After explaining some general characteristics of the different kinds of instrument, some specific instruments in the three fields of law will be introduced since it is evident that not all instruments can be discussed. A choice of the most important ones has been made including, in particular, recently drafted instruments, such as Principles, the application of which to cross-border relationships has not only been raised in legal literature but, more importantly, has been implemented already in legal practice.

The table on the next page indicates various aspects of our topic. Firstly, which organizations contribute to the harmonization of substantive private law (1st column), secondly, what kind of instruments have been adopted (2nd column), and thirdly, the fields of law in which the different organizations have been active so far (3rd-5th columns).

1. Organizations

47. Before describing the main characteristics of the respective instruments an overview should be pro-

vided of the organizations which are contributing to the harmonization of substantive law. Several organizations which are active in unifying substantive law, such as UNCITRAL, UNIDROIT, the European Union and the NCCUSL are also drafting and adopting instruments for the harmonization of substantive law. These organizations were introduced briefly at paragraph 1 in the previous chapter. In this chapter other organizations will be portrayed which do not have legislative power but, nevertheless, produce rules which are mainly based upon comparative research taking almost all European jurisdictions or — as far as the United States of America is concerned — all states into account.

Table 4. Harmonizing Substantive Law :
Organizations, Instruments and Areas of Law

Organizations	Instruments	Contracts	Delicts/torts	Family relations
European Union	Directives	yes	yes	no
International organizations	Model Laws	yes	no	no
	Principles	yes	no	no
NCCUSL (US)	Model Acts	yes	yes	no
American Law Institute	Restatements	yes	yes	no
	Principles	no	no	yes
European academic groups and commissions	Principles	yes	yes	no
	(Draft) Common Frame of Reference	yes	yes	no

1.1. European academic groups and commissions

48. It is not only at the European legislative level that the Europeanization of private law has been

attempted. For more than 30 years various projects have been undertaken by private groups and commissions to draft model rules based on comparative research and international co-operation in order to guide the interpretation and development of national legal systems in Europe and thus to pave the way for a gradual assimilation of these systems [82]. Since the end of the 1970s, when Ole Lando's Commission on European Contract Law commenced its work to restate the contract law laid down in the national legal systems in Europe [83], academic groups in other areas of private law have been popping up like mushrooms. Almost all fields of private law have been covered so far. To date, only in family law is there but one Commission whose activities are aimed at contributing to the further harmonization of the family law systems in Europe [84], whereas in the field of the law of obligations there are several groups [85] and commissions [86]. For an outside observer the picture might be confusing, since there are different projects, new groups have been established or merged and competition between the various groups also plays a role. The question is whose final results, in the form of Rules and Principles, provide the best models for legislators, adjudicators and parties alike ?

---

[82] R. Zimmermann, "The Present State of European Private Law", *American Journal of Comparative Law* (2009), 479-512 (482).

[83] See further Chapter IV, Section 2.4.

[84] See further Chapter IV, Section 1.1.2.

[85] See, e.g., the Project Group "Restatement of European Insurance Contract Law" (established in 1999) which drafted the Principles of European Insurance Contract Law ; www.Restatement.info.

[86] E. Hondius, "Towards a European *Ius Commune* : The Current Situation in Other Fields of Private Law", in K. Boele-Woelki (ed.), *Perspectives for the Unification and Harmonisation of Family Law in Europe*, European Family Law Series No. 4 (2003) 118-139.

1.1.1. The Commission on European Contract Law, the Study Group on a European Civil Code and the European Research Group on Existing EC Private Law

49. The Commission on European Contract Law was the first academic commission within Europe which commenced comparative research-based drafting of common Principles. The harmonizing project was finalized with the publication of the last part of the Principles of European Contract Law in 2003 [87]. The work of the Commission on European Contract Law has been continued and broadened by the Study Group on a European Civil Code which consists of a co-ordinating group and several working teams from across the European Union [88]. According to its aim the Study Group, which consists predominantly of academics, strives to produce a codified set of Principles of European Law for the law of obligations and core aspects of the law of property [89]. A significant step towards this aim consists of the publication in 2008 of a six-volume full edition of the Draft Common Frame of Reference (DCFR) which was drafted and compiled together with the European Research Group on Existing EC Private Law. This latter group, founded in 2002 [90], aims to arrange systematically existing

---

[87] frontpage.cbs.dk/law/commission_on_european_contract_law/survey_pecl.htm.

[88] These working teams cover : Sales, Services and Long-term Contracts, Extra-Contractual Obligations, Credit Securities, Transfer of Moveable Property, Trusts, Renting Contracts, Gifts, Loans and Insurance Contracts. See for an explanation of the working method : www.sgecc.net/pages/en/organisation/index.overview.htm.

[89] H. Schulte-Nölke, "Arbeiten an einem europäischen Vertragsrecht — Fakten und populäre Irrtümer", *Neue Juristische Wochenschrift* (2009) 2161-2167.

[90] www.acquis-group.org.

Community law which will help to elucidate the common structures of the emerging Community private law.

For this purpose, the group concentrates primarily upon existing EC private law which can be discovered within the *acquis communautaire*. The DCFR includes not only draft model rules but full comments and notes, which explain why a rule is formulated as it is, how it relates to other rules and where its roots lie in the European legal systems.

1.1.2. The European Group on Tort Law

50. The European Group on Tort Law was established in 1993. Currently, it consists of 23 scholars from several European jurisdictions ; however the United States of America, South Africa and Israel are also represented.

The Group's main objective is to provide material for the potential unification of the law of delict and tort within the European Union. To that end common Principles are drafted which might also influence legal science, courts of law and domestic legislatures [91].

1.1.3. The Commission on European Family Law

51. The Commission on European Family Law (CEFL) [92] established in 2001 is also a purely scientific initiative which is totally independent of any organization or institution.

---

[91] B. A. Koch, "The 'European Group on Tort Law' and its 'Principles of European Tort Law' ", *American Journal of Comparative Law* (2005) 189-205 ; G. Wagner, "The Project of Harmonizing European Tort Law", *Common Market Law Review* 2005, 1269-1312.

[92] www.ceflonline.net.

The CEFL consists of two groups : the Organizing Committee and the Expert Group. The Organizing Committee prepares and co-ordinates the work of the Commission as a whole.

The CEFL comprises 28 specialists in the field of family and comparative law from most of the European Union Member States with the involvement of experts from other European countries, such as Norway, Russia and Switzerland. The CEFL's main objective is the creation of Principles of European Family Law which aim to establish the most suitable means for the harmonization of family law within Europe [93].

1.2. The American Law Institute

52. In 1923, the American Law Institute (ALI) [94] was established by a group of practising lawyers to

"promote the clarification and simplification of the law and its better adaptation to social needs, to secure the better administration of justice, and to encourage and carry on scholarly and scientific work" [95].

The publication of large numbers of court decisions caused uncertainty and complexity as conflicts between courts became evident. To palliate the existing legal uncertainty, the ALI proposed the drafting of Restatements of the law which could function as authoritative sources. Thereby judges and lawyers are

---

[93] Boele-Woelki, *op. cit.*, footnote 17, 160-168.

[94] www.ali.org.

[95] Report of the Committee on the Establishment of a Permanent Organization for Improvement of the Law Proposing the Establishment of an American Law Institute, to be held 23 February 1923, in Washington, DC, 41.

told what the law is. Geoffrey C. Hazard, who served as Director of the American Law Institute from 1984 to 1999, in 1994 described the work of the Institute and its influence as follows :

"The Institute's work has received broad recognition and acceptance in the United States and elsewhere. The recognition is not always commendatory, for many of the Institute's formulations have been criticized, some of them very sharply so. However, even severe criticism constitutes recognition that the Institute's work product has authoritative force. Yet the Institute is not an agency of government. Its work product is strictly speaking merely private opinion. What is the dynamic by which legal formulations by a private organization of lawyers and judges assumes such positive legal significance ? The answer lies partly in the structure of the Institute, which has already been described : A selective membership drawn from members of the legal profession on the basis of their serious interest in improvement of the law, and an organization that is designed to focus on long-run objectives. However, the reception accorded the work of the Institute derives primarily from the procedures that the Institute employs in its drafting and deliberations. These procedures combine elements of intensive private discussion and open public debate, connected through meticulous drafting. . . . The authoritative influence of the Institute's Restatements and model legislation derives from these 'private' or intrinsic characteristics, not from the force of legal or political authority. The American Law Institute has no legal or political authority, but only such authority as others accord it."

In addition to the Restatements the ALI has collaborated with the NCCUSL in developing and monitoring

the Uniform Commercial Code for more than half a
century. In some areas, like family law and the law of
civil procedure the ALI has also drafted Principles, the
latter project was carried out in cooperation with
UNIDROIT.

2. Instruments

53. A great variety of instruments exists which are
aimed at harmonizing substantive private law. They are
drafted and adopted either by international or regional
organizations or by private initiatives in which, primarily, legal scholars from a great number of jurisdictions
are collaborating and acting as a team. Generally, these
instruments are characterized as "soft" law. The common feature of all harmonizing instruments is that they
can never obtain any binding force upon their own
motion. In order to acquire a binding effect a legislative act is required.

2.1. Directives

The harmonizing and unifying effects of EU Directives have been described in Chapter III, Section 2.3.

2.2. Model Laws and Model Acts

54. A Model Law suggests a set of legal propositions for law-makers and national Governments to consider adopting as part of their domestic legislation.
Both Model Laws adopted by an international organization and the Model Acts of the NCCUSL have no
binding effect. Their application depends on decisions
of national or state legislatures. They only contain a
recommendation that they be enacted into national or
state law. Given their lack of any enforceability, Model
Law and Model Acts must convince *imperio rationis*

instead of *ratione imperii* [96]. Countries and states are both free to adopt Model Laws and Model Acts in whole or in part or to adjust their content according to their specific needs. Generally, these instruments have been carefully considered ; they enjoy authority since they are drafted by experts who have, usually, also based their final decisions on comparative research. If a national legislator is inspired by the model solutions the decision not to take the whole package but to select only some parts of it and/or modify other parts instead should be well justified. Anyhow, their flexibility and the final say which national and state legislatures have, make Model Laws and Model Acts also highly attractive. They are drafted like codes or statutes. When they are used as model legislation no remuneration is requested.

On the contrary, the respective organizations support national and state legislatures if they decide to take the various "international products" as a model for their individual reform of the law. These kinds of initiatives are highly welcome to international organizations and the whole process will be monitored and reported by them. While the downside to the flexibility which Model Laws and Model Acts provide is that there is greater potential for divergence between various national and state laws, the upside is that they may encourage more countries and states to become involved in the harmonization process [97].

---

[96] Expression coined by A. Hartkamp, "Principles of Contract Law", in A. Hartkamp *et al.* (eds.), *Towards a European Civil Code* (2004) 125-143 (131).

[97] McAuley, *op. cit.*, footnote 28, 239 :

"There is no disincentive for failing to incorporate a Model Law into domestic law. While countries that do not ratify an international Convention may suffer the political stigma of not living up to their international obligations, countries can easily avoid incorporating a

2.3. Restatements

55. In the United States of America the private laws of the 50 states interact through the drafting of Restatements of Law which are comprehensive expositions of the law in specific subjects. A Restatement is formulated like a code, however it provides more information. The provisions state the rule followed by comments which explain the rule and by reporters' notes which provide references to decisions, statutes and treaties considered as supportive authority. Since its establishment the ALI has published many Restatements in various fields of law [98], contracts and torts included [99]. Family relationships, however, have never been addressed in a Restatement despite the fact that the family law systems of the 50 states also differ greatly. The Restatements are not legally binding. They are aimed at promoting consensus among the states' courts based on persuasive authority [100]. Restatements reflect the consensus of the American legal community as to what the law is and in some areas, what it should become. Many law professors, practising attorneys and

---

Model Law into domestic law without a genuine reason for doing so. Model Laws must rely on the promotion of the benefits of incorporating the particular Model Law into domestic law. In order for there to be widespread acceptance of the Model Law, countries must understand the associated benefits not only on a macro level, but also on a country-by-country basis."

[98] See for an overview of all ALI projects : www.ali.org/doc/past_present_ALIprojects.pdf.

[99] Three generations of Restatements are to be distinguished : the first period lasted from 1923 to 1944, the second period from 1952 to 1992 and the third period from 1995 to 2006.

[100] G. C. Hazard, "The American Law Institute : What It Is and What It Does", w3.uniroma1.it/idc/centro/publications/14hazard.pdf.

judges are contributing to the drafting process which takes many years. Therefore the decision whether or not to embark on a new Restatement is carefully considered.

2.4. Principles/rules

56. The Restatement technique has been copied, further adjusted to specific needs and elaborated by UNIDROIT and European academic groups in drafting their respective Principles. They are exponents of a new phenomenon of private law-making — some even call it private codification — where the work is carried out *without* the involvement of domestic legislatures.

2.4.1. UNIDROIT Principles of International Commercial Contracts

57. The first set of Principles was published by UNIDROIT. Almost 40 years ago the UNIDROIT Board of Directors decided to include in their working programme the "unification of general principles of the law on contracts" due to the considerable increase of international transactions worldwide. Based upon extensive comparative research UNIDROIT's efforts finally resulted in the adoption of the Principles of International Commercial Contracts in 1994. Ten years later they were supplemented by five new chapters [101]. Since then, various aspects of this new instrument in the field of international commercial law have been explained, explored, debated and criticised extensively. The amount of legal literature addressing the

---

[101] The 2004 edition contains 10 chapters : General Provisions, Formation, Validity, Interpretation, Content, Performance, Non-Performance, Set-Off, Assignment and Limitation Periods.

UNIDROIT Principles is enormous and no end is in sight [102]. Initially, the drafters of the UNIDROIT Principles indicated their activities as an attempt to "unify" international contract law. However, according to the view taken by this author, this goal has not been achieved and it is almost impossible that it will be reached. The UNIDROIT Principles have not been accepted by any diplomatic conference. They cannot become binding law, since they cannot be ratified by States' or other, regional, legislatures [103]. However, if national States adopt the Principles as their national law to be applied for international contracts or even internal contracts then, undoubtedly, in more countries the same rules are effective and applied. In this way a bottom-up unification of international commercial law takes place.

58. However, three aspects need to be taken into account : first of all, if a national State decides to enact the UNIDROIT Principles as their law for international contracts, generally the conflict of law rules require to be consulted as to whether this direct application of international substantive law is possible. The second aspect which requires specific consideration results from the fact that the UNIDROIT Principles only apply to business-to-business contracts and that they were not designed to establish a common law of contracts

---

[102] UNIDROIT maintains an excellent database which provides regular updates on the status quo of the Principles. See www.unilex.com.

[103] See H. Kronke, "A Bridge out of the Fortress : UNIDROIT's Work on Global Modernisation of Commercial Law and its Relevance for Europe", *Zeitschrift für Europäisches Privatrecht* (2008) 1-5 (5) who expresses the wish that Regional Economic Integration Organizations, in particular the European Community, following its accession to the Hague Conference on Private International Law, should also accede to the UNIDROIT Statute.

including, specifically, consumer contracts [104]. Thirdly, the emergence of a uniform contract law is hindered by the fact that to date not one single national legislature has adopted the UNIDROIT Principles in total. National interests lead to modifications, some parts are enacted and others are left out. Indisputably, it is to be welcomed that they have been used and continue to be used in a number of countries as a basis for the reform of their international contract law [105]. As a result, the differences between national contract law systems which have used the UNIDROIT Principles as a source of inspiration are becoming less pronounced and international business welcomes this development. In conclusion, whilst, in this author's view, the characterization of the UNIDROIT Principles as "uniform contract law" cannot be upheld, the description of their role in respect of recent reforms of national contract law, as "merely" providing a contribution to the harmonization

---

[104] In this respect I. Veillard, "Le caractère général et commercial des Principes d'UNIDROIT relatifs aux contrats du commerce international [The General and Commercial Character of the UNIDROIT Principles of International Commercial Contracts]", *Revue de droit des affaires internationales/International Business Law Journal* (2007) 479-492 (480) concludes that the adoption of the UNIDROIT Principles as provisions of a general section of the national law of contract is justifiable, as long as the national legislature is convinced that the substance of those principles meets the challenge posed by the precariousness of certain professionals and that, as a result, they offer a level of protection sufficient to be applied to all contractual relationships, regardless of the status for the parties to such contracts.

[105] Veillard, *op. cit.,* footnote 104, 484, who reports about influence on the Civil Codes in the Russian Federation (1995), Estonia and Lithuania (2001). Moreover the Principles have been used for the OHADA project. See S. K. Date-Bah, "The Preliminary Draft OHADA Uniform Act on Contract Law as Seen by a Common Law Lawyer", *Uniform Law Review* (2008) 217-222.

of contract law should not be seen at all to diminish their enormous value for the approximation of international commercial law.

2.4.2. Principles of European Contract Law

59. Almost in parallel to the elaboration of the UNIDROIT Principles, pioneering efforts were put into a similar project in Europe. Despite their regional orientation the Principles of European Contract Law have gained world fame. Drafted between 1980 and 2001 and based upon extensive comparative research and international co-operation they constitute an entire new and comprehensive contract law for B2B and B2C relationships which in essence is based on the CISG rules [106]. The Principles of European Contract Law are so designed as to be acceptable to the legal profession in Europe, while the UNIDROIT Principles aim at no less than the world. Both sets are non-binding. Force of conviction and authoritativeness are their only weapons in the struggle for recognition, and both of these they possess thanks to the alliance of the continental legal tradition with the principles of the common law. As far as the Principles of European Contract law are concerned they are aimed at guiding the interpretation and development of the national legal systems in Europe thus paving the way towards a gradual assimilation of these systems [107]. The legal literature on the

---

[106] O. Lando and H. Beale (eds.), *Principles of European Contract Law Parts I and II* (1999), O. Lando, E. Clive, A. Prüm and R. Zimmermann (eds.), *Principles of European Contract Law Part III* (2003). According to Zimmermann, *op. cit.*, footnote 82, 482, they do not provide the blueprint for a codification of (general) contract law.

[107] Zimmermann, *op. cit.*, footnote 82, 482, who notes that there are, in fact, a number of encouraging examples

Contract Principles already fills whole libraries with monographs, commentaries and articles. The discourse about their content, value, applicability and competitiveness is passionate. Moreover, they constitute the building blocks of the Model Rules which are contained in the Draft Common Frame of Reference [108].

2.4.3. *Principles of European Tort Law*

60. In the law of delict and tort the increasing trend, of contributing to the harmonization of private law in Europe through the drafting of Principles, is also reflected. However, the systems of delict and tort law in Europe differ considerably. There is not only the traditional border line between the common law and the continental civil law countries but also, the continental systems vary to a great extent amongst themselves.

These differences in the law of delict and tort explain why there has long been no attempt to harmonize the entire field of delict and tort law in a consistent manner.

However, this situation has changed since 2005 when the Principles of European Tort Law were published [109]. According to their draftsmen they address the fundamental questions underlying every system of the law of delict and tort. In identifying these prin-

---

of how the European Contract Principles have been used as a source of inspiration for legislators, legal writers, and courts of law.

[108] Study Group on a European Civil Code/Research Group on EC Private Law (Acquis Group), *Principles, Definitions and Model Rules of European Private Law* (2009).

[109] The European Group on Tort Law (ed.), *Principles of European Tort Law : Text and Commentary* (2005).

ciples and searching for a common law of Europe the Tort Law Principles — which are available in 16 different languages — might be used for a European civil code, once it would come into existence [110].

2.4.4. Principles of European Family Law

61. Principles of European Family Law are drafted by the CEFL. The Divorce and Maintenance between Former Spouses Principles were published in 2004 [111], the Parental Responsibilities Principles in 2007 [112]. Currently, the CEFL is preparing Principles regarding the Property Relationship between Spouses. They are planned to be launched in 2011. All sets of principles have been prepared and drafted according to the same method which was considered carefully at the outset following the establishment of CEFL [113].

---

[110] H. Koziol, "Die 'Principles of European Tort Law' der 'European Group on Tort Law'", *Zeitschrift für europäisches Privatrecht* (2004) 234-259 ; N. Jansen, "The State of the Art of European Tort Law", in M. Bussani, *European Tort Law* (2007) 15-45, and J. Blackie, "The Torts Provisions of the Study Group on a European Code", in M. Bussani, *European Tort Law* (2007) 55-80.

[111] K. Boele-Woelki, F. Ferrand, C. González Beilfuss, M. Jänterä-Jareborg, N. Lowe, D. Martiny and W. Pintens, *Principles of European Family Law Regarding Divorce and Maintenance between Former Spouses*, European Family Law Series No. 7 (2004).

[112] K. Boele-Woelki, F. Ferrand, C. González Beilfuss, M. Jänterä-Jareborg, N. Lowe, D. Martiny and W. Pintens, *Principles of European Family Law Regarding Parental Responsibilities*, European Family Law Series No. 16 (2007).

[113] K. Boele-Woelki, "The Working Method of the Commission on European Family Law", in K. Boele-Woelki (ed.), *Common Core and Better Law in European Family Law*, European Family Law Series No. 10 (2005) 14-38.

2.4.5. American Principles on Family Dissolution

62. An American Restatement on Family Law does not exist; instead in 2000, Principles of the Law on Family Dissolution were finalized under the auspices of the ALI [114]. This enormous project, which started in the early 1990s, is aimed at harmonizing certain aspects of family law in the United States [115] because the exercise by the courts of their wide discretionary power in family disputes has been perceived as causing uncertainty and inequality. According to ALI Chief Reporter Ira Mark Ellman [116],

---

[114] Principles of the Law on Family Dissolution: Analysis and Recommendations, as Adopted and Promulgated by the American Law Institute on 16 May 2000, 2002. According to the drafters of the ALI Principles of Family Dissolution

"the work is described as 'Principles' rather than 'Restatement' because 'Principles' is the better designation for a project that carefully, explores and clarifies the fundamental assumptions — about the best interests of children, fairness to divorcing wives and husbands, and the legitimate economic claims of unmarried partners — upon which the legal rules must rest. Many of these Principles, nevertheless, restate and clarify present law, while others recommend directions for implementation by courts, legislatures, and other appropriate decision makers. The result is a coherent legal framework, sensitive to both the traditional value systems within which most families are formed and the non-traditional realities and expectations of other families, a framework the earlier drafts of which have already begun to influence both courts and legislatures."

[115] R. Fretwell Wilson, "The Harmonization of Family Law in the United States", in K. Boele-Woelki and T. Sverdrup (eds.), *European Challenges in Contemporary Family Law* (2008) 27-49 (34).

[116] I. M. Ellman, *Inventing Family Law*, University of California (1999) 855-886 (870-871). Interestingly he mentions child support rules which in his view only exist

"alimony, custody, and even property allocation are effectively governed in most states by a family law version of Rule 1 : decide as you see fit. The legislatures and appellate courts leave basic policy choices up to the trial judge deciding each case. Most people think there is something unfair about having the governing legal principles change from judge to judge and from case to case."

3. Does the Harmonization of Substantive Law Have the Future ?

63. In the field of commercial and finance law the number of soft law instruments drawn up by UNIDROIT and UNCITRAL has been steadily growing during the last 25 years. The respective instruments which are aimed at harmonizing substantive law at a global level consist of Model Laws, rules, principles and legal guides. At the regional level the American Restatements are still highly respected. More significantly, the Restatement technique has inspired the working methods of many academic groups and commissions in Europe. Generally, however, the European Principles have gone one step further since they not only restate the law in the various fields of private law but also propose better law solutions [117] or, to put it dif-

---

"because they were pushed on the states by Washington lawmakers concerned primarily with their potential value in reducing the federal contribution to welfare payments" (856).

[117] Schulte-Nöltke, *op. cit.*, footnote 89, 2162 :

"Regeln [können] so abgefasst werden, dass sie Gemeinsamkeiten der untersuchten Rechtsordnungen wiedergeben ('common rules') oder eine nach Auffassung ihrer Verfasser vorzugswürdige Lösung aus dem vorgefundenen Spektrum auswählen ('best rules')."

See also Boele-Woelki, *op. cit.*, footnote 113, 14-38, and Wagner, *op. cit.*, footnote 91, 1281-1284.

ferently, unconventional solutions have been adopted which can be described as a progressive development from the common core [118]. This method has been applied in respect of the law of obligations and family relations respectively.

64. Evidently, the choice of the right instrument constitutes the crucial step in the unification and harmonization process. Whereas international organizations and the European legislator really have a choice between hard law (Conventions, Regulations, Directives) and soft law (Model Laws, Restatements, Rules and Principles), the choice of academic groups or organizations established by legal scholars and practitioners is clearly restricted. They can only draft and propose non-binding instruments. Unmistakably, the drawbacks of Conventions, however, are being seen to outweigh the disadvantages of Model Laws and Principles, since international organizations are tending also to focus their activities increasingly on the drafting of non-binding rules. This is the general trend. The advent of Principles has caused a change of paradigms. Unification and harmonization is being "privatized" and is no longer the exclusive domain of instruments adopted between States in the shape of Conventions. The drafters of Principles, in opting for the Restatement technique which has been complemented by a better law approach, have to a great extent been responsible for this development [119].

---

[118] Zimmermann, *op. cit.*, footnote 82, 483.
[119] Boele-Woelki, *op. cit.*, footnote 14, 659.

CHAPTER V

WHICH INSTRUMENT FOR WHICH PURPOSE ?

1. The Rationale for Unifying and Harmonizing
Substantive Law Instruments

65. It is been submitted, rightly, that the pursuit of
harmonization and unification as a goal in itself —
rather than as a means to an end — is both futile and a
waste of valuable resources. The reasons for unifying
or harmonizing whatever law is to be subjected to such
processes need to be expressed and carefully assessed.
The respective projects must not only propose reform
of the existing legal framework, but must demonstrate
that the existing system is genuinely deficient [120]. In
addition, the underlying rationale for unifying or harmonizing certain areas of the law is also considered to
be a key ingredient towards encouraging a more active
involvement of various interested parties in the law-
making process.

Is there a need for uniform or harmonized law ? Is it
useful and desirable ? For each field of law these questions need to be discussed meticulously and answered.
What is the incentive to embark on long-lasting
research projects involving representatives from many
different jurisdictions ? Within the global setting of
international organizations almost 200 different jurisdictions are represented, within the United States of
America in some areas like family law more than 50
systems are to be taken into account and within Europe
it depends whether we consider the greater Europe,
like the Council of Europe, where 46 States are taking

---

[120] In this sense McAuley, *op. cit.*, footnote 28, 233.

part or the European Union with only 27 Member States.

66. Several arguments in favour of more unification and harmonization of substantive private law have been used to justify the drafting and adoption of instruments such as Conventions, Model Laws, Uniform Laws or Principles. Commonly reference is made to developments in the following areas of the current world legal situation :

1. The process of further globalization [121]
2. Differences between national laws which causes extra costs for cross-border relationships
3. Insufficiencies of national law to regulate effectively cross-border relationships
4. Problems in the mutual understanding of law where it is written predominantly in the English language
5. Demand by legal practitioners for more transnational rules.

All these different aspects, or a combination of one or more thereof, have been and are used as a reasoned basis for, and in order to justify, the drafting and adoption of transnational and /or European-wide instruments, in addition to national substantive law. It goes beyond the purposes and scope of this book to discuss the different aspects of, and underlying motivations, for each instrument in any great detail, however some further explanations of the different backgrounds will be provided when the various instruments come to be introduced briefly.

---

[121] Heidemann, *op. cit.*, footnote 23, 36 :

"The process of globalisation with fewer trade barriers, interlocked financial markets and multi-national enterprises acting as 'global players' who are able to transfer workers, ideas, materials and products all around the world makes it in some cases hard to even establish the place (state) of their seat."

2. *Upsides and Downsides of the Various Instruments*

67. Which technique should be selected as that most suited to the harmonization of a certain area of law ? This is the primary question for international organizations, academic groups and law institutes alike when starting a new project. What instruments intended to harmonize the substantive law do have in common is that they cannot be ratified and States are not bound to enact them. This also applies to those parts of EU Directives which do not contain rules which must be implemented into the law of the Member States and in respect of which the Member States are free to adopt, modify or reject the proposed rules. If States decide to enact Model Laws, Uniform Laws, Principles or Rules they are free to modify substantially the rules of the selected instruments in accordance with their own sovereign interests. Hence, instruments which harmonize the substantive law clearly lack the enforceability of ratified and enacted Conventions. They serve as a source of inspiration. The rules ultimately should convince *imperii rationes* instead of *rationes imperii*. In addition, it is generally acknowledged, that "there is no disincentive for failing to incorporate such harmonising substantive law instruments into domestic law" [122]. While countries which do not ratify an international Convention may suffer the political stigma of not living up to their international obligations, countries can easily avoid incorporating a Model Law into domestic law without the necessity of having to offer a genuine reason for not doing so nor incurring the collective opprobrium of the international legal community.

68. From a State's perspective, a major advantage of many instruments which set out to harmonize sub-

---

[122] In this sense McAuley, *op. cit.*, footnote 28, 238.

stantive law is their high level of flexibility. Countries are free to adopt either the full content of the instrument or only some parts or modifications thereof. The harmonizing substantive law instruments offer their rules and, as regards their adoption, it all boils down to the motto : "Take it or leave it !" However, the success of the instruments is not only to be measured by the frequency and different degrees whereby each is used by international, regional and national law-makers, but also how often private parties have used them in the drafting of contracts, for instance, or how often they have been used by courts or arbitral tribunals. Monitoring of the extent of use of such instruments is predominantly carried out by the organizations or academic groups which drafted and adopted the instruments concerned. They report on the various "achievements" and "progresses" which have been made.

69. Further distinctions can be discerned among the various instruments. The final products are either indicated to be Model Laws, Uniform Laws, Principles or Rules. Often, however, the title description is less important than the structure and content of the instrument. Model Laws, for instance, regulate all aspects of a specific area of law. They can be compared to a code which a national legislature has enacted. Further, before drafting begins, a decision has to be taken as to whether the substantive text of the harmonization instrument should be broad and non-specific, resulting in Principles, or more concrete and precise, resulting in Rules. One would expect Principles to provide only general guidelines, the basic concepts and fundamental guarantees which have to be transformed into specific legislation ; whereas Rules — like Model Laws — are similar to statutory rules. The content of Rules is clear and precise and, as they contain a high level of specificity, further implementation or redrafting is not necessary for legislative purposes. However, the detailed

character of the Principles, which have been approved in the fields of contract, delict and tort and family law, makes it difficult to draw a clear demarcation line between this type of harmonizing substantive law instrument and Rules, on the one hand, and Model Laws, on the other. It is often submitted that such Principles provide a "model" or a "frame of reference" which national legislatures can take into account when reforming their internal law. Moreover, in point of fact, they do not really differ from commonly adopted Rules. However, the American law Institute/UNIDROIT joint project on the harmonization of transnational civil procedure has made a distinction between the one and the other. That project employs both the Principles approach and the Rules approach in order to enable States to choose one of them [123].

3. Unifying and Harmonizing Effects

70. Undoubtedly substantive law instruments intended to unify the law can also have a positive effect on the harmonization of the law, whilst those aimed at harmonizing substantive law can lead to a certain degree of uniform law. For our purposes these side effects of unification and harmonisation are of less importance. Nevertheless it is worthwhile to be aware of these corollaries since, despite the fact that the terms "unification" and "harmonization" are often used as synonyms, this is, however, inaccurate since, quite evidently, they have different meanings.

The CISG, for instance, with its 74 signatories, is a role model. It has had significant influence on interna-

---

[123] Th. Pfeiffer, "The ALI/UNIDROIT Project : Are Principles Sufficient, without the Rules ?", *Uniform Law Review* (2001) 1015-1033 (1017). See also McAuley, *op. cit.*, footnote 28, 238.

tional, regional (in Africa and Europe) and national law-making. Countries which are not bound by this Convention nevertheless can seek inspiration from the Convention rules in their quest to reform their domestic sales law [124], whereas — to provide another example — the fundamental elements of the Uniform Commercial Laws of the OHADA which bind 16 African States have been provided by the UNIDROIT Principles of International Commercial Contracts [125].

Both objectives — unification and harmonization — are, also, often pursued by legislative acts of the European Union. In the case of Directives, implementing measures are to be taken by the Member States within a certain period after the adoption of the Directive by the European Institutions. Generally, Directives contain both minimum rules which are to be transformed into the domestic law of the Member States (unification) and proposed rules as to how the specific area addressed by the Directive can be further regulated (harmonization). The Member States may adopt, reject or modify these rules.

71. In examining the question as to whether a law other than national law may be applied in cross-border relationships, the distinction between unification and harmonization remains, nonetheless, indispensible irrespective of any side effects which might arise eventually.

This distinction focuses on the main objectives of the respective instruments which in turn enables us to classify them into those which, first and foremost, aim at unifying substantive law and those which are intended primarily to harmonize substantive law.

---

[124] I. Schwenzer and P. Hachem, "The CISG — Successes and Pitfalls", *American Journal of Comparative Law* (2009) 457-478 (461-463).

[125] See further Chapter VII, Section 3.2.

Tables 5 and 6. Effects of Unifying
and Harmonizing Substantive Law Instruments

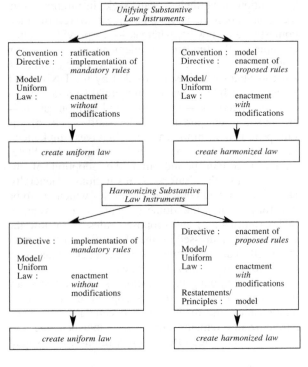

Convention : ratification	Convention : model
Directive : implementation of *mandatory rules*	Directive : enacment of *proposed rules*
Model/ Uniform Law : enactment *without* modifications	Model/ Uniform Law : enactment *with* modifications
create uniform law	*create harmonized law*

Unifying Substantive Law Instruments

Harmonizing Substantive Law Instruments

Directive : implementation of *mandatory rules*	Directive : enacment of *proposed rules*
Model/ Uniform Law : enactment *without* modifications	Model/ Uniform Law : enactment *with* modifications
	Restatements/ Principles : model
create uniform law	*create harmonized law*

4. *Choice of Instruments*

72. The success of any harmonization or unification
depends on the choice of instrument for the purpose.
Undoubtedly, this choice affects the level of compliance and acceptance of the final result. As has been
indicated   above   harmonization   instruments   vary
according to their level of formality, flexibility and
enforceability. The objectives of the drafters will determine which of the instruments will be selected as most

Table 7. Comparison of the Main Objectives
and Effects of International and Regional
Substantive Law Instruments

Instrument	Unifying effect	Harmonizing effect
Convention		
Regulation		
Directive		
Model Law		
Uniform Law		
Restatement		
Principles		

eligible for their purpose. Furthermore, not all instruments are available to all law-making organizations, institutions and groups alike. Whereas States co-operating actively within the framework of an international organization may have a great variety of instruments at their disposal, academic research groups or the American Law Institute, perceptibly, can only contribute to the harmonization process through the drafting of model or uniform laws (ALI), common rules or principles. When considering the question as to which specific type of instrument to select, it is striking to observe that international organizations in the field of international commercial law (UNIDROIT and UNCITRAL) increasingly focus their activities on Model Laws, Rules and Principles rather than on the drafting and adoption of international Conventions which are aimed at unifying substantive law. Evidently, States are often hesitant to ratify Conventions which do not provide clear benefits for their national interests. The lack of many ratifications of Conven-

tions on the one hand and the enormous success of
Model Laws [126], Principles and Rules on the other
might suggest a preference for the latter over the
former. It should be noted that, so far, the European
legislator has not yet turned its attention towards
Model Laws, Principles and Rules.

5. Developments and Trends in the Various Areas of Law

73. Whereas in the field of commercial law, more
specifically among those active in the business world,
all efforts to unify or harmonize international trade law
have been easily accepted, welcomed and greatly supported, the situation in respect of family relationships
looks completely different. Here, family law and comparative law experts have discussed extensively — at
least in Europe — whether any harmonization in the
form of common rules of family law is desirable, feasible and possible [127], since family law traditionally
belongs to the domain of national legislators. Also, in
the United States of America, family law has been
developed separately in each state by its own local
courts and local legislature: "As a result, American
family laws vary significantly in both substance and
procedure from one state to another." [128] Nevertheless,

---

[126] E.g., the UNCITRAL Model Law on International
Commercial Arbitration has been adopted, albeit with spe-
cific modifications, all around the world.
[127] See K. Boele-Woelki (ed.), *Perspectives for the
Unification and Harmonisation of Family Law in Europe*,
European Family Law Series No. 4, (2003).
[128] See L. D. Wardle and L. C. Nolan, "United States
of America" (latest update 1998), in W. Pintens (ed.),
International Encyclopaedia of Laws, Vol. 4, *Family and
Succession Law*, No. 11, 37:

"Of course, no state has developed its family law
entirely independently. However, there are many

within the United States, attempts to harmonize family law have also been undertaken. Some of these initiatives have turned out to be highly successful. The Uniform Child Support Act, for example, has been adopted by all States. Other projects, such as the American Law Institute's (ALI) Principles of Family Dissolution, which have not yet really been used as a model when reforming family law, have hardly fulfilled their major aims and objectives.

74. Another aspect which is worthy of reflection concerns the existence of the different instruments in terms of their age. Viewed from a global perspective unifying substantive law instruments are not only more numerous than the instruments whose intention is to harmonize substantive law but they have also been in existence for rather longer. Probably the Nordic initiatives for co-operation in family law, which started almost a hundred years ago, are amongst the oldest unification projects. About 50 years later the Hague Uniform Sales Laws were adopted and these were themselves replaced some 30 years ago by the extremely successful CISG. In contrast, harmonizing sub-

---

homogenizing cultural influences in the United States that create a tendency of similarity, if not harmony and consistency. For example, persuasive sister-state judicial opinions, new legislation enacted in other states that proves to be effective or popular, proposals for uniform legislation, programs of federal government providing support and incentives for states to take particular policy position, federal constitutional standards, the national news and entertainment media, and special interests that operate nationally have produced many multi-state and national trends in the family laws of the various states. Due to the homogenizing influences, students and teachers of family law in the United States often — look for and find — trends, and general principles that are shared and prevailing rules and practices . . ."

stantive law instruments began to be drafted and adopted at a far later stage. The first Model Laws of UNCITRAL [129] containing substantive law rules were only adopted between 1992 and 1994 [130] whereas the UNIDROIT Principles of International Commercial Contracts of 1994 and the Principles of European Contract Law of 1995 [131] are still teenagers. Their brothers and sisters in family law [132] and in the law of delict and tort [133] are, even, a good deal younger. Academic initiatives in the field of family law started only at the beginning of this century, whereas comparable projects in the law of obligations are years ahead of them.

75. Within the United States of America, however, the situation is different. Afraid of chaos in a legal world of, the then, 48 states and toying with the possibility of official codification but unable to take such a step, the American Law Institute created the Restatements. Since the establishment of the ALI in 1923

---

[129] The famous Model Law on International Commercial Arbitration (amended in 2006) was adopted in 1985.

[130] Model Law on International Credit Transfers adopted 15 May 1992. Based on the principles of this Model Law the Directive of the European Parliament and of the Council of the European Union was issued on 27 January 1997. Model Law on Procurement of Goods and Construction with Guide to Enactment adopted 16 July 1993 and Model Law on Procurement of Goods, Construction and Services adopted 15 June 1994. Legislative texts based on, or largely inspired by, this Model Law have been adopted in some 20 countries.

[131] Part I of the Principles dealing with performance, non-performance and remedies was published in 1995. Parts I and II were published in 1999 and Part III in 2003.

[132] The Principles of European Family Law Regarding Divorce and Maintenance between Former Spouses and Regarding Parental Responsibilities were published in 2004 and 2007 respectively, *op. cit.*, footnotes 111 and 112.

[133] The Principles of European Tort Law were published in 2005. See www.egtl.org.

numerous Restatements in various fields of law have been issued and been replaced subsequently by new ones, whereas the National Conference of Commissioners on Uniform State Laws (NCCUSL) had already begun its work in 1892. Since then a great number of uniform laws have been adopted with varying degrees of success. It is worthwhile mentioning that one of the areas of effort of this organization, with its enduring authority, is aimed at reducing the need for individuals and businesses to deal with different laws as they move to and from, and do business, in different states.

76. In the overall discussion about the inter-relationship between the various instruments the time element is of the essence, in particular as far as the Principles of Contract, Delict/Tort and Family Relations are concerned. Compared with the "older generation" represented by uniform law Conventions they belong to the "younger generation". Just as in daily life, the "young ones" provide fresh ideas and challenge the "establishment". They might be responsible for any changes as far as the application of a law other than national law in cross-border relations is concerned.

CHAPTER VI

CONFLICT OF LAWS

77. Since it is the interrelationship between unifying and harmonizing substantive law rules and conflict of law rules which is being investigated, it is appropriate also to provide a brief overview of legal sources pertinent to the latter. For our purposes a distinction is to be made between three levels : the international level, the European level and the national level which consists of statutory rules and/or case law. The conflict of law rules adopted and enacted at these different levels are to be applied in accordance with a generally accepted hierarchy. If a country is bound by an international Convention it will not apply its national conflict of law rules unless the legal issue does not fall within the Convention's scope of application. The same holds true for the relationship between European Regulations on the one side, and national rules, on the other, as far as the European Union is concerned. If the European Regulation applies — that is if the relevant legal question falls within the scope of application — national conflict of law rules cannot be consulted. The expectation that the hierarchy of precedence as between international Conventions and European Regulations might be similar in the sense that the higher level (international) takes priority over the lower level (regional) is, however, not justified. In this respect a one-size-fits-all answer cannot be provided since each specific European Regulation itself determines whether or not, in relation to the contracting States of an international Convention, preference is to be given to either European or (existing) Convention rules [134].

---

[134] Article 28 of the Rome II Regulation, for example, provides in respect of the relationship to existing international Conventions :

Table 8. Conflict of Law : Organizations,
Instruments and Areas of Law

Organizations	Instruments	Contracts	Delicts/torts	Family relations
International organizations	Convention	yes	yes	yes
European Union	Regulation	yes	yes	yes
National legislatures and courts	Statutes and case law	yes	yes	yes

1. Multilateral Conventions

78. The unification of private international law through Conventions commenced with the establishment of the International Conference on Private International Law which took place on 12 September 1893 in The Hague. T. M. C. Asser, a member of the Dutch Council of State, who had devoted over 20 years to propagating and putting into practice the idea of

---

"(1) This Regulation shall not prejudice the application of international Conventions to which the Member States are parties when this Regulation is adopted and which, in relation to particular matters, lay down conflict-of-law rules relating to non-contractual obligations.

(2) However, this Regulation shall, as between Member States, take precedence over Conventions concluded exclusively between two or more of them in so far as such Conventions concern matters governed by this Regulation."

Article 25 of the Rome I Regulation contains a similar provision. In respect of the European Regulation on property relations between spouses and succession it is to be expected that preference will be given to the European rules and not the rules of the Hague Convention on matrimonial property of 1978 and the Hague Convention on the law applicable to succession of 1989 respectively.

codifying private international law at an international level, was appointed Chairman. At the ceremonial opening of this first conference, which may be considered to be the real birth of the Hague Conference on Private International Law [135], T. M. C. Asser voiced his delight in the opening address as follows [136] :

> "I do not wish to hide from you the deep emotion I feel on asking you to begin your work. This is one of the dreams of my youth which now, if the signs do not deceive us, has started to become a reality. Thanks to your participation, knowledge and experience, I have no doubt that we shall succeed in drafting uniform rules which will lend themselves to adoption by legislatures, thereby creating a basis for the codification of private international law."

In respect of the Conference's objectives, and particularly the question as to what kind of rules should be unified, he provided the following guideline [137] which to this very day has been applied by the Hague Conference on Private International Law [138] :

> "We shall respect the sovereignty and the autonomy of states. We do not aspire to a general unification of private law. On the contrary, it is precisely

---

[135] www.hcch.net.

[136] Derived from G. J. W. Steenhoff, *Avec patience et courage, A History of the Foundation of the Hague Conference on Private International Law*, Dutch Ministry of Justice 1993, 5.

[137] Steenhoff, *op. cit.*, footnote 136, 53.

[138] See Article 1 of the Statute of the Hague Conference on Private International Law which entered into force on 15 July 1955 : "The purpose of the Hague Conference is to work for the progressive unification of the rules of private international law." See H. Van Loon, "Unification of Private International Law in a Multi-forum Context", in E.-M. Kieninger (ed.), *Denationaliserung des Privatrechts ?* (2005) 33-52.

the diversity of national laws which renders a uniform resolution of international conflicts of laws necessary. The programme of this Conference is thus itself a tribute to national autonomy."

79. During Asser's lifetime three more conferences took place and several Conventions were adopted in the field of marriage and divorce, the guardianship of minors, the effects of marriage, and the property relations between spouses and their estates. Only after World War II was the conference put on a permanent footing and since then 36 Conventions and two Protocols have been adopted. Not all instruments address all three parts of private international law (jurisdiction, applicable law and recognition and enforcement). Some focus exclusively on the issue of applicable law, others on international procedural law. It is worth noticing that for almost 30 years — since the adoption of the Hague Convention on international child abduction — the area of administrative co-operation between contracting States has been included in the Conventions dealing with family matters.

It is only since 2009 that the harmonization of private international law has also been added to the conference's activities. The development of a non-binding instrument is envisaged, its principal aim being to establish a global model for conflict of law rules which are applicable to contracts [139].

2. European Regulations

80. Private international law is not only unified by the ratification of international Conventions but also by European law-making [140]. However, European Regu-

---

[139] See *infra* Chapter X, Section 6.
[140] Struycken, *op. cit.*, footnote 1, 122-179.

lations in the field of cross-border relationships containing conflict of law rules [141] are of a much younger age.

More than 10 years ago — as a result of the entry into force of the Amsterdam Treaty of 1997 [142] — the European Community [143] acquired its own competence to legislate in matters concerning co-operation in civil matters having cross-border implications [144]. The first two Regulations which contain uniform conflict of law rules are the Rome II Regulation on the law applicable to non-contractual obligations and the Rome I Regulation on the law applicable to contractual obligations. The former has only been in force since 11 January 2009, the latter since 17 December 2009. International procedural law (jurisdiction and recognition and enforcement) are regulated in several Regulations which cover issues such as civil and commercial mat-

---

[141] K. Boele-Woelki, "Unification and Harmonization of Private International Law in Europe", in J. Basedow, I. Meier, A. K. Schnyder, T. Einhorn and D. Girsberger, *Private Law in the International Arena, From National Conflict Rules towards Harmonization and Unification, Liber Amicorum Kurt Siehr* (2000) 61-77. See also J. Harris, "Understanding the English Response to the Europeanisation of Private International Law", *Journal of Private International Law* (2008) 347-395.

[142] The Amsterdam Treaty of 18 June 1997 entered into force for the then 15 Member States on 1 May 1999. The Treaty amended the Treaty on European Union (Treaty of Maastricht of 7 February 1992) and the three Community Treaties (European Coal and Steel Community (ECSC), European Atomic Energy Community (EAEC) and the European Community (EC). The amendments primarily concerned the Treaty on European Union (TEU) and the EC Treaty (TEC).

[143] On 1 December 2009 the European Community was replaced by the *Union* which succeeded it and took over all its rights and obligations.

[144] Article 65 EC Treaty.

ters [145], divorce and parental responsibilities [146], and insolvency and specific procedural matters [147]. Two Regulations which, in addition to private international law issues address in detail international co-operation of administrative bodies are the Brussels II *bis* Regulation and the Maintenance Regulation [148]. Rules which determine the law to be applied, however, are

---

[145] Council Regulation (EC) No. 44/2001 of 22 December 2000 on jurisdiction and the recognition and enforcement of judgments in civil and commercial matters ("Brussels I").

[146] Council Regulation (EC) No. 2201/2003 of 27 November 2003 concerning jurisdiction and the recognition and enforcement of judgments in matrimonial matters and the matters of parental responsibility, repealing Regulation (EC) No. 1347/2000 ("Brussels II *bis*").

[147] Council Regulation (EC) No. 1346/2000 of 29 May 2000 on insolvency proceedings. In addition to Regulations concerning jurisdiction and recognition and enforcement the following instruments have been adopted : Regulation (EC) No. 1206/2001 of 28 May 2001 on Co-operation between the Courts of the Member States in the Taking of Evidence in Civil or Commercial Matters ; Regulation (EC) No. 805/2004 of the European Parliament and of the Council of 21 April 2004 creating a European Enforcement Order for Uncontested Claims ; Regulation (EC) No. 1896/2006 of the European Parliament and of the Council of 12 December 2006 Creating a European Order for Payment Procedure ; Regulation (EC) No. 861/2007 of the European Parliament and of the Council of 11 July 2007 establishing a European Small Claims Procedure ; Regulation (EC) No. 1393/2007 of the European Parliament and of the Council of 13 November 2007 on the service in the Member States of judicial and extrajudicial documents in civil or commercial matters (service of documents), and repealing Council Regulation (EC) No. 1348/2000.

[148] Council Regulation (EC) No. 4/2009 of 18 December 2008 on jurisdiction, applicable law, recognition and enforcement of decisions and co-operation in matters relating to maintenance obligations. The Regulation is due to apply from 18 June 2011.

not contained in the latter instrument itself. Instead reference is made to the Hague Protocol of 23 November 2007 on the law applicable to maintenance obligations.

All Member States — with the exception of Denmark, the United Kingdom and Ireland — will be bound by the Hague Protocol if the European Union, which in 2007 became a Member of the Hague Conference on Private International Law [149], ratifies it. This is a new form of co-operation resulting in a division of tasks between the global and the regional legislator which is greatly to be welcomed [150].

81. The Lisbon Treaty has enlarged the Community's competences in the field of private international law. Article 81 TFEU provides that measures in the field of judicial co-operation in civil measures shall be

---

[149] By depositing the instrument of acceptance of the Statute of the Hague Conference. This admission of the European Community (since 1 December 2009 replaced by the European Union) to the Hague Conference comes in addition to the individual membership of all 27 EU Member States, all of which are already Members of the Hague Conference. See H. Van Loon and A. Schulz, "The European Community and the Hague Conference on Private International Law", in B. Martenczuk and S. Van Thiel (eds.), *Justice, Liberty, Security : New Challenges for EU External Relations* (2008) 257-299. They predict that the Hague Conference on Private International Law will continue to be a major forum for the elaboration and monitoring of private international law treaties linking the European Community and its Member States with the other States of the world (299).

[150] W. Duncan, "The Hague Convention of 23 November 2007 on the International Recovery of Child Support and Other Forms of Family Maintenance, Comments on Its Objectives and Some of Its Special Features", *Yearbook of Private International Law* (2008) 313-331 ; A. Bonomi, "The Hague Protocol on the Law Applicable to Maintenance Obligations", *Yearbook of Private International Law* (2008) 333-357.

adopted, "particularly when necessary for the proper functioning of the internal market" whereas Article 65 EC Treaty required that the measures were to be taken "in so far as necessary for the proper functioning of the internal market". The decision to adopt measures on the basis of Article 81 TFEU thus no longer only depends on the internal market criterion [151]. Furthermore, the position of Denmark has changed. Just as Ireland and the United Kingdom already had under Protocol 4 to the Amsterdam Treaty, Denmark has acquired the possibility to opt in into the adoption of the measures taken under Title V of the TFEU.

82. Since within the European Union private international law has become European law [152], the European Court of Justice is competent to interpret the respective Regulations and it is worthwhile mentioning that this regional court acquires competence in respect of some of the Hague Conventions once they will have entered into force for the European Union [153]. To date, no decisions on the interpretation of conflict of law rules contained in Regulations have been delivered [154].

---

[151] G.-R. De Groot and J.-J. Kuipers, "The New Provisions on Private International Law in the Treaty of Lisbon", *Maastricht Journal of International and Comparative Law* (2008) 113-118 (111).

[152] K. Boele-Woelki and R. Van Ooik, "The Communautarization of Private International Law", *Yearbook of Private International Law* (2002) 1-36.

[153] R. Wagner, "Die Haager Konferenz für Internationales Privatrecht zehn Jahre nach der Vergemeinschaftung der Gesetzgebungskompetenz in der justiziellen Zusammenarbeit in Zivilsachen", *Rabels Zeitschrift für internationales und ausländisches Privatrecht* (2009) 215-240 (238-239).

[154] The first private international law decisions of the European Court of Justice concern the interpretation of provisions of the Brussels I and Brussels II *bis* Regulations.

However, shortly before the Rome Convention of 1980 on the law applicable to contractual obligations had been transformed into the Rome I Regulation the Protocol establishing the competence of the European Court of Justice to interpret the Rome Convention entered into force [155]. The decisions of the Court regarding provisions of the Rome Convention are of equal importance for the application and interpretation of the Rome I Regulation as far as similar provisions are concerned [156].

Prior to Lisbon, the ability of a national court to refer a case for a preliminary ruling to the European Court of Justice was limited to national courts against whose decision there was no legal remedy.

The Treaty of Lisbon made the normal preliminary procedure of Article 267 TFEU (formerly Article 234 TEC) also applicable in cases concerning Title V on the Area of Freedom, Security and Justice to which Chapter 3 on Judicial Co-operation in Judicial Matters belongs. The Treaty of Lisbon will thus have the effect that every national court may request a preliminary ruling.

3. *National Statute Law and Case Law*

83. The general assertion that private international law is merely private law and is thereby, in principle, national law emanates from days of old. It requires modification [157]. The more unification takes place at the international and regional level, the less important,

---

[155] The Protocol entered into force on 1 August 2004 for the old 15 Member States.

[156] The ECJ judgment of 6 October 2009, C-133/08, concerning the interpretation of Article 4 (5) of the Rome Convention 1980 is also relevant for Article 4 (3) of the Rome I Regulation.

[157] Boele-Woelki, *op. cit.*, footnote 141, 61.

in terms of their restricted application, do national private international law statutes become, at least as far as the legal systems of the Member States of the European Union are concerned. At the national level the codification of private international law is either part of the (introductory part of) the national Civil Code or the Civil Code of Procedure or is laid down in independent statutes.

84. In Europe, the most recent national statutes on private international law have been enacted in 2004 in Belgium [158] and in 2005 in Bulgaria [159]. Following the example of the Swiss legislator in 1987 these codifications contain all three aspects of private international law (jurisdiction, applicable law and recognition and enforcement), whereas in other countries with older codifications the different parts are divided among several legal sources. In October 2009, the bill for a Dutch Private International Law statute was introduced. It merely contains rules of applicable law since it will become Book 10 of the Dutch Civil Code [160]. In some jurisdictions — predominately in the common-law systems — not all private international law issues are regulated by statute but are rather decided by the courts (judge-made law). The courts develop the rules on applicable law by referring to precedents or — as far

[158] J. Erauw, "Brief Description of the Draft Belgian Code on Private International Law", *Yearbook of Private International Law* (2002) 145-161.

[159] Z. Jordanka and V. Stanceva-Minceva, "Gesetzbuch über das Internationale Privatrecht der Republik Bulgarien", *Rabels Zeitschrift für ausländisches und internationales Privatrecht* (2007) 398-456.

[160] Handelingen der Tweede Kamer (Parliamentary documents) 32137. See K. Boele-Woelki and D. van Iterson, "The Dutch Private International Law Codification : Principles, Objectives and Opportunities", Contribution to the International Academy of Comparative Law, Washington, D.C., July 25 to August 1, 2010.

as the United States of America is concerned — to
Restatements, such as the Restatement Second on
Conflict of Laws [161].

---

[161] Between 1984 and 1988 the American Law Institute developed revisions of selected portions of the 1971
text of Restatement Second, Conflict of Laws. The revisions obtained final approval in May 1988.

PART II

THE INTERACTION

85. Two questions, at least, arise as regards the relationship between instruments designed to unify or harmonize substantive law on the one hand and those containing conflict of law rules on the other : how do these instruments interact with, and are they interdependent on, each other ? How does each fulfil its designated tasks without distressing the other ? These questions are explored in this Part in which we examine the issues at the core of this book. In Chapter VII the scope of application of unifying and harmonizing substantive law instruments is analysed. It will be demonstrated that unifying substantive law instruments partially make use of conflict of law rules with the purpose of prescribing their scope of application whereas harmonizing substantive law instruments cannot draw on conflict of law rules. The answers provided by various conflict of law rules to the question whether unifying and harmonizing substantive law rules can be applied in cross-border relationships are investigated in Chapter VIII.

CHAPTER VII

THE SCOPE OF APPLICATION OF UNIFYING
AND HARMONIZING SUBSTANTIVE LAW
INSTRUMENTS

86. The central theme addressed in this lecture
focuses on the possibility of applying a law other than
national substantive law in cross-border relationships.
The previous chapters contain information about which
kind of instruments may be taken into account. In this
chapter the following questions will be analysed :

(1) What are the requirements for the application of
    unifying and harmonizing substantive law instru-
    ments ?
(2) Does it make a difference whether the instrument
    is aimed at unifying or harmonizing substantive
    law ?

This part of the investigation starts by observing that,
particularly for the unification of private law, both the
enactment of uniform law by States as well as the
application of uniform law in legal practice depend
decisively on the requirements which, according to the
relevant instrument, must be fulfilled. Both these situations can be seen as indications of "acceptance" of the
application of a law other than national substantive law
and in this context it has been argued that probably
such a technical framework of uniform law — the prescription of its scope of application — is even more
important for its reception than the content of the
instrument [162].

---

[162] U. G. Schroeter, "Schaffung und Akzeptanz einheitlichen Privatrechts in Europa", *Lehren aus der Anwendung des UN-Kaufrechts für ein Europäisches Vertragsrecht*, Internationale Juristenvereinigung Osnabrück,

1. One Side of the Coin : How to Regulate the Scope of Application ?

87. Many international Conventions have regulated, distinctively, the circumstances under which they are to be applied. The drafters of both the UNIDROIT Principles and the Principles of European Contract Law have also indicated those requirements which must be met in order to apply these Principles in cross-border relationships. Evidently, the issue of applicability is one of the first issues to be addressed in the various respective instruments. Whether the conflict of law rules of the forum accept the applicability of the Principles, for example, is a different question. This could not and cannot be decided by those organizations and academic commissions which have been drafting and adopting instruments aimed at harmonizing substantive law. In this respect there is a clear difference between unifying and harmonizing substantive law instruments. States decide whether to ratify an international Convention containing uniform substantive law. They decide whether to enact a Model Law or — considering the situation in the United States — a uniform law. Finally, States decide, according to their conflict of law rules, whether a law other than national substantive law — which might not be uniform law — can be applied. This latter question, for instance, gave rise to a profound debate when the Rome I Regulation on the law applicable to contracts [163] was being drafted and adopted [164].

Jahresheft 2007 (2008) 35-58 (36). He discusses European contract law as a "Regelwerk, das in Form eines Gemeinschaftsrechtsaktes erlassen wurde. Auf die genaue Rechtsform und den genauen Inhalt kommt es dabei zunächst nicht entscheidend an."

[163] (EC) No. 593/2008, *Official Journal of the European Union* 2008, L 177/6.

[164] See *infra* Chapter VIII, Section 3.1.2.

Other instruments, such as the Principles of European Tort Law, the Principles of European Family Law or the American Restatements, lack provisions which specify the circumstances under which they are to be applied. For various reasons the drafters did not have in mind that their instrument might be applied as the law governing a cross-border relationship. Instead, the instruments only focus on their probable harmonizing effect on substantive law in the various individual jurisdictions.

88. In respect of the potential creation of a European law of obligations [165], for example, the question arises as to how such a uniform law could be applied in practice. This question should definitely not be neglected by those who are currently drafting this new European contract and delict/tort law. If, eventually, the European legislator were to adopt such a new law as European law in the form of a Regulation, the question of its application would have to be answered.

Ignoring this aspect would result in problems since the absence of the appropriate application rules would simply aggravate the tendency for uniform law to produce a rich hunting-ground for doctoral theses, which, for decades, result in a huge amount of publications, but remain a dead letter as far as legal practice is concerned [166]. Moreover, however splendid the law might be "in the books", it may simply be an illusion of progress were the administrative machinery to give this law a degree of force in practice not to be put in place [167].

---

[165] See *infra* Chapter VII, Section 5.

[166] In this sense see P. Schlechtriem, *Einheitliches Kaufrecht — wissenschaftliches Modell oder praxisnahe Regelung ?* (1978) 7, cited by Schroeter, *op. cit.*, footnote 162, 38-39.

[167] R. Cranston, "Theorizing Transnational Commercial Law", *Texas International Law Journal* (2007) 597-617 (616).

2. The Key Question : Replacement,
Opt-Out or Opt-In

89. When investigating the question whether unifying and harmonizing substantive law instruments can be applied in cross-border relationships, the key question is *how* they can be applied — instead of national substantive law — as the law governing the cross-border relationship. What approaches are available ? Which rules determining the applicability of the various instruments are currently effective ? Which approach should be chosen for future instruments ? What are the pros and cons of selecting one above the other ? Which interests are at stake ? Hence, many questions arise when the scope of application of an instrument is to be determined or the applicability of an instrument is investigated. This depends on various aspects.

Essentially, three options are available :

1. States replace national substantive law by uniform substantive law which is to be applied in cross-border situations (the *stand-in approach*).
2. The unifying substantive law instruments are applicable to cross-border relationships subject to the parties' exclusion of their applicability (the *opt-out approach*).
3. The parties determine that unifying or harmonizing substantive law instruments should govern their cross-border relationship (the *opt-in approach*).

In the following paragraphs all three options will be discussed, exemplified and compared.

3. Uniform Substantive Law Replaces National Substantive Law

90. The most far-reaching option is that where national substantive law is totally replaced by uniform

substantive law [168]. This decision is taken by States, for example, which ratify an international Convention containing uniform substantive law rules. Another frequently discussed scenario within the framework of the creation of a European law of obligations is that where the European legislature enacts substantive law rules which belong to the *acquis communautaire* [169]. Consequently, they are effective in all European Member States bound by them. In both situations two approaches are to be distinguished : first, national substantive law is only replaced or, at best complemented, by uniform rules which only apply to international relationships. In such a case internal relationships are still governed by national substantive law. As a result, two sets of substantive law rules exist alongside each other : substantive law rules derived from the international or regional legislator for international relationships and substantive law rules derived from the national legislature for internal relationships. Second, uniform law rules replace those of national law and apply to both international and domestic relationships.

In the following paragraphs examples are provided of co-operation at international and regional levels with a focus on the most important instruments which have been or will be adopted.

---

[168] S. Leible and M. Müller, "Der 'blue button' für den Internetshop, Ein optionales Instrument für den E-Commerce ?", *Kommunikation und Recht* (2009) 7-14 (10-11), indicate this option as a "Vollharmonisierung".

[169] The Community *acquis* is the body of common rights and obligations which bind all the Member States together within the European Union. It comprises not only Community law in the strict sense, but also all acts adopted under the second and third pillars of the European Union and the common objectives laid down in the Treaties. Derogations from the *acquis* are granted only in exceptional circumstances and are limited in scope. See europa.eu/scadplus/glossary/community_acquis_en.htm.

3.1. International co-operation in the field of contract law

91. The CISG provides the best example of the dual existence of substantive law. States which have ratified this Convention apply, on the one hand, for international sales contracts, international substantive law rules subject to the parties' exclusion of the Convention rules [170], and on the other, for internal sales contracts, national substantive rules [171]. A similar approach is applied in the UNIDROIT Conventions on International Financial Leasing and International Factoring concluded on 28 May 1988 [172].

92. The rules of the Leasing Convention are to be applied if the lessor and the lessee have their places of business in different States and those States, and the State in which the supplier has its principal place of business, are contracting States (Art. 3 (1) *(a)*) or both the supply agreement and the leasing agreement are governed by the law of a contracting state (Art. 3 (1) *(b)*), subject however to the parties' exclusion of the Convention rules (Art. 5). The option under Article 3

---

[170] Online databases such as the one of Pace University or CISG online make a majority of cases available. The analysis and categorization of these cases, in the form of regular overviews covering the courts of all signatories and also arbitral tribunals, increases the CISG's familiarity. See I. Bach, "Neuere Rechtsprechung zum UN-Kaufrecht", *Praxis des internationalen Privat- und Verfahrensrechts* (2009) 299-306.

[171] The scope of application of the CISG is explained in more detail in Chapter VIII, Section 1.

[172] See, for an exhaustive overview of substantive uniform law in the field of contracts, U. Magnus, "Europäisches Vertragsrecht und materielles Einheitsrecht — künftige Symbiose oder störende Konkurrenz", in H.-P. Mansel, Th. Pfeiffer, H. Kronke, Ch. Kohler and R. Hausmann (eds.), *Festschrift für Erik Jayme*, Vol. 2 (2004) 1307-1321 (1313-1315).

(1) *(b)* is of particular importance if the parties have designated the law of a contracting State. If the requirements of the scope of application of the Convention are met, the uniform substantive law rules of the Convention are to be applied. They replace domestic rules if the leasing relationship has cross-border elements.

93. The International Factoring Convention prescribes its scope of application in a different way but the effect is identical. The substantive law rules of the Convention apply whenever the receivables assigned pursuant to a factoring contract arise from a contract of sale of goods between a supplier and a debtor whose places of business are in different States and those States and the State in which the factor has its place of business are Contracting States (Art. 2 (1) *(a)*) or both the contract of sale of goods and the factoring contract are governed by the law of a Contracting State (Art. 2 (1) *(b)*), unless the parties have not excluded the Convention regime (Art. 3).

3.2. *The OHADA co-operation in the field of contract law*

94. The total replacement of national substantive law by uniform substantive law for both kinds of relationships, internal as well as international, constitutes another approach. This form of legal integration eliminates the differences between the national provisions by replacing them with a unique and identical text for all the States involved in the legal integration process [173].

---

[173] Mancuso, *op. cit.*, footnote 51, 159 :

"This process can be pursued in two different ways : the text is submitted to national parliaments who may adopt it as it is, modify it or even reject it, or the

The OHADA [174], provides a good example of this technique. This African collaboration aims to implement a modern legal framework in the area of business law in order to promote investment and develop economic growth. The Treaty calls for the elaboration of Uniform Acts to be directly applicable in Member States, notwithstanding any provision of domestic law [175]. The OHADA has set up a significant infrastructure with a single court and a growing number of uniform acts in which the issue of contract law has been addressed. Book 5 of the Uniform Act of 1997 Relating to General Commercial Law is dedicated entirely to commercial sales, namely "to contracts of sale of goods between traders, be they natural persons or corporate bodies" [176]. It should be noted, in this respect, that in the area of commercial sales, none of the African States party to the OHADA Treaty have signed the CISG. More importantly, at the request of UNIDROIT, a member of the UNIDROIT Study Group for the Preparation of the Principles [177] drafted the OHADA Uniform Act on Contract Law which, in 2004 [178], was submitted to the OHADA Permanent Bureau [179]. This Act also draws heavily upon the CISG and as a result

---

adopted text contains the principle of supra-nationality, by which the uniform norm is directly integrated into the domestic legal order."

[174] See Chapter III, Section 1.3.1.

[175] Mancuso, *op. cit.*, footnote 51, 165.

[176] www.jurisint.org/ohada/text/text.02.en.html.

[177] This task was performed by Marcel Fontaine. See S. K. Date-Bah, "The Preliminary Draft OHADA Uniform Act on Contract Law as Seen by a Common Law Lawyer", *Uniform Law Review* (2008) 217-222 (219).

[178] Hagge, *op. cit.*, footnote 79.

[179] The UNIDROIT Principles have been taken as a model. See M. Fontaine, "The OHADA Uniform Act on Contract Law, Explanatory Notes to the Preliminary Draft", www.unidroit.org/english/legalcooperation/

illustrates how regional and international unification of the law can co-operate. The provision determining the scope of application of this Act (Art. 00/1) recommends that it should be applied to all contracts both commercial and non-commercial. Furthermore, no distinction is made between domestic and international contracts [180].

3.3. *European co-operation in the field of private law*

95. The situation in the European Union is different. Within the framework of the creation of a European law of obligations the idea to replace the 27 national systems [181] by one single European Civil Code has been proffered but, allegedly, this option will not become reality due to current lack of political support [182]. However, according to the Chairman of the

---

OHADA%20explanatory%20note-e.pdf. See also the contributions and documents to the Colloquium at Ouagadougou (Burkina Faso), 15-17 November 2007, in *Uniform Law Review/Revue de droit uniform* (2008). Furthermore, see extensively on the preparation by UNIDROIT of the OHADA Uniform Act on Contract Law, www.unidroit.org/english/legalcooperation/ohada.htm.

[180] E. Hondius, "CISG and a European Civil Code, Some Reflexions", *Rabels Zeitschrift für ausländisches und internationales Privatrecht* (2007) 99-114 (111). He considers the OHADA to be one of the most promising parts of the world where the regional harmonization of sales law is realized.

[181] One could probably better speak of 29 legal systems within the European Union since the United Kingdom comprehends three different systems : England and Wales, Northern Ireland and Scotland of which the latter is distinct from the other two as a result of having its origins in the civil (French and Roman-Dutch) law tradition.

[182] Ch. Von Bar, "A Common Frame of Reference for European Private Law — Academic Efforts and Political Realities", 12.1 *Electronic Journal of Comparative Law* (2008) 1-10 (3-4) www.ejcl.org.

Study Group on a European Civil Code, Christian von Bar, no sleep should be lost over the question whether or not the drafting of the Common Frame of Reference for European Private Law is, "in reality", all about the creation of a European Civil Code. In his view the "reality" is that it does not matter whether one responds to this in the positive or in the negative sense [183]. The century-old civil law codifications in Germany or France, for instance, which have recently been reformed, or the new codifications of civil law in the new EU Member States, which acceded to the European Union in 2004, will not be replaced by one

---

[183] Von Bar, *op. cit.*, footnote 182, 3. He continues :

"It clearly has to be answered in the negative if by a 'European Civil Code' we mean a legislative instrument like the *Code Napoléon,* the *Codice civile* or the *Bürgerliches Gesetzbuch.* That is definitely not the idea, not even mine ! (My reasons for that, however, would have nothing to do with political or 'diplomatic' considerations of any sort ; I simply believe that such a major step requires more time and more detailed knowledge about each other's systems than we possess today.) But the question of the European Civil Code could equally be answered in the positive if the Common Frame of Reference were to become a success and be used at least for some of the purposes I mentioned earlier."

In respect of these latter purposes Von Bar refers, among other things, to the integration of all the relevant EU instruments, to the possibility of teaching students from all over Europe on the basis of an identical text and to the assistance which Europe, as the home for private law, can offer to non-European countries in their quest to modernize their private law systems. But see S. Grundmann, "La structure du DCFR : quelle forme pour un droit européen des contrats ?", *Revue de droit international et de droit comparé* (2009) 423-453 (425-427), who argues that the core members of the Study Group on a European Civil Code see the DCFR as a potential model for a European Civil Code.

new single European instrument. Attempts to impose such a uniform system on all Member States are not to be expected [184].

96. If, instead, European civil law rules will only be enacted alongside national substantive law it is also highly questionable whether, in the long run Member States will eventually replace their national substantive law by the European system. This depends on the "success" or, as has been indicated earlier, the "acceptance" of these rules. But how can they be tested ? Only by comparing the European solutions with national solutions, a task to be carried out predominantly by legal scholars ? To this author's knowledge the precise effect of legal writings on any law-making process has not yet been measured empirically. However, even if the European rules were to be given, generally, a positive evaluation, their direct use and application in legal practice would be needed also since they would be intended ultimately to regulate specific legal relationships and to provide solutions for disputes if they arise.

Obviously, the drafters of the European rules on the law of obligations would like not only that national legislators should take them as a model when reforming their law, but also that the courts would take notice of, gain inspiration from or, even, apply these rules ; they want the rules to "percolate" into national systems. Drafting the rules for academic purposes only would not be acceptable. In addition to the purpose of a European private law to provide a model for interna-

---

[184] See the Communication from the Commission to the European Parliament and the Council, A more Coherent European Contract Law, An Action Plan, COM (2003) 68 final No. 92. In particular from the viewpoint of electronic consumer contracts the idea is rejected by Leible and Müller, *op. cit.*, footnote 168, 7-14.

tional, regional and national legislators alike, direct
application of these rules is envisaged.

97. Consequently, the time will come for the water
to be tested as regards both objectives and, given the
fact that a European law of obligations should be
drafted from a truly pan-European perspective, cross-
border relationships are the best test-case scenarios for
this purpose. It depends on the instrument to be
adopted whether conflict of law rules are to be consulted : should they allow the application of norms
other than national norms ?

This question attracts our main interest. In Chapter
VII, Section 5, the idea of applying a set of European
substantive law rules as the twenty-eighth or thir-
tieth [185] legal system within the European Union, next
to national substantive law rules, will be taken further
by investigating which cross-border relationships are
suitable for fulfilling this aim and who is to decide on
their applicability.

3.4. *Nordic co-operation in the field of family law*

98. Another example of legal integration removing
differences between national systems is provided by
the initiatives for Nordic co-operation in the field of
family law which is mainly confined to provisions on
marriage, divorce, maintenance and matrimonial property [186]. Between 1909 and 1927 major law reforms
took place in the Nordic countries (Denmark, Finland,
Iceland, Norway and Sweden) [187]. This co-operation

---

[185] See footnote 181, *supra*.

[186] S. Blomstrand, "Nordic Co-operation on Legislation in the Field of Private Law", *Scandinavian Studies in
Law* (2000) 59-77 (69-71).

[187] I. Lund-Andersen, "Approximation of Nordic Family
Law within the Framework of Nordic Cooperation", in
M. Antokolskaia (ed.), *Convergence and Divergence of*

led to the enactment, in the years from 1913 to 1927, of rules for married couples (Act on Contraction and Dissolution of Marriage and the Act on the Legal Effects of Marriage in Denmark, and corresponding legislation in Norway and Sweden) which were based on the recommendations of the Nordic committees. Interestingly, these enactments were characterized as unifications since the Nordic co-operation produced texts which the different parliaments adopted with only minor amendments, hence the creation of uniform texts was the goal. The overall result was legislation which was almost identical in both structure and wording in the various Nordic countries. In this context it has been suggested that the argument in the Nordic debate of today for or against harmonization is more of a series

---

Family Law in Europe, European Family Law Series No. 18 (2007) 51-61 (52-56), provides a brief historical overview of the Nordic Cooperation :

"In 1872, the Nordic Lawyers Meetings was established which every three years met in order to discuss a number of the most current legal issues are discussed *[sic]*. After World War II there was a great desire to strengthen cooperation between the 5 Nordic countries. Two official bodies were established, both having the development of legal cooperation as one of their aims. In 1952 the *Nordic Council* was set up ; this is a body for promoting cooperation between the parliaments of the Nordic countries. And in 1971, as an addition to this, the *Nordic Council of Ministers* was set up, to promote cooperation between governments. In addition, in the area of family law, since 1980 a *Nordic Family Law Seminar* has been held each alternate year. This is an association for cooperation on family law in the Nordic countries. The seminars are arranged in turn in one of the Nordic universities and last for 2-3 days. The number of participants is limited to a maximum of 40 specially invited family law experts. In addition to legal academics, the participants include advocates and representatives from government ministries with responsibilities for family law."

of debates for or against a higher degree of unification [188]. The quasi-unified rules on marriage, divorce, maintenance and matrimonial property were applied in internal and inter-Scandinavian relationships ; later, in the 1980s and 1990s the five Nordic countries amended separately the Nordic "uniform" family laws [189].

3.5. Comparison : various stages and levels of success

99. In conclusion it can be stated that the question whether uniform substantive law is to be applied in cross-border relationships is evidently decided by States. Based on international treaties they can either ratify a substantive law Convention or enact Uniform Acts. The CISG has taken the lead in respect of the number of contracting States. However, it is still the situation that many countries with comparatively strong economies are not yet bound by the Convention regime, examples being the United Kingdom, Portugal and Brazil. The OHADA Uniform Acts exemplify how, within a short period of time, the law of contract has been unified successfully in 16 African States. In respect of the Nordic co-operation it has been questioned whether the Uniform Acts can be considered to have been a success, given the fact that the Nordic countries modified them individually and enacted new statutes. Within the framework of the European Union

---

[188] P. Lødrup, "The Reharmonisation of Nordic Family Law", in K. Boele-Woelki and T. Sverdrup (eds.), *European Challenges in Contemporary Family Law*, European Family Law Series No. 23 (2008) 17-26 (18).

[189] For this reason it has been questioned whether the Nordic co-operation really was a success. See E. Örücü, "A Family Law for Europe : Necessary, Feasible, Desirable ?", in K. Boele-Woelki (ed.), *Perspectives for the Unification and Harmonisation of Family Law in Europe*, European Family Law Series No. 4 (2003) 551-572.

it is up to the European Institutions to decide whether and, if so, how to legislate in the field of substantive law.

In some policy areas, regional legislative measures in the form of Directives have already been taken. In addition, the legal basis for a European Regulation containing substantive law has been provided by Article 308 EC Treaty (Article 352 Treaty of Lisbon), although indisputably it will be carefully scrutinized as to whether such legislation has any, or no, substantial connection with the internal market [190]. All legislative activities lie in the future. It is beyond doubt that the question as to how well a European unification of substantive law is doing will be evaluated in terms of the scope and content of the rules, information about its existence and its application in actual practice.

4. Unifying and Harmonizing Substantive Law Competes with National Substantive Law : How to Solve the Issue of Concurrence/Coincidence

100. The following two approaches as to how a law other than national law can be applied in cross-border relationships have been discussed extensively during the preparation of a Community instrument containing substantive law rules for the law of obligations [191]. It all started in 2003 with a Communication from the Commission to the European Parliament and the

---

[190] See, for instance, House of Commons, European Scrutiny Committee, Article 308 of the EC Treaty, Twenty-ninth Report of Session 2006-07, www.publications.parliament.uk/pa/cm200607/cmselect/cmeuleg/41-xxix/41-xxix.pdf.

[191] J. M. Smits, "Europese integratie in het vermogensrecht : een pleidooi voor keuzevrijheid, Preadvies Nederlandse Juristen-Vereniging 2006", in 136 *Handelingen Nederlandse Juristen-Vereniging* (2006) 57-104.

Council requesting a more coherent European contract law.

The idea of an optional instrument was born [192] :

> "The Commission will examine whether non-sector-specific-measures such as an optional instrument may be required to solve problems in the area of European contract law. It intends to launch a reflection on the opportuneness, the possible form, the contents and the legal basis for possible action of such measures. As to its form one could think of EU wide contract law rules in the form of a regulation or a recommendation, which would exist in parallel with, rather than instead of national contract laws. This new instrument would exist in all Community languages. It could either apply to all contracts, which concern cross-border transactions or only to those which parties decide to subject to it through a choice of law clause. The latter would give parties the greatest degree of contractual freedom. They would only choose the new instrument if it suited their economic or legal needs better than the national law which would have been determined by private international law rules as the law applicable to the contract."

This idea of an optional instrument has been considered substantially since the submission of the original Communication [193]. In a further Communication to the European Parliament and Council of 10 June 2009 the European Commission has developed the idea by

---

[192] See the Communication from the Commission to the European Parliament and the Council, A More Coherent European Contract Law, An Action Plan, COM (2003) 68 final No. 92.

[193] J. M. Smits, *The Need of a European Contract Law* (2005) 155-179.

stating that, in the area of freedom, security and justice serving citizens, consideration could be given to an optional, specifically European, system of rules open to companies.

This system would be similar to those devised for other areas of the internal market, such as the European company, the European economic interest grouping or the Community trade mark, and would encourage the development of intra-Community trade and establish a single, directly applicable, legal framework [194].

101. The more far-reaching option, namely, to apply a European substantive law instrument automatically in all cross-border cases, as does the CISG, is not yet excluded [195].

The pertinent policy questions to be considered and decided are as to whether the parties should only have the possibility to exclude the application of the rules in such an instrument (the *opt-out approach*) or — to choose a less far-reaching option — should such a set of European rules only apply if the parties express jointly that their relationship should be governed by these rules (the *opt-in approach*) and what should happen if the parties only determine that instead of national substantive law general principles of (contract or delict/tort) law should be applied ?

Both approaches will require to be discussed and tested in relation to any proposal for a substantive uniform law intended to be adopted, eventually, by the European legislator. In respect of this future instrument

---

[194] COM (2009) 262 final.
[195] P. Mankowski, "CFR und Rechtswahl", in M. Schmidt-Kessel (ed.), *Der Gemeinsame Referenzrahmen, Entstehung, Inhalte, Anwendung* (2009), 391-433 (416), considers this option to be utopian from a political point of view.

some legal scholars have already proffered several appealing ideas and the issue is highly topical. A discussion of the recent idea, submitted by other legal scholars, to draft a new global uniform code in international sales law [196], given that the CISG has been unsuccessful in attaining its goal of uniformity [197], will

---

[196] Ch. Sheaffer, "The Failure of the United Nations Conventions on Contracts for the International Sales of Goods and a Proposal for a New Uniform Global Code in International Sales Law", *Cardozo Journal of International and Comparative Law* (2007) 461-495 (494). According to the author's view

"the CISG is a perfect starting point for an international commercial code ; it simply should be reformed. With UNCITRAL in a position to act as a regulatory council, it could easily issue advisory opinions and provide guidance for interpretation. UNIDROIT has already drafted what could be the official commentary to accompany the new statutory text. Finally, CLOUT and UNILEX make international decisions easily accessible to both courts and scholars, permitting the evaluation of prior decisions to render well-reasoned, uniform judgments with highly persuasive authority."

[197] The idea is supported by G. Cuniberti, "Is the CISG Benefiting Anybody", *Vanderbilt Journal of Transnational Law* (2006), 1511-1550 1550) :

"the flaws of the CISG may disappear one day. The CISG may have been just the first step towards complete harmonization. . . . Retrospectively, the CISG will appear as a transition towards a better world. It will have been a necessary evil."

See also J. E. Bailey, "Facing the Truth : Seeing the Convention on Contracts for the International Sale of Goods as an Obstacle to a Uniform Law of International Sales", *Cornell International Law Journal* (1999) 273-317, and O. Lando, "CISG and Its Followers : A Proposal to Adopt Some International Principles of Contract Law", *American Journal of Comparative Law* (2005), 379-401 (401) :

"The present troika of contract rules in the CISG,

not be undertaken, however interesting that idea might be [198].

5. *The Future European Substantive Law Instrument for Cross-border Relationships*

102. In view of the possibility of the coming into existence of a new comprehensive European instrument containing substantive law rules (hereafter : the European instrument) [199] — most likely in the field of

---

    UPICC and PECL has set a model for the future World Contract Law, which is now in sight, first as a 'creeping and informal codification' and later as a Global Code of International Commercial Contracts. The rapidly growing world trade and communication are in need of that."

And O. Lando, "Principles of European Contract Law and UNIDROIT Principles : Moving from Harmonisation to Unification ?", *Uniform Law Review/Revue de droit uniforme* (2003) 123-133 (132-133). From a different angel it has been argued that the UNIDROIT Principles should be considered as a general part of transnational contract law. See Michaels, *op. cit.*, footnote 6, 885-887.

[198] M. J. Bonell, "Towards a Legislative Codification of the UNIDROIT Principles ?", *Uniform Law Review/Revue de droit uniforme* (2007) 233-245 (244) :

    "UNCITRAL may prepare, in co-operation with other interested international organisations a 'Global Commercial Code' to be adopted in the form of a Model Law which refers to the UNIDROIT Principles as its 'general contract law' applicable to the specific contracts covered by the Code unless otherwise agreed by the parties. The UNIDROIT Principles, however, should not be transformed into binding legislation in the form of an international Convention since it is 'neither feasible nor recommendable'."

[199] The choice of the most suitable instrument has been discussed in the Communication from the Commission to the Council and the European Parliament on European Contract Law, COM (2001) 398 final : a Directive would,

contract [200] delict and tort [201] and the law of property —
it is worthwhile reflecting upon the likely interaction
of such an instrument with conflict of law rules [202]
since, for good reasons, it would be used not only as a
model for national or international law-makers but it
would be applied also as regards cross-border relationships [203]. In this context it should be mentioned that the
EU Treaty does not limit the European Union to take
measures only in cross-border cases or disputes.
According to Article 81 TFEU the European Union can
take measures in "matters having cross border implications". It is therefore

---

on the one hand, give Member States a certain degree of
flexibility to adapt the respective provisions of the implementation law to their specific national economic and legal
situation. On the other hand, it may allow differences in
implementation which could constitute obstacles to the
"proper" functioning of the internal market. A Regulation
would give the Member States less flexibility for its integration into the national legal systems, but on the other
hand it would ensure more transparent and uniform conditions for economic operators in the internal market
whereas a Recommendation could only be envisaged if a
purely optional model is chosen.

[200] S. Grundmann and M. Schauer (eds.), *The Architecture of European Codes and Contract Law* (2006) 3-30,
and Grundmann, *op. cit.*, footnote 183, 423-453. But see
C. Kessedjian, "Uniformity v. Diversity in Law in a Global
World — the Example of Commercial and Procedural
Law", *Hellenic Review of International Law* (2008) 319-
333 who concludes that, for the time, being there is no
hope for a uniform system of contract law in Europe.

[201] Critically, N. Jansen, "Negotiorum gestio und Benevolent Intervention in Another's Affairs : Principles of
European Law ?", *Zeitschrift für Europäisches Privatrecht*
(2007) 958-991 (958-959).

[202] Mankowski, *op. cit.*, footnote 195, 393 : "Die Frage
(ob man den CFR oder den Draft CFR) wählen kann, ist
eine fundamentele Frage, und sie wird sich noch für eine
ganze Weile in voller Schärfe stellen."

[203] Schroeter, *op. cit.*, footnote 162, 35.

"legally possible to adopt legislation which also applies to situations which are being referred to as 'domestic', provided that the subject-area of the legislation is one with cross-border 'implications' and the proposed measures respect the principles of proportionality and subsidiarity" [204].

103. In a short study for the European Parliament on the different options for a future instrument on the Common Frame of Reference in EU contract law, in particular the legal form of, and the legal basis for, any future optional instrument, the authors concluded that it seems likely that Article 352 TFEU (formerly Article 308 EC Treaty) could provide a legal basis for adopting one or more optional instruments on subjects of contract law which are particularly relevant to the operation of the Internal Market. From the perspective of the legal basis it would not make a difference whether the optional instruments would be applicable to B2B, B2C or to both, nor whether they would apply only to cross-border contracts or also to purely internal contracts [205].

104. The Preamble to the Rome I Regulation, which is based on Article 65 EC Treaty, states explicitly in its recital (14) that "[s]hould the Community adopt, in an appropriate legal instrument, rules of substantive contract law, including standard terms and conditions, such instrument may provide that the parties may choose to apply those rules" [206]. No similar

---

[204] F. Frattini, "European Area of Civil Justice — Has the Community Reached the Limits ?", *Zeitschrift für Europäisches Privatrecht* (2006) 225-235 (231).

[205] M. W. Hesselink, J. W. Rutgers and T. De Booys, *The Legal Basis for an Optional Instrument on European Contract Law*, Centre for the Study of European Contract Law Working Paper Series (2007) No. 04, 71-72.

[206] (EC) No. 593/2008, *Official Journal of the European Union* 2008, L 177/6.

recital is contained in the Rome II Regulation [207] ; however, it has been proposed that a future optional instrument which covers non-contractual obligations should be made available to the parties so that they can choose it as the *lex delicti* [208]. The adoption of such a European instrument — will it even be a Code [209] ? — lies in the future ; however, the essential components already exist in the form of the Draft Common Frame of Reference which will be followed by a Common Frame of Reference [210] to be created by the European institutions [211]. It had already been concluded in 2002

---

[207] (EC) No. 864/2007, *Official Journal of the European Union* 2007, L 199/40.

[208] S. Leible, "Rechtswahl im IPR der ausservertraglichen Schuldverhätnisse nach der Rom II-Verordnung", *Recht der Internationalen Wirtschaft* (2008) 257-264 (261).

[209] D. Wallis, "Is it a Code ?", *Zeitschrift für Europäisches Privatrecht* (2006), 513-514 ; Grundmann, *op. cit.*, footnote 183, 423-453 ; Hondius, *op. cit.*, footnote 180, 99-114 ; Schulte-Nölke, *op. cit.*, footnote 89, 2167 :

> "Der DCFR schafft lediglich eine neue Grundlage für eine europäische Diskussion, die Gemeinsames und Trennendes offenlegt und gegenseitige Kenntnis fördert. Eine europäische Rechtswissenschaft ist in Sicht — und damit die Voraussetzung für die organische Entwicklung einer europäischen Rechtsordnung."

[210] See, on the difference between the one and the other, Ch. Von Bar, H. Beale, E. Clive and H. Schulte-Nöltke, "Introduction", in *Principles, Definitions and Model Rules of European Private Law*, *Draft Common Frame of Reference* (DCFR) (2008) 1-38.

[211] But see Zimmermann, *op. cit.*, footnote 82, 512 who states that

> "the respective parts of the Draft Common Frame of Reference cannot claim to be a 'Restatement', or to represent a 'common core' of European law. They may be used to kick off the debate about an authoritative European reference text but they cannot be regarded as constituting such a reference text themselves."

that it was a vocation of our times to create a uniform European contract law and that research and the institutions were moving cautiously — obviously with a safety-belt — towards legislation [212], the catalyst being that the European Community as a regional organization was gaining more importance. In turn, the European Community would have to be integrated into existing international law-making bodies and their instruments [213]. Accession to the UNIDROIT Statute, for instance, would also be highly welcomed [214].

105. If a future European substantive law instrument were to apply specifically in international legal relationships it would be essential to define, from the outset, which cross-border relationships should fall within the scope of application of that European instrument [215]. Would it provide that it should be applied if the legal relationship is connected to :

---

[212] F. Blase, "A Uniform European Law of Contracts — Why and How", *Columbia Journal of European Law* (2002) 487-491 (491). See also U. Mattei, "Hard Code Now !", *Global Juris Frontiers* (2002) www.bepress.com/gj/frontiers/vol2/iss1/art1 :

> "The new European Code should be hard, minimal, not limited to contracts, and process-oriented. It should aim to reflect the social fabric of European capitalism. The European codification process should look beyond the frontiers of fortress Europe and locate itself in the global dynamic of lawmaking."

[213] J. Basedow, "Worldwide Harmonisation of Private Law and Regional Economic Integration — General Report", *Uniform Law Review* (2003) 31-52 (35) ; Mankowski, *op. cit.*, footnote 195, 419.

[214] Kronke, *op. cit.*, footnote 103, 5.

[215] It has been proposed that the European instrument should also apply to purely domestic contractual relationships, see S. Leible, "Was tun mit dem Gemeinsamen Referenzrahmen für das Europäische Vertragsrecht ? — Plädoyer für ein optimales Instrument", *Betriebs Berater* (2008) 1469-1475 (1472).

(a) One Member State — (internal relationship) ?
(b) Two different Member States — (regional relation-
    ship) ?
(c) One Member State and a non-Member State —
    (regional-international relationship) ?
(d) Two different non-Member States — (international
    relationship) ?

106. In respect of *situation (a)* — in cases where
the relationship in point is connected exclusively to
one Member State — the question arises whether that
State should be allowed to select the European substantive law instrument. At least two arguments have been
put forward in favour of such a solution [216]. Firstly,
complete competition of legal systems should be
allowed. Why exclude European law which is, in any
case, a part of national law ? Secondly, big companies
could use one single standard form for all transactions
within the Union. They would no longer need to adjust
their contracts to conform to each national law. If the
parties were to be permitted to choose the European
substantive law instrument, even in circumstances
which are connected exclusively to one State, then
situation (a) should be included within the scope
of application of the instrument.

107. The inclusion of *situation (b)* described above
within the scope of application will be, presumably,
ineluctable. It would make sense, clearly, to provide,
specifically, that such a European instrument would be
applicable to cases involving more than one EU State,
since all the Member States would be bound by the
instrument if Denmark, Ireland and the United Kingdom were to opt in.

---

[216] S. Leible, "Choice of the Applicable Law", in E.
Cashin Ritaine, A. Bonomi (eds.), *Le nouveau règlement
européen "Rome I" relatif à la loi applicable aux obligations contractuelles* (2008) 61-75 (71).

108. It is possible to include the relationship indicated under *situation (c)*. However, a choice would fall to be made between a wide or a restricted scope of application. The latter approach would be achieved by the adoption of a provision which establishes that the conflict of law rules determine that the law of a Member State is to be applied [217]. If the drafters opt for copying the CISG technique [218] the next question which arises is as to whether the designation of the law of a Member State automatically leads to the application of the European instrument if a dispute is to be decided by a court in a Member State [219].

109. In respect of the relationship under *situation (d)*, in which none of the parties is located in one of the Member States, the question as to whether the European instrument is to be applied might arise if the parties have selected this European uniform law to apply to their legal relationship.

The conflict of law rules of the competent forum (within or outside the EU) must be consulted as to whether such a choice will be permitted. The choice of the law of a Member State raises the same question as in *situation (c)*.

5.1. The opt-out approach

110. If the European uniform law were to be applicable automatically in clearly prescribed situa-

---

[217] See Article 1, Section 1 under *(b)* of the CISG.

[218] Article 1, Section 1 under *(b)*.

[219] Lando, *op. cit.*, footnote 197, 133 :

"If a World Code of Contract applicable to international commercial transactions will be adopted, the European Civil Code will be a national system operating within the EU. A contract between a party inside and a party outside the EU will then be governed by the World Code, unless the parties agree that it shall be governed by the European Civil Code."

tions [220] the "opt-out" approach potentially would have the potential to set aside domestic substantive law unless the parties were to agree to the contrary [221]. When they have expressly opted out of the European instrument its rules could not be applied unless they were to do nothing or were to select the national law of a Member State. In the latter case it would fall to be decided whether or not such a choice is sufficient to exclude the European instrument's application. Answering this question in the positive would, as a corollary, lead to the application of the national substantive law of the Member State.

110. Obviously, the "opt-out" method would result in a stronger position for the European instrument than the "opt-in" technique. The instrument would be recognized as "the" European substantive law which, in respect of cross-border relationships, should always be consulted. The CISG, which has been praised as the veritable world sales law [222], perfectly illustrates how such a system works. It belongs to the common knowledge of every lawyer that if the conditions of Article 1 of the CISG are fulfilled, the Convention rules govern the relevant international sales contract, unless the parties have excluded, explicitly, the application of the Convention in accordance with Article 6.

111. Apparently application of the Convention is excluded regularly [223], because, it seems that the parties

---

[220] According to Mankowski, *op. cit.*, footnote 195, 414, this option requires courage, "wie ihn die politischen Organe der Gemeinschaft bisher nicht ansatzweise gezeigt haben".

[221] Proposed by Leible, *op. cit.*, footnote 216, 70-71.

[222] M. J. Bonell, "The CISG, European Contract Law and the Development of a World Contract Law", *American Journal of Comparative Law* (2008) 1-28 (1).

[223] N. Voser and Ch. Boog, "Die Wahl des Schweizer Rechts – was mann wissen sollte", *Recht der interna-*

and, particularly, their legal advisers are often unfamiliar with the Convention rules and prefer to select their own law (the homeward trend) [224]. Empirical comparative research to investigate the question as to how often and why the parties have excluded application of the Convention has, so far, scarcely been undertaken [225], regardless of the fact that entire libraries have been filled with publications on the CISG and several documentation systems exist [226].

It has been reported, however, that almost two decades after the CISG was enacted as effective American law, it has yet to gain wide acceptance as the

---

tionalen Wirtschaft (2009) 126-139 (136), who conclude that the standardized exclusion of the CISG is to be rejected, whatever the reasons might be. In their view it is advisable that if a choice is to be made between, for instance, German sales law, which is more permissive for the buyer, and Swiss sales law, which puts the seller into a better position, the CISG as a neutral and balanced law should be selected.

[224] I. Schwenzer, "The Application of the CISG in Light of National Law", *NYU and Journal of Private International Conference on Private International Law*, April 17-18, 2009. She distinguishes three different forms : (1) no application of the CISG where it should have been applied ; (2) interpretation of the CISG provisions according to existing or merely presumed domestic counterparts ; and (3) undermining the CISG by resorting to concurring domestic remedies. See also F. Ferrari, "Homeward Trend : What, Why and Why Not", in A. Jansen and O. Meyer (eds.), *CISG Methodology* (2009) 171-206.

[225] F. Ferrari (ed.), *The CISG and Its Impact on National Legal Legislation* (2008). The book analyses the Convention's impact on the practice of law, the style of court decisions as well as the domestic legislation in the area of contract law in 25 contracting States.

[226] See, for instance, the Pace Database on the CISG and International Commercial Law, www.cisg.law.pace. edu. Schwenzer, *op. cit.*, footnote 224 : "the literature on the CISG by now is abundant".

preferred choice of law for international transactions for the sale of goods [227]. The degree of familiarity with the CISG is still very low which seems to be reinforced by prejudices being nourished especially by US scholars [228]. Domestic attorneys in the United States feel more comfortable with the Uniform Commercial Code than the provisions of the Convention, which are not only less familiar to them, but also to courts in the United States called upon to interpret and construe these provisions [229]. For these reasons it has been suggested that the CISG should be enacted as federal legislation,

> "which would eliminate any confusions as to its application and would unequivocally notify U.S. courts, lawyers and businesses of its application"

and, even, that the title of the CISG should be modified to "The Convention for International Contracts Involving the Sale of Goods and Related Services." [230]

112. In Germany, an empirical study was undertaken in 2004. Some 42 per cent of the 500 legal practitioners who were interviewed indicated that they advise their clients to exclude the CISG. On the other hand, increasing acceptance has been noticed [231]. Similar experiences have been reported in other con-

---

[227] M. Reimann, "The CISG in the United States: Why It Has Been Neglected and Why Europeans Should Care", *Rabels Zeitschrift für ausländisches und internationales Privatrecht* (2007) 115-129.

[228] Schwenzer, *op. cit.*, footnote 224.

[229] G. V. Philippopoulos, "Awareness of the CISG among American Attorneys", *Uniform Commercial Code Law Journal* (2008) 357-371 (371). Confirmed by Sheaffer, *op. cit.*, footnote 196, 494.

[230] Bailey, *op. cit.*, footnote 197, 315.

[231] J. Meyer, "UN-Kaufrecht in der deutschen Anwaltspraxis", *Rabels Zeitschrift für ausländisches und internationales Privatrecht* (2005), 457-486 (471, 486).

tracting States [232]. A comparison of awareness of the CISG in different jurisdictions [233] shows that increasing acceptance in practice [234]

> "is true for most civil law countries, especially in Western Europe, which do apply the CISG in a rapidly growing number of cases, but it remains highly questionable with regard to the common law world which has shown much greater reluctance in that regard. The paucity of American case law is probably the most significant manifestation of this reluctance." [235]

All in all, however, it has been concluded recently, that the story of the CISG has been one of world-wide success. Criticism could either be rejected as largely unfounded or met by a correct interpretation of the Convention [236].

5.2. The opt-in approach

113. Contrary to the "opt-out" or "yes, unless" approach the applicability of a European instrument

---

[232] Ferrari, *op. cit.*, footnote 225.

[233] M. Wethmar-Lemmer, "When Could a South African Court Be Expected to Apply the CISG ?", paper delivered on 2008-01-21 at the Society of Teachers of Law of Southern Africa and the Southern African Society of Legal Historians Conference held at the University of Pretoria from 21 to 24 January 2008.

[234] Schwenzer and Hachem, *op. cit.*, footnote 124, 463-467.

[235] Reimann, *op. cit.*, footnote 227, 129. In respect of other common law jurisdictions their reluctance towards the CISG has also been confirmed in respect of the law of Australia, New Zealand and Canada by P. Butler, *The Doctrines of Parol Evidence Rule and Consideration − A Deterrence to the Common Law Lawyer ?*, Collation of Papers at UNCITRAL-SIAC Conference, 22-23 September 2005, Singapore International Arbitration Centre.

[236] Schwenzer and Hachem, *op. cit.*, footnote 124, 478.

choosing the "opt-in" approach would depend on the
parties to the cross-border legal relationship. The
instrument itself will not prescribe any objective scope
of application. If the parties express, explicitly, that
their relationship should be governed by the European
instrument, their choice of a law other than national
law should — from the outset — be recognized, since
otherwise their designation of the applicable law
makes no sense whatsoever. As a result, any opt-in provision goes hand in hand with conflict of law rules
allowing the parties to select the law governing their
relationship. The one cannot function without the other :
an opt-in provision stating that parties may determine
that their relationship should be governed by non-State
law depends, on the one hand, on the recognition of
such a choice by the conflict of law rules whereas, on
the other hand, the effectiveness of conflict of law
rules allowing the parties to choose non-national law
depends on the availability of a set of rules which can
be chosen as a law governing the relationship. Consequently, the non-State law to be chosen must be of a
certain quality [237].

In Chapter VIII, Section 3, we will investigate further as to whether or not choice of law rules can only
allow the choice of an instrument which contains an
opt-in possibility or whether the choice of law rules
can and probably should also allow the choice of a set
of rules, that is uniform rules, which lack such an
explicit "invitation". If the parties do not opt in,
national substantive law is to be applied, either on the
basis of the parties' choice (subjective determination of
the applicable national law) or on the basis of the
objective determination of the applicable law by the
court in the case of a dispute. As a result, the opt-in

---

[237] This question will be addressed in Chapter IX,
Section 2.

approach, which might result in the application of a law other than national law, actually requires two steps : first, the State allows the application of non-state norms through its conflict of law rules and, secondly, parties make a positive choice in favour of these norms.

5.2.1. *Experiences of the past*

114. To date, the opt-in approach has been scarcely used by instruments which contain uniform substantive law rules. The CISG, for instance, does not contain a rule which determines that the Convention rules are to be applied when the parties have opted for their applicability [238]. Instead, the drafters of this Convention determined that the scope of application depends on the factual situation that the parties have their principal places of business in different contracting States and if this requirement is not fulfilled the private international law rules of the forum are to be consulted as to whether these rules determine that the law of a contracting State is to be applied. The Convention itself does not provide the possibility for the parties to opt in. Consequently, conflict of law rules determine whether such a choice is to be recognized since the Convention does not prohibit such a positive choice [239].

---

[238] According to Mankowski, *op. cit.*, footnote 195, 416, the choice of an international Convention can only be qualified as a *materiellrechtliche Verweisung*.

[239] The Convention can also be applied if the requirements for its application according to Article 1 are not fulfilled. See F. Ferrari, in P. Schlechtriem and I. Schwenzer (eds.), "Kommentar zum einheitlichen Kaufrecht (2008) Art. 1 no. 85", where reference is made to the Arbitration Institute of the Stockholm Chamber of Commerce, 5 April 2007 CISG online 1521 : application of the CISG as the "law" chosen by the parties.

115. The predecessor of the CISG, the Hague Uniform Sales Law of 1964, provided ratifying States, however, with the possibility of deciding whether they wanted the uniform sales law to be applied on the basis of an opt-in declaration by the parties or automatically with the option for the parties to opt out. That Law, which was effective in only nine European countries, was replaced by the CISG. The scope of application was redrafted and the previous possibility for ratifying States to make a reservation in respect of the scope of application — that the uniform rules on sales law were only to be applied when the parties had opted explicitly for their application — was not retained. The United Kingdom, which to date is still not a contracting State to the CISG [240], made the opt-in reservation when ratifying the Hague Uniform Sales Law since they did not want it to influence the work of London lawyers, courts and arbitrators who jointly had, and still have, an enormous interest — legal as well as commercial — in applying English law. That this goal has been achieved through the making of the opt-in reservation can be demonstrated by the fact that, to date, English courts have still not decided one single case on the basis of the Hague Uniform Sales Law because it has never been chosen by the parties and their legal advisers [241].

5.2.2. *Questions for the future*

116. In view of the opt-in approach, which requires that parties to an international relationship determine

---

[240] See, extensively, on the British refusal to ratify the CISG, J. Linarelli, "The Economics of Uniform Law and Uniform Lawmaking", *Wayne Law Review* (2003) 1387-1447 (1426-1439).

[241] This has been reported by Schroeter, *op. cit.*, footnote 162, 55.

actively the applicable law, the following scenarios illustrate how many questions need to be addressed and, more importantly, should be provided with an answer. Suppose that A, who has his principal place of business in Member State AA, contracts with B, who has his principal place of business in Member State BB. They can agree :

1. to not include a choice of law clause in their contract
2. to determine that their contract should be governed by :
   (a) a national law which is not further specified
   (b) law Z (the law of a non-Member State)
   (c) law C (the law of a third Member State)
   (d) law AA or law BB
   (e) the European substantive law instrument.

117. In *scenario 1* the parties for various reasons — deliberately or because of negligence — "agree" not to designate the applicable law. The law to be applied will then be determined by the conflict of law rules of the forum in the case of litigation. A Member State's court has to apply Article 4 of the Rome I Regulation on the law applicable to contractual obligations and, depending on the qualification of the contract as a sale of goods or service contract, for instance, the law is objectively determined.

118. In *scenario 2 (a)* the parties prefer the application of a national substantive law rather than the new European substantive law with which they are probably not familiar. They cannot decide which national law to choose, but they have no confidence in the application of the European instrument. This scenario is definitely not unrealistic considering the practice under the CISG. It is known generally that uniform sales rules are excluded *en masse,* not least due to the persistent use of model contract forms which are rarely adapted

to new contracts since they have proved their practical functionality in the past. Apart from this experience, it should be noted that the choice made by the parties in *scenario 2 (a)* is both negative and positive. European substantive law is excluded from its application (negative) and instead the application of a national substantive law, which is not further specified, is favoured (positive). Undoubtedly, the will of the parties should be recognized not only when they litigate but also when a dispute is to be decided by an arbitral tribunal.

119. The choice of the parties in *scenario 2 (b)* should generally be recognized if the forum has to apply the Rome I Regulation which allows the parties to select any *lex contractus*. A reasonable relationship with the chosen law and the contract is not required [242]. In international arbitration the choice of law by the parties will always be recognized.

120. In *scenarios 2 (c)* and *2 (d)* the parties select the law of a Member State, being AA, BB or C. The question arises how this choice of the law of a Member State should be interpreted. As has been mentioned earlier, it is to be expected that the European instrument will contain a provision to the effect that it can be applied in cross-border cases. The questions arising here are should the choice of the European instrument only be recognized if the parties have explicitly expressed this intention or should the choice of the law of a Member State also be sufficient ? These questions should definitely be answered by the terms of the new European instrument if it comes to be adopted. Should the drafters opt for a restrictive approach, which means that only the parties' express choice of the European

---

[242] Under American conflict of law rules, however, such a choice will only be recognized if the contract is sufficiently connected with the law of the selected jurisdiction.

instrument could lead to its application, or should they select a more open approach which would lead to the application of the European instrument if the law of a Member State is chosen ? If the latter approach is favoured a clear provision would be necessary to determine those circumstances under which the European instrument can be applied. This latter approach is taken by the CISG and in respect thereof a huge amount of case law confirms that the choice of the national law of a contracting State is not sufficient to exclude the application of the Convention. This experience should be taken into account.

121. A choice of the parties to apply the rules of the European instrument *(scenario 2 (e))* to the exclusion of national substantive law would require that the relevant conflict of law rules admit the application of such kind of rules. Either the European instrument itself will contain a provision such as : "The rules of this . . . (regulation) are applicable if they have been chosen by the parties to a cross-border relationship", or — and this is to be preferred in view of other unifying and harmonizing substantive instruments — the Rome I and Rome II Regulations explicitly allow the parties to determine that their relationship is governed by non-State norms, such as European substantive law rules.

122. Conceivably other scenarios could exist, for instance where one of the parties has its principal place of business in a Member State and the other in a non-Member State or both parties are located outside the European Union but agree that the law of a Member State should be applied or that the European instrument should govern their relationship. There is no problem when arbitrators decide the dispute. They will recognize either choice. If a Member State court were to determine the applicable law the European instrument would only be used as the *lex contractus* if it clearly

stated that it is irrelevant where the parties' principal places of business are situated. The parties' express choice in favour of the European instrument would be sufficient and also, in accordance with the Rome I Regulation, should be allowed [243].

123. So far only business transactions have been addressed. Would the above analysis also hold good in the case of a consumer transaction ? It has been submitted that any future European substantive law instrument should be applicable — as far as contracts are concerned — not only to contracts between enterprises (B2B), but also between private persons (C2C) and between enterprises and private persons/consumers (B2C). Such a broad scope of application would require at least that parties may not deviate from or modify certain mandatory rules [244] which protect the weaker party [245]. This proposal is based on the assumption that a future European instrument would only be an optional instrument. However, a closer look at those whose interests might be at stake by the instrument might provide some new insight and shed some light in the current darkness.

5.3. Weighing the interests of stakeholders

124. What are the interests which fall to be taken into account in the discussion on whether to select the opt-in or opt-out solution for a European instrument containing substantive law ? More precisely, what are the interests of those to whom the rules are directed [246] ?

---

[243] Mankowski, *op. cit.*, footnote 195, 391-433.

[244] Extensively on the relation between both European and Member State consumer law : Mankowski, *op. cit.*, footnote 195, 422.

[245] Leible, *op. cit.*, footnote 215, 1475.

[246] The following analysis is inspired by Schroeter, *op. cit.*, footnote 162, 42-57. From now till 2011 two Dutch

5.3.1. Enterprises and their legal advisers

125. In international trade, the contracting parties are free to choose the law governing their relationship which best suits their interests. This chosen law governs those issues not expressly settled by the parties even in lengthy and meticulously drawn-up contract documents. The parties will be looking for a law which grants the largest party autonomy possible since they will be interested in being able to choose, to the desired extent, a law which best suits their interests and so making the "right" choice of law is therefore essential [247]. One would expect each of the contracting parties to propose a law to its prospective contracting partner which promises the highest expected benefits for itself [248] which, in turn, might lead to the so-called "battle of the forms", a clash of standard contract terms containing each party's choice of law clause [249]. However, do operators have time to understand, do they have the capability to acquire knowledge of the different legal systems potentially applicable to a transaction and do they make an enlightened choice of the law best suited to their needs [250] ? In the following paragraphs

---

legal scholars (Hesselink and Smits) will "explore the resistance that exists against European integration in the field of private law by looking at two reasons for such resistance : nationalist ideology and the behaviour of firms and consumers." See www.hiil.org/research/other-research-projects/the-europeanisation-of-private-law.

[247] C. Fountoulakis, "The Parties' Choice of 'Neutral Law' in International Sales Contracts", *European Journal of Law Reform* (2006) 303-329 (304).

[248] S. Voigt, "Are International Merchants Stupid ? — Their Choice of Law Sheds Doubt on the Legal Origin Theory", *Journal of Empirical Legal Studies* (2008) 1-20 (10).

[249] Fountoulakis, *op. cit.*, footnote 247, 305.

[250] Kessedjian, *op. cit.*, footnote 200, 323.

there will be outlined a few considerations aimed at explaining various aspects of this problematic.

126. An economic analysis of the differences between national systems, for instance, reveals that, in particular for businesses contracting across borders, transaction costs should be higher than for those who, contracting only within their own jurisdiction, can offer their products at a lower price [251]. Transaction costs consist of, for instance, information costs relating to the different contract laws. It has been stated that there is no way of disputing the fact that cross-border trade in Europe would be cheaper if all countries applied the same set of rules [252]. Likewise, differences in systems of delict and tort law may impose transaction costs which can be reduced [253]. The question arises whether, based upon the information available, enterprises decide which national law contains the most benefits for them. Which law favours the seller, which law puts the buyer in a better position ? This would finally influence the parties when subjecting their contracts to a specific national law. According to Stefan Voigt [254] the following aspects possibly play a role :

---

[251] C. P. Gillette and R. E. Scott, "The Political Economy of International Sales Law", *International Review of Law and Economics* (2005) 446-486 (446, 448), cited by Schroeter, *op. cit.*, footnote 162, 43.

[252] Wagner, *op. cit.*, footnote 91, 1272.

[253] W. Van Boom, *Harmonizing Tort Law : A Comparative Tort Law and Economic Analysis*, Rotterdam Institute of Private Law Working Paper Series (2008) 1-16 (10) http://papers.ssrn.com/sol3/papers.cfm ?abstract_id=1156739. See also J. Albert, *Compensation of Victims of Cross-Border Road Traffic Accidents in the EU : Comparison of National Practices, Analysis of Problems and Evaluation of Options for Improving the Position of Cross-border Victims* (2008) http://ec.europa.eu/civiljustice/news/docs/study_compensation_road_victims_en.pdf.

[254] Voigt, *op. cit.*, footnote 248, 10.

(1) *Familiarity* with a private law system. A high
    degree of familiarity involves the incurring of
    lower additional transaction costs.
(2) The *quality* of the law in the sense that some par-
    ticular legal order promises to regulate specific
    transactions in ways which suit all the contracting
    partners better than other legal orders, for example,
    because it is highly developed.
(3) The *predictability* of decisions by courts and arbi-
    trators based on the respective law which, in turn,
    depends on the precision of the relevant laws.
    Predictability further depends on the stability of
    the relevant law.
(4) The *perceived neutrality* of the relevant laws. Ex-
    ante, parties do not know whether they will ever be
    plaintiffs or defendants, which means that they
    have incentives to consent to a law that which does
    not unduly favour one of the parties.

Other benefits of divergent legal rules — from a law
and economics point of view — are that the competition between legal orders allows a greater number of
preferences to be satisfied and also enables the development of learning processes for businesses and their
legal advisers [255].

127. However, despite the extensive literature
which indicates that higher costs are usually involved
in the case of cross-border contracting, no empirical
evidence exists which demonstrates that either big or
small enterprises really consider this aspect of the substantive law to be relevant and, more importantly, that
they expressly make a choice for the most favourable
contract law as being most propitious to furthering

---

[255] R. Van den Bergh and L. Visscher, "The Principles
of European Tort Law : The Right Path to Harmonization ?", *European Review of Private Law* (2006) 511-543
(516).

their interests [256]. On the contrary, European enterprises, at least in their respective standard contract forms, almost always designate their own law, the law which applies at their principle place of business or, alternatively, they choose a neutral law [257]. However, there is also no reliable comparative empirical evidence which would confirm that "seemingly the content of the various national legal systems in view of the interests of one of the parties or the specific transaction is totally irrelevant" [258]. Only in respect of some jurisdictions has this kind of research been undertaken [259]. Furthermore, it has been demonstrated that it is impossible to calculate either the costs of legal diversity or the costs of uniform law since a quantitative analysis cannot provide an answer [260].

128. A parallel can be drawn with the experience provided by the documentation of more than 2,100 judicial and arbitral decisions which have been ren-

---

[256] Extensively on this point with further references : Schroeter, *op. cit.*, footnote 162, 42-45.

[257] Fountoulakis, *op. cit.*, footnote 247, 303-329. See also Voser and Boog, *op. cit.*, footnote 223, 126-139.

[258] In this sense Schroeter, *op. cit.*, footnote 162, 45.

[259] Voigt, *op. cit.*, footnote 248, 1-20. He compares the use of the substantive law of four jurisdictions (England, France, Switzerland and the United States) concerning cases that were decided by the ICC in Paris. See for the situation in the Netherlands, T. Q. De Booys, E. J. A. De Volder and D. Raic, *Bestaat er behoefte aan een gemeenschappelijk referentiekader voor Europees contractenrecht*, Hague Institute for the Internationalisation of Law (HiiL) (2009) www.justitie.nl.

[260] Smits, *op. cit.*, footnote 193, 178-179. Instead the question should be rephrased : "Would the savings in transaction costs through the removal of legal diversity be greater than the losses caused by the termination of competition between legal systems", since this question would allow an analysis on the basis of qualitative arguments ?

dered since the CISG entered into force. If the contract contains one or more choice of law clauses, more often than not the national law of the principal place of business of one of the parties is chosen ; the parties seldom agree to apply the CISG directly. Only in some branches of commerce has it become common practice to select a specific national law, such as English law, for shipping contracts and the commodity trade, and the law of New York, for international financial contracts. It is apparent that the idea that enterprises impose the application of a particular foreign law, because it contains more favourable provisions for them than for the other contracting partner, is more theoretical than based on reality [261]. Besides, very often, traders do not themselves think about including any clause as to choice of forum and law in the contract. It is usually only upon the recommendation of their legal advisers that such "safety mechanisms" are included eventually, but not always at the very end of the process of negotiating and drafting the contract. It may be that the contracting parties consider that it seems rude and distrustful to be thinking about the possibility that a dispute may arise later under the contract just at the point when they have, ultimately, — often after long negotiations — reached an agreement. Additionally, when this moment has been reached and the bottles of champagne are about to be opened, almost nobody cares about the law to be applied in the case of a disagreement. The insertion of a clause as to jurisdiction and choice of law depends heavily on legal advisers who, in many cases, do not compare the various available contract systems but prefer to play safe resulting most frequently in the choice of their and their client's own national law. Apparently, also, a comparison of the CISG and of national contract law is not even

---

[261] Schroeter, *op. cit.*, footnote 162, 45.

attempted probably due to lack of knowledge concerning the uniform sales law even though, depending on which contractual obligation must be fulfilled, this might lead to a better position for one or other of the parties [262]. The lack of knowledge of the CISG has another downside or — seen from a positive angle — upside. If its application has not been properly excluded it falls to be applied, *ex officio,* if the requirements of Article 1 are met and, for those who state that they do not care about the CISG and that they only contract on the basis that their own law is chosen, it may come as a surprise if this "own law" is the law of a contracting State. Eventually, in such circumstances they would end up being introduced, willy-nilly, to the CISG [263].

In conclusion, in view of the experience with the opt-out system of the CISG and the preferred application of national contract law in international transactions, it can be suggested that international traders are most likely to favour a European instrument which is applicable only if the parties have chosen it explicitly as the law governing their relationship. Generally, for them only the opt-in approach would be acceptable.

5.3.2. Consumers

129. Consumer contracts, at least in Europe, are governed generally by the law of the habitual residence of the consumer because she/he is considered to be the weaker party to the contract. It is assumed that the consumer will be familiar with the law of the place where he lives and, accordingly, the choice of the applicable

---

[262] Voser and Boog, *op. cit.*, footnote 223, 135-136.
[263] See with further references Schroeter, *op. cit.*, footnote 162, 49.

law is restricted in order to protect the consumer. It is to be expected that were the European instrument to be adopted it would be applicable not only in cross-border business to business transactions but also in the case of international consumer contracts. The choice between the opt-in and opt-out approach, from a consumer perspective, depends positively on the content of the rules of the European substantive law to be adopted. Should the rules of the European instrument indeed be consumer-friendly [264] — that is to say that at least all the existing rules of the Directives relating to consumer contracts would be incorporated — the opt-out approach might be the best way to protect consumer interests. It is doubtful whether consumers will make the effort to investigate the pros and cons of the application of a European instrument in order to propose to the other contracting party a clause making the European uniform law applicable [265]. Besides, many con-

---

[264] M. Hesselink, "European Contract Law : A Matter of Consumer Protection, Citizenship, or Justice ?", *European Review of Private Law* (2007) 323-348.

[265] See also the recent Report on Cross-Border E-Commerce in the EU, Commission Staff Working Document, Brussels, 5 March 2009, SEC(2009) 283 final, which identifies e-commerce trends and potential cross-border obstacles in order to analyse the direction that cross-border e-commerce is taking in the EU. It states (50-51) :

"The minimum harmonisation approach used by Member States in implementing consumer protection regulations has resulted in a patchwork of national laws. On one hand, some respondents said that consumers often complain of the lack of transparency of the contract terms in relation to the applicable law. On the other hand, some respondents argued that consumers are often ill-informed about their rights and that legal considerations do not seem to influence their purchasing decision beforehand. Consumers are more concerned with the possibility of obtaining redress in case

sumer contracts are not concluded in writing. Enterprises selling their products and services to consumers might also select an opt-out approach. This would be advantageous for them since they would then have to deal, and become familiar, with only one single law instead of the great variety of contract laws in Europe with which they currently have to cope.

Hence, it can be assumed reasonably that both parties to a B2C contract are likely to have a preference for the automatic application of a European instrument, unless they have opted out.

5.3.3. Judges and arbitrators

130. How would the choice between an opt-in and an opt-out instrument be decided by judges and arbitrators ? Would they also, like parties to a B2B transaction, favour the opt-in method ? Past experience might allow some predictions to be hazarded as to which option they might prefer. In this context the CISG again provides interesting insights. Apparently, case law deriving from most of the European jurisdictions demonstrates that, despite the existence of the opt-out mechanism, there is no clear evidence of the emergence of the so-called homeward trend [266]. The interpretation by the courts of the requirements for the exclusion of the CISG according to Article 6 is extremely stringent. This conclusion is based upon three commonly acknowledged conditions : first, parties need to express their clear intention to opt out of the

---

they encounter a problem with the seller. In addition, the law applicable to distance contracts should always be the law of the country of the consumer."

[266] Schwenzer, *op. cit.*, footnote 224, who addresses the homeward trend (e.g., uniform interpretation) by domestic courts when applying the CISG from a global perspective.

CISG [267]. Second, the choice of the national law of a contracting State does not exclude the application of the CISG since it is also part of the national law. Third, even the exclusion of the old Hague Uniform Sales Law has not been recognized as an exclusion of the CISG [268]. In some jurisdictions courts are uniform-law-minded and this is due to various reasons. In those jurisdictions where foreign law has to be determined *ex officio* by the courts [269], the application of the CISG avoids seeking costly and time-consuming expert opinions on foreign law [270]. It might be important for several jurisdictions that many commentaries and case-law overviews have been published. Easily accessible databases might also have contributed to the courts' positive approach towards the CISG [271]. Moreover, international arbitration, too, provides a fertile ground for the application of the CISG [272].

---

[267] But see the decision of the French Cour de cassation, 26 June 2001 — CISG online 598 — which held that pleading a case in court under French law amounted to a subsequent implicit exclusion of the CISG irrespective of whether the parties were aware or not that the CISG applied to their contract.

[268] Schroeter, *op. cit.*, footnote 162, 50-52.

[269] M. Jänterä-Jareborg, "Foreign Law in National Courts, A Comparative Perspective", *Recueil des cours* (2004) Vol. 304, 185-385 (272-285).

[270] According to Schroeter, *op. cit.*, footnote 162, 52, in other jurisdictions also, where foreign law has to be proved by the parties, no homeward trend to the detriment of the CISG can be detected.

[271] See however Schwenzer, *op. cit.*, footnote 224, who illustrates the point that even after 21 years of the Convention having been in force it is still hard work to achieve even a basic level of uniformity in the application and interpretation of the CISG.

[272] L. Mistelis, "CISG and Arbitration", in A. Janssen and O. Meyer (eds.), *CISG Methodology* (2009) 375-395, who provides interesting statistics based upon the a review

Based upon the stringent interpretation of a "CISG exclusion clause" which is commonly applied, courts and arbitrators are seemingly uniform-law-minded. It is to be expected that if they were to be consulted — which is admittedly impossible on such a huge scale — they would prefer the opt-out method for a European instrument to be adopted in the field of substantive law.

5.3.4. Community institutions and Member States

131. Finally, what are the interests of those legal institutions which would be taking the decision to adopt the European instrument ? Based upon a proposal by the European Commission, the Member States can influence the decision of the European Council which, in co-decision with the European Parliament, could decide to adopt such a European instrument. A decision to do so is a political one which makes it difficult to weigh the legal interests involved. It has been suggested that the institutions of the Community would probably favour an opt-out instrument, since their actual power would increase if a European substantive law were to be applied frequently [273]. This goal would

---

of published awards. See also A. Mourre, "Application of the Vienna International Sales Convention", *International Court of Arbitration Bulletin* (2006) 43-50.

[273] M. Kenny, "The 2003 Action Plan on European Contract Law : Is the Commission Running Wild ?", *European Law Review* (2003) 538-550 (549) :

"Yet the final contents of both the frame of reference and the optional instrument(s) will be decided neither by the trading parties nor the interested academics, but in the horse-trading that is EC law-making. Given this combination of result-orientation and sausage-making, parties interested in shaping the process should be aware of the risks : their capacity to influence the Commission is limited. Those not within reach of EC funding will be in a poor position to provide any critical input."

probably not be achieved if a European opt-in set of rules co-exists alongside the 27 or so national laws. If it would turn out to be necessary that the European instrument were to be amended all the European institutions would be involved and the highest court with interpretative competence would be the European Court of Justice. The idea of a central European State supports such a scenario. With legal unification, a truly European legal system would be created [274].

132. At this point it is useful to elucidate briefly what the effects of the enactment of such a European instrument, for instance in the form of a Regulation, would be [275]. Depending on its geographical scope of application it would bind all, or most of, the Member States. The binding nature of the instrument as law would be beyond doubt since it would acquire full authority as Community law [276]. Neither reservations nor modifications of that law by any Member State would be possible. It would be European law in its classical meaning. Both the European substantive law and the domestic substantive law would be able to be quali-fied as national substantive law [277]; however, there is a difference between the one and the other [278] if we consider only the position of the highest courts of the Member States on the one side and the European Court of Justice on the other. Only the latter can interpret European substantive law whereas the highest court of a Member State would be able to interpret

[274] Blase, *op. cit.*, footnote 212, 490.
[275] Favoured by Mankowski, *op. cit.*, footnote 195, 413.
[276] Mankowski, *op. cit.*, footnote 195, 413, 414.
[277] *Ibid.*, 414.
[278] Contrary : Mankowski, *op. cit.*, footnote 195, 415 : "Die Option zu Gunsten des CFR wird damit eine Option zur Auswahl zwischen zwei Teilen des nationalen Rechts. Man scheint nur innerhalb des nationalen Rechts zu operieren."

both sets of rules. Moreover, the legislative processes to reform the substantive rules are totally different.

133. European institutions — one may blame them for being selfish — would be most likely to advocate strongly the opt-out method[279]. However, Member States also have a say in the whole process. They hold a key position[280]. Would they be interested only in sustaining an optional European instrument in order to protect their own national law[281]? From a conflict of laws perspective it is open to question whether States gain any profit from the application of their domestic law. However, choice of law clauses are often combined with jurisdiction clauses and frequently the selected forum and the selected law are in one and the same place. In "big money" cases this might be attractive for legal advisers and attorneys. In any case, the interests of Member States may differ. Currently, 23 EU Member States are CISG contracting States. They are familiar with the opt-out technique. The United Kingdom, Ireland, Portugal and Malta stand to one aside. If the European instrument were to address not only sales law but contract law in its entirety, or even the law of obligations as a whole, this might be considered as a threat, although it should be borne in mind that the European substantive law rules might only be applicable in cross-border cases.

5.4. The final decision

134. All things considered, it should come as no surprise that there is a high likelihood that the final

---

[279] Schroeter, *op. cit.*, foot note 162, 53-54.

[280] O. Remien, "On the Trend Towards Recodification and Reorientation in Private and Business Law", 12.3 *Electronic Journal of Comparative Law* (2008), who hopes that national codifications will continue to blossom in Europe.

[281] Schroeter, *op. cit.*, foot note 162, 54.

decision as to whether any European instrument
(1) should be applied automatically [282], unless the parties exclude its application, or whether it (2) might
be applied only if the parties have expressly opted for
this [283], is going to be very difficult. Not all Member
States, and certainly not least the United Kingdom,
where "legal London" is considered to be an important
aspect of the economy [284], will support the first option [285]
which, however, would be supposed to be received
favourably by consumers, enterprises contracting with
consumers, courts and arbitrators and the European
institutions alike. However, a two-step approach might
also be an option. If sufficient practical experience
were to be gained in applying an optional instrument
the degree of obligation could be raised by a transition
from opt-in to opt-out [286].

---

[282] Supported by Schroeter, *op. cit.*, footnote 162, 58.

[283] Supported by Leible, *op. cit.*, footnote 215, 1475.
See also J. M. Smits, "Europees Burgerlijk Wetboek mag
enkel een optionele code zijn", *Nederlands Juristenblad*
(2007) 2487-2488 :

> "An optional code is a perfect way to determine
> whether there is a need to adopt uniform law. If parties
> frequently refer to them because they consider it
> favourable, this is great. Instead, if they prefer their
> national law, this is fine too : Uniform private law
> should not be imposed."

[284] Wallis, *op. cit.*, footnote 209, 513. Little has
changed since 1852 when Charles Dickens wrote in *Bleak
House*, Bantam Classic reissue November 2006, 579 :
"The one great principle of the English law is, to make
business for itself. There is no other principle distinctly,
certainly, and consistently maintained through all its nar-
row turnings."

[285] R. Goode, "The Harmonization of Dispositive Contract and Commercial Law — Should the European Community Be Involved ?", in E.-A. Kieninger, *Denationalisierung des Privatrechts ?* (2005), 19-32 (32), favours an
optional instrument.

[286] Callies, *op. cit.*, footnote 22, 483.

6. Harmonizing Substantive Law Instruments Which "Offer" Their Application

135. In this section we look primarily at Principles. Some of them clearly state that they may be applied in cross-border relationships, others do not contain any suggestion to that end. The question arises whether this makes any difference. The clear distinction between Principles which "offer" their application, on the one hand, and Principles which remain silent in this respect, on the other, determines the structure of the following analysis.

136. In respect of US Uniform Acts — quite apart from whether or not they have been enacted by states — and Restatements, it has never been proposed that they should be applicable in inter-state or international relations. According to the common law approach a court may look into these kinds of soft law in order to obtain inspiration if the state law designated by the conflict of law rules does not provide for a solution to the dispute. Under the current 2nd Restatement on Conflicts of Law this issue is not addressed [287]. Even in the largely uncodified American system, in which the choice of law is determined by judges rather than legislators, the applicability of Restatements or Uniform Acts, in inter-state relationships at least, has never been considered.

However, within the framework of the recent discussion on the drafting of a Restatement 3rd on Conflict of Laws [288], the position of soft law/non-

---

[287] S. C. Symeonides, "Contracts Subject to Non-State Norms", *American Journal of Comparative Law* (2006) 209-231.

[288] S. C. Symeonides, "A Third Restatement for Choice of Law, Why Not?", *Bi-Annual Conference the Journal of Private International Law*, New York, 17-18 April 2009.

national law, whereby a distinction is to be made between the choice of the applicable law by the parties and the submission of the relationship to non-national law by the court, will, most likely, be addressed.

6.1. Contract Principles

137. It is interesting to see that both the UNIDROIT Principles of International Commercial Contracts and the Principles of European Contract Law define their scope of application. In short, two purposes are to be distinguished. They may be used as a model for law-makers and they may be used as the law governing a contract, whereby no distinction is made between internal and international contracts. In the Preamble to the UNDIROIT Principles and Article 1:101 of the Principles of European Contract Law it is determined that they shall be applied when the parties have agreed that their contract should be governed by them or by general principles of law, the *lex mercatoria* or the like, and that they may be applied even when the parties have not chosen any law to govern their contract.

The drafters suggest that the Principles provide applicable norms when parties select them as the applicable law and even when they have not selected any law to be applicable [289]. Is this instruction, directed as

---

[289] F. K. Juenger, "The UNIDROIT Principles of Commercial Contracts and Inter-American Contract Choice of Law", *Contratación international, Comentarios a los Principios sobre los Contratos Comerciales Internationales del Unidroit*, Unversidad Nacional Autónoma de México — Unversidad Panamericana (1998) 229-236 (229) :

"At first glance, the objectives listed in the UNIDROIT Principles' Preamble appear remarkably modest . . . Implicit in this provision is the real purpose of the drafters' endeavor : to codify the new law merchant, the supranational commercial law of our times."

it is towards the contracting parties and adjudicators, to be considered as an opt-in provision ? Does this actual prescription of the Principles bind them ?

138. In respect of the UNIDROIT Principles — the same applies with respect to the European Contract Principles — it has been submitted rightly that this purpose, that of actual prescription of their scope of application, poses a two-fold challenge to traditional conceptions of law. First, Conventionally, only the law of States as competent law-makers can be applied in cross-border relationships. To date, an autonomous law of commerce, a *lex mercatoria*, has been rejected, for the most part, as the applicable law, at least in State courts ; the situation is however somewhat different in arbitration [290]. The Principles share the unofficial status of *lex mercatoria* [291]. In contrast to this, previously vague, concept they provide — and this is considered highly attractive — detailed rules. Second, whether or not the Principles are applicable in a given legal system [292] is determined by that system's own conflict of law rules [293]. In particular this aspect implicitly dis-

---

[290] It lacks the elements of structure, systemization, and transparency. These significant deficiencies seriously speak against choosing it as the law applicable to a contract. The need for foreseeability and reliability in the law cannot be safeguarded. See Fountoulakis, *op. cit.*, footnote 247, 329.

[291] Confirmed by P. Perales Viscasillas, "The Role of the UNIDROIT Principles and the PECL in the Interpretation and Gap-filling of CISG", in A. Janssen and O. Meyer (eds.), *CISG Methodology* (2009) 287-317 (313).

[292] On the question as to whether the *lex mercatoria* is law or not see T. Schultz, "Some Critical Comments on the Juridicity of *Lex Mercatoria*", *Yearbook of Private International Law* (2008) 667-710.

[293] R. Michaelis, in S. Vogenauer and J. Kleinheisterkamp (eds.), *Commentary on the UNIDROIT Principles*

applies construction of the Principles as enabling an opt-in approach since they are completely dependent upon their "acceptance" by virtue of the conflict of law rules, at least when a dispute is decided by State courts. The Principles themselves cannot prescribe their own application and, therefore, use the wording "shall" or "may be applied" [294]. As a corollary, if the conflict of law rules do not allow their use as the law governing the contract, parties can only incorporate the text of the Principles in whole or in part into their contract *(materiellrechtliche Verweisung)*. If the contractual provisions do not provide a solution in the case of a dispute, the national substantive law, which has been designated according to the forum's choice of law rules, is to be consulted. Whether these rules can allow or support the application of non-national law, as laid down in harmonizing substantive law instruments, will be discussed in Chapter VIII. Again, it should be emphasized that, in the case of arbitration, more flexibility exists in this respect.

139. It is appropriate to mention at this stage that, in respect of the extent to which the UNIDROIT Principles can be applied in cross-border cases, it has been submitted that the following distinctions ought to be made [295] :

---

of International Commercial Contracts (2009), Preamble No. 7. Critically, about this commentary, Kessedjian, *op. cit.*, footnote 200, 325-326.

[294] See Michaelis, *op. cit.*, footnote 293, Preamble No. 7, who refers to M. J. Bonell, "The UNIDROIT Principles a Decade after Their First Appearance : What Have They Achieved and What Are Their Prospects for the Future ?", in E. Cashin Ritaine and E. Lein (eds.), *The UNIDROIT Principles 2004 : Their Impact on Contractual Practice, Jurisprudence and Codification* (2007) 259, 260, who has explained that the use of "may" rather than "shall" is an expression of self-restraint and modesty.

[295] Michaelis, *op. cit.*, footnote 293, Preamble No. 8.

1. Insofar as the Principles fulfil their Restatement purpose and provide an accurate description of all actual laws, they can be said to be valid merely as a systematization, since their application would not contradict any national laws which are otherwise applicable.
2. Where they fulfil their model purpose and present a superior law, they can guide the decisions of an adjudicator, but only within the limits of otherwise applicable law ; these limits are stricter for courts than for arbitrators.
3. Where the Principles fulfil neither the Restatement nor the model purpose, their application is not justified except to the degree that they are applicable within the limits established by the law which is otherwise applicable.

140. Admittedly, these distinctions do make sense ; however, is it always practical to assess the various rules as to whether they fall under one of the three distinguished categories ? And how should conflict of law rules respond ? Should they also take these distinctions into account ? It can be argued that the determination of the law to be applied will become quite complicated if each Principle is to be categorized and tested as to its applicability as the law governing each specific contractual aspect. Conceivably in any one dispute, several Principles might fall to be applied. Would their different characterizations then lead to *dépeçage* ? If so the result would be that some aspects of the dispute would fall to be decided according to the Principles, whilst for other aspects a national law would require to be consulted. The assessment of whether each Principle is in compliance with the otherwise applicable law makes the choice of the Principles, as a whole, less attractive for the contracting parties, who might have opted for them because they have been designed specifically for

international contracts, whereas national contract laws have been adopted first and foremost to regulate internal contracts. Moreover, it depends on the adjudicating body how each Principle will be characterized. Interpretations may differ and, the more they do, so the more legal uncertainty increases. All in all, it is highly questionable whether the classification of each Principle in terms of its applicability in a concrete dispute, as in the distinctions indicated above, should be supported.

6.2. *Principles in the field of delict/tort and family relations*

141. Neither the Principles of European Tort Law nor the Principles of European Family Law contain any recommendation as to their application in cross-border situations. Also parties are not reminded to make a choice for their application. The drafters deliberately restrained themselves from suggesting this objective. Instead, both sets of Principles have been drafted primarily with the aim of being able to contribute to furthering the harmonization, within Europe, of the law of delict and tort and family law respectively. This is expressed explicitly in the Preamble to the Principles of European Family Law [296], whereas the primary pur-

---

[296] The Preamble reads :

"Recognising that, notwithstanding the existing diversities of national family law systems, there is nevertheless a growing convergence of laws ;

Recognising that the free movement of persons within Europe is hindered by the remaining differences ;

Desiring to contribute to the harmonisation of family law in Europe and to facilitate further the free movement of persons within Europe ;

Desiring to balance the interests of spouses and

pose of the Principles of European Tort Law was to present a common framework both for the further development of national laws and for uniform European legislation. Therefore, the Principles are not intended to serve as a model code ; even drafting them required a wording which often resembles a statutory text [297]. This is the most fundamental difference from the work of the Study Group on a European Civil Code, which addresses both contractual and non-contractual obligations.

142. In respect of (international) family law, the freedom of the parties is much more restricted. Only in some areas do a number of jurisdictions allow the determination of the applicable law by the parties. Furthermore, when the Commission on European Family Law began the comparative, research-based, drafting of common Principles its activities were not welcomed by everybody [298] ; some family law experts demonstrated great scepticism [299]. Strategically, it was advisable not to be too ambitious, although during the course of the last few years the scepticism has slightly changed. It has been acknowledged, firstly, that it is possible to draft common principles despite the great variety of family law systems. Secondly, the Principles of European Family Law have been assessed and empirically tested by other family law legal experts and it has been concluded generally that they are indeed accept-

---

society and to support actual gender equality, taking into account the best interests of children,

The Commission on European Family Law recommends the following Principles : . . ."

[297] Koch, *op. cit.*, footnote 91, 191.
[298] M. Antokolskaia, "Family Law and National Culture, Arguing against the Cultural Contraints Argument", *Utrecht Law Review* (2008) 25-34.
[299] See the various contributions in Boele-Woelki, *op. cit.*, footnote 127.

able and/or regarded as an improvement on existing family laws with which they were compared [300].

143. It should be borne in mind that there is a great difference between the two family law sets of Principles which have been drafted to date. The first set, published in 2004, regarding divorce and maintenance between former spouses is, as elaborated, more in line with the concept of Principles [301] than the second set regarding parental responsibilities, published in 2007, which contains very detailed rules. Apart from this difference it has been suggested by this author that for this reason both sets of rules might contribute to the European frame of reference which is being prepared currently [302]. Moreover, if courts refer increasingly to the CEFL Principles as a source of inspiration in international family disputes [303], the idea of applying the family law principles in cross-border cases gains

---

[300] E. Örücü and J. Mair (eds.), *Juxtaposing Legal Systems and the Principles of European Family Law on Divorce and Maintenance*, European Family Law Series No. 17 (2007), and E. Örücü and J. Mair (eds.), *Juxtaposing Legal Systems and the Principles of European Family Law on Parental Responsibilities*, European Family Law Series No. 26 (2009).

[301] W. Pintens, "Materielles Familienrecht in Europa — Rechtseinheit oder — vielfalt ?", in R. Freitag, S. Leible, H. Sippel and U. Wanitzek (eds.), *Internationales Familienrecht für das 21. Jahrhundert* (2006) 137-150 (146-150).

[302] K. Boele-Woelki, "Building on Convergence and Coping with Divergence in the CEFL Principles of European Family Law", in M. Antokolskaia (ed.), *Convergence and Divergence of Family Law in Europe*, European Family Law Series No. 18, 253-269 (269).

[303] See the advisory opinion of the Advocate General of the Dutch Supreme Court, Hoge Raad 25 April 2008, LJN BC5901. Further K. Boele-Woelki, "Umzug von Kindern aus den Niederlanden in die Schweiz : die niederländische Perspektive", *Praxis des Familienrechts* (2009) 381-396.

increasing attention. Admittedly, from a conflict of laws perspective, a huge difference remains between "law" used as a source of inspiration — this might also be the domestic law of another jurisdiction — and the "law" which governs the relationship. Another possible route consists of the inclusion of family law issues in the Common Frame of Reference to be adopted. However, in the field of family law it has also been demonstrated that the unification of international family law, at least in Europe, maintains the great variety of family law systems. Only the unification of family law in the form of an optional instrument would be an effective remedy for this situation [304]. This would require such an optional instrument to be drafted and finally adopted by the European institutions. It could then be chosen by the parties as the law governing their marriage or partnership, their general rights and duties, their property relations, their divorce and their maintenance obligations after separation. Based jointly upon the extensive comparative work which the CEFL has undertaken, one of its experts will soon finalize an individual research project containing a set of rules to be applied in cross-border European family marriages [305]. Another option would be the adoption of a Convention which attains a similar importance and reputation as the CISG [306]. However, this idea, which was suggested almost 15 years ago, has yet to be pursued further.

---

[304] G.-R. De Groot, "Op weg naar een Europees personen- en familierecht ?", *Ars Aequi* (1995) 29-33.

[305] N. Dethloff, "Die Europäische Ehe", *Zeitschrift für das Standesamtswesen* (2006) 253-260.

[306] N. Dethloff, "Arguments for the Unification and Harmonisation of Family Law in Europe", in K. Boele-Woelki (ed.), *Perspectives for the Unification and Harmonisation of Family Law in Europe*, European Family Law Series No. 4 (2002) 37-64 (54).

6.3. *Do the different approaches matter ?*

144. To conclude : in the field of contract law both the UNIDROIT Principles and the Principles of European Contract Law initiated the discussion on their potential application in cross-border contracts. This path has not been followed by those academic groups which started similar projects in the field of delict, tort and family law. This is somewhat surprising in view of the Principles of European Tort Law. Evidently, the question arises whether it is necessary, in order for that to happen, that the harmonizing substantive law instrument should itself suggest its application in cross-border cases. Finally, it all depends on the conflict of law rules whether it is possible to apply non-State norms. Do they fulfil the requirements to be recognized as "law" ? Yet it is important to keep in mind that the more ambition is demonstrated, in respect of the suitability of the Principles for application in cross-border relationships, the more should law-makers at the national, regional and international levels take their explicit suggestions into account. They should consider whether their conflict of law rules should accept or reject these recommendations since they have the legislative power to do so. In this way the Principles are capable of challenging conflict of law rules. The question as to whether and, if so, in how far they do so, is addressed in Chapter VIII on the determination of the application of substantive law instruments by conflict of laws rules.

7. *The Other Side of the Coin : How do Conflict of Law Rules Respond ?*

145. In this chapter an attempt is made to clarify the requirements which several unifying and harmonizing substantive law instruments pose in respect of their

application in cross-border relationships. It has been demonstrated that, in respect of this aspect, unifying and harmonizing substantive law instruments differ to a large extent. The first category imposes application of its rules whereas the latter only encourages this.

Table 9. The Applicability of Unifying
and Harmonizing Substantive Law Instruments
in Cross-border Relationships

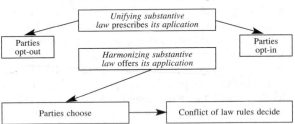

However, this is only one side of the coin. The other side consists of the conflict of law rules — how do they respond to the possibilities of applying a law other than national law ? This is further explored in the next chapter.

CHAPTER VIII

THE APPLICATION OF A LAW OTHER THAN
NATIONAL SUBSTANTIVE LAW

146. As has become evident from the previous
chapter, the applicability of non-national substantive
law in cross-border situations is dependent, to a very
large extent, on the effect of rules in conflict of laws
systems. Several situations are to be distinguished. In
the first place, it is essential to know whether a dispute
is decided by arbitration or litigation. Courts must consult their conflict of law rules, whereas arbitrators are
not obliged to apply any (which [307] ?) conflict of law
rules. This major difference should be taken into
account, in particular in international transactions
where the parties have the choice either to litigate or
go to arbitration. Generally, this choice is not available
to parties in a cross-border family relationship who can
only resort to the courts. However, alternative dispute
resolution mechanisms are used increasingly, in particular in child abduction, contact and relocation cases
with cross-border elements. If the parties agree on
seeking a resolution by mediation, for instance, it may
be possible to take the solutions provided by the

---

[307] Perfectly illustrated by Juenger, *op. cit.*, footnote 289, 231 :

"But in contrast to judges, whose courtrooms are
decorated with national symbols that remind them of
the loyalty they owe to domestic laws and constitutions,
an arbitral panel consisting of, say, a Mexican, an
American and a Swedish arbitrator who listen to the
parties' allegations in a Geneva hotel room will not feel
beholden to the law of any particular state or nation."

Principles of European Family Law regarding Parental Responsibilities, or the ALI Principles on Family Dissolution, into account.

147. The following distinction is equally apparent. Unifying substantive law instruments, in the form of international Conventions or Uniform Acts, prescribe their scope of application principally without the assistance of conflict of law rules. If the parties are situated in different contracting states or EU Member States — if we include a reference to the emergence of a European uniform law instrument — the uniform substantive law is to be applied. In order to extend its applicability, uniform law often uses conflict of law rules which may determine that the law of a contracting State or a Member State is to be applied. This is the well-known CISG technique.

148. In contrast, harmonizing substantive law instruments lack the possibility to prescribe their application in cross-border cases. It has been illustrated above (Chapter VII, Section 6) that they may indeed "offer" their applicability, but, if the parties litigate, the final decision is taken by virtue of the application of conflict of law rules. How far does party autonomy reach? Does the parties' agreement as to the law to be applied include non-State norms? What effects flow from a choice for Principles, in particular? Moreover, should it not also be possible to select a uniform substantive law as the law governing the relationship?

150. Consequently, in this chapter we explore the following issues: the application of non-national law in case of litigation and ADR including arbitration and mediation. Within these forms of dispute resolution two situations are dealt with: first, where the parties have chosen non-State law; second, in the case of a lack of a choice of law, where the court or arbitral tribunal submits the relationship to non-national law. The extension of the application of uniform law by the use

of conflict of law rules is analysed before we focus on aspects of just how far the competence of the parties, on the one hand, and of judges and arbitrators, on the other, to choose or, as the case may be, determine which law can be applied, reaches.

1. Conflict of Law Rules Determine the Scope of Application of Uniform Substantive Law

151. The CISG autonomously prescribes its scope of application in Article 1 (1) *(a)*. In the case of a dispute, conflict of law rules are *not* to be consulted if the buyer and the seller have their places of business in different contracting States [308]. This represents an exception from the steps generally to be taken since as soon as a private relationship is connected to more than one jurisdiction where private international law questions — which court or arbitral tribunal has jurisdictional competence, which is the law applicable or how is recognition and enforcement of a resulting decision to be achieved — need to be addressed and need to be answered. As a matter of fact, without answering these questions a dispute cannot, generally, be decided or a status (marriage, adoption) obtained. A legal relationship without law does not exist [309]. Logically, the characterization of a private relationship as an international sales contract cannot but exclude the application of conflict of law rules whereas the competence of a court to decide an international sales dispute is to be decided according to the rules on jurisdictional competence of the forum which has been seised. Methodologically, it is therefore incorrect to consult conflict of law rules in

---

[308] A. Kampf, "UN-Kaufrecht und Kollisionsrecht", *Recht der internationalen Wirtschaft* (2009) 297-301.

[309] See extensively Gannagé, *op. cit.*, footnote 18, 275-308.

the first place when the law governing an international sales contract is to be determined [310]. Instead, Article 1 (1) *(a)* CISG determines the law to be applied, at least in those legal systems which are bound by this Convention. If the requirements for their application are fulfilled the Convention rules are directly applicable, without further ado, unless the parties have exercised their autonomy to exclude their application. The application of the CISG, which is based on Article 1 (1) *(a)*, has been characterized, therefore, as the "autonomous way of application" [311].

152. In addition to this direct prescription, Article 1 (1) *(b)* contains an "alternative way of application" which requires the *Zwischenschaltung* of conflict of law rules. If the parties are not located in different CISG States, the uniform rules are still to be applied if the conflict of law rules determine that the law of a contracting State is to be applied.

As a result, if one of the parties has its, or even both have, their place of business in a non-contracting State, the CISG rules may govern the sales contract. Under Article 1 (1) *(a)* conflict of law rules are excluded whereas under 1 (1) *(b)* conflict of law rules are needed [312]. In both cases the formal scope of application of the CISG rules is defined.

Consulting conflict of law rules, which eventually lead to the application of the law of a contracting State,

---

[310] K. Boele-Woelki, "Geünificeerd materieel recht gaat vóór een conflictenrechtelijke toets", in S. C. J. J. Kortmann, J. M. M. Maeijer, A. J. M. Nuytink and S. Perrick (eds.), *Op Recht, liber amicorum A. V. M. Struycken* (1996) 11-18. But see Kampf, *op. cit.*, footnote 308, 298-300.

[311] Ferrari, *op. cit.*, footnote 239, Vor Arts.1-6, No. 5 with further references.

[312] See also Article 3.1.b and Article 2.1.b of the UNIDROIT Conventions on International Financial Leasing and International Factoring of 1988 respectively.

results in a broader scope of application than if no resort is had to these rules. This idea was not supported by all national delegations during the drafting stages of the Convention and as a result — a compromise had to be achieved — States when ratifying the CISG may exclude the conflict-of-law mechanism of Article 1 (1) *(b)* [313].

153. It is worthwhile noticing that in reality conflict of law rules concerning sales contracts indirectly *lead to and support* the application of rules of uniform substantive law. They do not determine the application of these rules in a direct way and, admittedly, they restrict themselves to the designation of national substantive law. More precisely, if the national contract law to be applied is the law of a contracting State, conflict of law rules do not intervene further. To this author's knowledge nobody has ever questioned whether this result is desirable or not, nor whether conflict of rules should not always have the final say about which specific substantive rules are to be applied. This means that the control in deciding which law is applicable is taken away from the conflict of law rules which the court or, as the case may be, arbitral tribunal, has applied. It is up to the State concerned which laws have been designated by conflict of law rules to determine whether or not [314] this designation will lead to the application of the CISG. The law of that State finally decides. Conflict of law rules are used and needed but the ultimate decision lies with whichever national substantive law has been designated. The role which conflict of law

---

[313] Article 95 CISG : Any State may declare at the time of the deposit of its instrument of ratification, acceptance, approval or accession that it will not be bound by subparagraph (1) *(b)* of Article 1 of this Convention.

[314] Only States which have made a reservation according to Article 95 will apply the national contract law whereas all others will apply the CISG.

rules play in Article 1 (1) *(b)* can be characterized metaphorically by quoting from the work of Friedrich Schiller from 1783 : *Der Mohr hat seine Schuldigkeit getan, der Mohr kann gehen* [315]. "The Moor has done his work, the Moor may go." [316]

154. However, the provisions of Article 1 (1) *(a)* and *(b)* CISG illustrate perfectly how uniform substantive law and conflict of law rules get along, how the one depends on the other, how they co-exist and how they fulfil their designated tasks without disturbing each other. One might argue that the discussion about the interaction between uniform substantive law and conflict of laws is not an issue since the ratification of the CISG leads to the existence of two "national" contract laws. However, the decision as to which of the two contract laws — the international or the domestic — is to be applied is not taken by the application of the conflict of law rules whereas traditionally this is their main duty. If, and in so far as, uniform substantive law claims its own applicability with no need for help from conflict of law rules, the task of the latter is restricted.

2. Conflict of Law Rules Determine Whether a Law Other than National Law May Be Applied

155. May a law other than national substantive law be applied as the law governing a cross-border relationship [317] ? Primarily, conflict of law rules decide this

---

[315] Die Verschwörung des Fiesko zu Genua (1783) 3. Aufzug (4. Szene).

[316] *The Works of Frederick Schiller, Early Dramas and Romances*, translator Henry G. Bohn (1873) 189.

[317] F. Blase, *Die Grundregeln des Europäischen Vertragsrechts als Recht grenzüberschreitender Verträge* (2001) ; López Rodríguez, *op. cit.*, footnote 71.

question. The issue is highly controversial. It all started with the publication of the first set of Principles in the field of contract law [318] and currently the emergence of a European substantive law instrument has made the debate even sharper [319].

156. In respect of contract law — which has always been a front-runner or pacemaker — the subject-matter was extensively addressed at the 17th Conference of the International Academy of Comparative Law under the title *"Le contrat sans loi en droit international privé*/The contract without Law in Private International Law"* [320].

The expression *sans loi* is actually misleading — though frequently used [321] — since a legal relationship, by definition, is governed by law. More precisely it should therefore be questioned what kind of law is meant. Do only national legal rules fall under this term and not, for instance, the UNIDROIT Principles of International Commercial Contracts ? What separates the one from the other ? In the discussion on non-national legal rules, such as the *lex mercatoria*, general principles of law or substantive uniform law rules which may govern a legal relationship, the views expressed in the discussion differ greatly. Scholarly opinion can be divided into the *traditional* and the *liberal* approach. According to the *traditional* approach a relationship may only be governed by national legal

---

[318] Boele-Woelki, *op. cit.*, footnote 14, 652-678.

[319] Mankowski, *op. cit.*, footnote 195, 391-433.

[320] Gannagé, *op. cit.*, footnote 18, 275-308.

[321] F. De Ly, "Choice of Law Clauses, Unidroit Principles of International Commercial Contracts and Article 3 Rome Convention : The *Lex Mercatoria* before Domestic Courts or Arbitration Privilege ?", in F. Lefebvre (eds.), *Etudes offertes à Barthelemy Mercadal* (2002), 133-145 (134, 137). In this context one should probably prefer the expression *contrat sans loi mais pas sans droit*.

rules [322], whereas the *liberal* approach also accepts non-national legal rules for this purpose [323]. Both camps provide interesting arguments which we will compare and evaluate. Since the application of a law other than national law largely depends on party-autonomy, the following questions are relevant : first, have the parties chosen the applicable non-national law ; second, may courts and arbitrators, in the absence of any choice by the parties, subject a relationship to non-national law ?

157. In the following sections, in which the topics are subdivided into contracts, on the one hand, and delict/tort and family relationships, on the other, the conflict of law stance towards non-national law will be analysed by reference to various private international law instruments. Admittedly, the vast majority of private international law instruments, which operate effectively, refer indisputably to national substantive law only. The Inter-American Convention on the Law Applicable to International Contracts alone allows explicitly the application of non-national law, whereas in respect of the new Rome I and Rome II regimes it is highly controversial whether this is possible, feasible and desirable. From a global perspective these instruments definitely represent a minority and one might argue that their selection, for purposes of this discussion, is unbalanced. However, new developments only emerge in specific areas such as contract law. Whereas innovative ideas and solutions might well be rejected in other areas, such as in delict/tort and family relation-

---

[322] Passionately defended by Mankowski, *op. cit.*, footnote 195, 396-411. See also M. Bogdan, "The Rome I Regulation on the Law Applicable to Contractual Obligations and the Choice of Law by the Parties", *Nederlands Internationaal Privaatrecht* (2009) 407-410 (407-408).

[323] De Ly, *op. cit.*, footnote 321, 133-145.

ships, they might there also be copied, intensified or be subject to follow-up.

3. Application of Non-national Substantive Law in Case of Litigation

158. Much of the discussion about the application of non-national law is focused on whether Principles can become "the applicable law" on the basis of a choice by the parties. In litigation their use as "applicable law", when there has been no choice by the parties, has gained only very modest attention, although — considering the Contract Principles — such use seems to be much more in tune with their purposes and character [324].

3.1. Displacement of mandatory rules by the parties ?

159. Party autonomy is an internationally accepted principle in the area of choice of law [325]. More specifically, it is almost universally recognized that promoting party autonomy in international contracts corresponds to a real need for international business operators. In the great majority of jurisdictions the parties may choose a national law to govern their contractual relationship [326] and, generally, they may change their choice at any time [327]. In all European jurisdictions they may even choose a national law which has no objective link *(ratione materiae* or *ratione per-*

---

[324] Rightly observed by Michaelis, *op. cit.*, footnote 293, No. 49.
[325] A. V. M. Struycken, *op. cit.*, footnote 1, 369 : "Party autonomy is a matter of business interests : respectable interests, but not a dogma of a superior order."
[326] Article 3, Section 1, Rome I Regulation.
[327] Article 3, Section 2, Rome I Regulation.

sonae) [328] with the contract, whereas the choice of law doctrine in the United States still requires, in respect of some contracts [329], a reasonable relationship between the selected law and the contract [330]. According to European conflict of laws rules parties may select different national laws for different parts of the contract *(dépeçage)* [331]. Moreover, in some jurisdictions parties may freeze the applicable national law as it is at the time of contracting (stabilization clause) [332]. Furthermore, it is generally acknowledged that the parties may agree on almost everything. They may "incorporate" common principles into their specific contract (incorporation clause). All these different aspects lie at the heart of party autonomy.

160. The main issue of interest to us is the question as to what effects may be given to a clause providing for the application of non-national legal rules. Do these

---

[328] Kessedjian, *op. cit.*, footnote 7, 112.

[329] In 2004 the requirement of "reasonable relation" was removed except for when one of the parties to a transaction is a consumer, Uniform Commercial Code Section 1-301. See also Section 187 of Restatement (Second) of Conflict of Laws providing a general approach to be followed in determining choice of law questions involving contracts.

[330] Mo Zhang, "Party Autonomy and Beyond : An International Perspective of Contractual Choice of Law", *Emory International Law Review* (2006) 511-561 (515). See also G. Rühl, "Konvergenzen im Internationalen Vertragsrecht ?, Zu jüngeren Entwicklungen im US-amerikanischen und europäischen Kollisionsrecht", *Zeitschrift für Rechtsvergleichung* (2006) 175-182 (177-179).

[331] Article 3 (1), last sentence Rome I Regulation. See Kessedjian, *op. cit.*, footnote 7, 109, who reports that in practice this possibility is rarely used by the parties, as it may be a dangerous method leading to contradictions in the interpretation of the contract.

[332] De Ly, *op. cit.*, footnote 321, 137. Article 3 Rome I Regulation is, however, silent about these clauses.

rules govern the contract to the exclusion of national law ? Is it of importance how the parties refer to contract principles, since the effect is to be decided by the application of conflict of law rules ?

UNIDROIT, for instance, proposes two different approaches as expressed in the following clauses :

(1) This contract shall be governed by the UNIDROIT Principles, except as to Articles . . .
(2) This contract shall be governed by the UNIDROIT Principles, except as to Articles . . ., supplemented when necessary by the law of jurisdiction . . .

161. Only in the second clause is reference made to national law and then only as an after-thought application by necessity [333], whereas in both clauses, from the perspective of the application of the Principles, the wording "shall be governed by" is used, which indicates that first and foremost the drafters wanted the Principles to be applied to the exclusion of national contract law. But this is not — it has been emphasized — for them to decide. If the drafters' mission were to succeed, through the application of the choice of law rules of the forum, in the case of litigation, or by arbitrators, the reference to non-national rules would have the effect of replacing the national law, including its mandatory rules, which would have been otherwise applicable without a choice of law clause. This effect is generally indicated as the so-called *kollisionsrechtliche Verweisung* (choice of law designation) since the mandatory rules of the otherwise applicable national law are set aside by the parties' choice of law. As a consequence non-national law and national law are left on the same footing. If this effect is *not* granted to the parties' choice of non-national law the application of this law takes place within the limits and by virtue of

---

[333] De Ly, *op. cit.*, footnote 321, 136.

the (objectively to be determined) applicable national
contract law. This is the so-called *materiellrechtliche
Verweisung* (substantive law designation). In terms of
this restricted effect the incorporation of, for instance,
the UNIDROIT Principles of International Commercial
Contracts into a contract does not reveal any problems.
The court which has jurisdiction, or the arbitrator who
has been appointed, will solve the dispute in accordance with the UNIDROIT Principles as being part of
the contract. However, there are two situations where
reference to a national contract law is deemed necessary : (1) the transnational rules do not provide a solution for the specific legal issue which is under dispute,
and (2) mandatory rules of the national law applicable
to the contract are to be applied [334]. The special category of overriding mandatory rules *(lois de police,
Eingriffsnormen)* [335] is left apart since these norms,
under certain conditions, are always to be applied irrespective of the law governing the relationship.

162. It is up to conflict of law rules to determine
whether the parties' choice of non-national law should
not go one step further. It might be argued that if the
non-national law provides for a gap-filling mechanism [336] and contains mandatory provisions, the appli-

---

[334] F. Diedrich, "Rechtswahlfreiheit und Vertragsstatut
— eine Zwischenbilanz angesichts der Rome I-Verordnung", *Recht der internationalen Wirtschaft* (2009) 378-
385 (384).

[335] Article 9 (1) of the Rome I Regulation defines
"overriding mandatory provisions" as "provisions the
respect for which is regarded as crucial by a country for
safeguarding its public interests, such as its political,
social or economic organisation, to such an extent that
they are applicable to any situation falling within their
scope, irrespective of the law otherwise applicable to the
contract" under the Regulation.

[336] "Gap-filling" — is needed if a certain matter is
governed, but not expressly settled nor covered, by the

cation of the otherwise applicable national contract law is no longer necessary. Provided that these two conditions are fulfilled, the choice of non-national law can then be considered also to be a *kollisionsrechtliche Verweisung* [337].

This is the *pièce de résistance* which leads to the divide between the traditional and the liberal approach. It has been the focus of intense debate and, seemingly, the different interpretations are unbridgeable. Admittedly, both the gap-filling mechanism and the mandatory rules are two important components of a "law" to be applied. They are both contained in the CISG, the UNIDROIT Principles of International Commercial Contracts [338] and the Principles of European Contract Law. If these two aspects are provided by unifying and harmonizing substantive law

---

instrument, containing substantive law rules, which is to be applied. Generally, the instrument provides that the gap is to be filled according to the general principles on which it is based. Another option is that domestic law is taken into consideration. See B. Zeller, *CISG and the Unification of International Trade Law* (2007) 33.

[337] Struycken, *op. cit.*, footnote 1, 393 questions :

"Legislators should be keen on not losing contact with the shop floor. If highly qualified and respected non-governmental international organisations, such as the International Chamber of Commerce, Paris, offer comprehensive bodies of rules which are widely applied, why should the forum hesitate to approve parties to an international contract to choose those rules as the governing law for the part of their contract covered by such rules ?"

[338] But see with further references Schultz, *op. cit.*, footnote 292, 685 :

"The juridicity of a norm follows from its belonging to a legal system. Rules that do not form part of any legal order are not legal, as for instance the UNIDROIT principles are not legal rules."

instruments [339] the question arises how the respective rules are to be applied if one adheres to the incorporation theory *(materiellrechtliche Verweisung)* since the problem of a potential clash between different kinds of rules must then be solved [340]. In this context it should be mentioned, that the practical difference between the two approaches (as between that of conflict of law and designation of substantive law) has been considered as being limited since there are not many mandatory rules in the field of commercial law. Moreover, there is a growing tendency to consider the few mandatory rules — such as the entitlement of commercial agents to indemnity or compensation on termination of the agency contract — as overriding mandatory rules *(Eingriffsnormen)* which are applicable irrespective of the *lex contractus* [341].

163. In particular in respect of the CISG, it has been illustrated convincingly that it is worth choosing it as the law governing an international sales contract since the uniform sales law is genuinely neutral law, provides a well-balanced concept for both buyer and seller, is flexible, has rationalization potential and gives rise to only negligible costs of examination given that it is very well documented. Therefore, from a conflict of law rules perspective, a choice for the CISG does not raise any difficulties since it is a Convention and, as such, "hard law" with the same authoritative quality as any chosen domestic sales law [342]. For transnational rules of law, such as the Contract Principles, it is doubtful, to a certain extent, whether they qualify as

---

[339] See for the UNIDROIT Principles De Ly, *op. cit.*, footnote 321, 139-141. Contrary, Michaels, *op. cit.*, footnote 6, 872-873.

[340] Extensively on this point De Ly, *op. cit.*, footnote 321, 137-142.

[341] Michaels, *op. cit.*, footnote 6, 870.

[342] Fountoulakis, *op. cit.*, footnote 247, 314, 329.

a valid choice of law in litigation proceedings. However, under US choice of law rules, their potential application has been illustrated [343]. First, according to the governmental interest analysis, the UNIDROIT Principles could be applicable to situations in which no US state is interested in the application of its own law ; second, they qualify as international law for the purpose of the Restatement (2nd) on Conflict of Laws ; and, third, for the better-law theory, according to which the substantive quality of a law is a criterion for the choice of a law, they are a candidate to be the law applicable insofar as they perform a model function.

164. The recommendation to establish, for truly international facts, substantive rules which enjoy universal recognition, or at least seem compatible with the laws of the States directly interested in the settlement of the case at hand, is an acknowledgment, by conflict of laws scholars, that a localization of truly international contracts is a solution of embarrassment [344]. However, far less intense is the debate about the applicability of a law other than national law if the parties have not designated the applicable law. Does the objective conflict of laws approach allow the application of world-wide known and applied collections of rules or should their applicability always be made dependent on a clause in the contract to that effect ? As a result they would be applicable unless it is clear, in any particular case, that they should not apply [345]. This is possible under the Inter-American Convention on the Law Applicable to International Contracts, whereas the

---

[343] Michaels, *op. cit.*, footnote 6, 880-883, who also explains the meaning of the "government interests analysis" which refers to policies underlying competing laws.

[344] Oser, *op. cit.*, footnote 6, 162.

[345] Proposed by Struycken, *op. cit.*, footnote 1, 394.

Rome I Regulation merely connects the contract with the law of a country in the absence of a choice of law by the parties. In contrast, within the Swiss context, it has been argued that, under Article 19 (2) as read with Article 15, of the Swiss Private International Law Act, the UNIDROIT Principles may become applicable in the absence of a choice therefore by the parties and that, generally, this approach should be adopted [346].

3.1.1. *The progressive approach of the Inter-American Convention on the Law Applicable to International Contracts*

165. On 17 March 1994 the Fifth Inter-American Specialized Conference on Private International Law of the Organization of American States (OAS [347]), meeting in Mexico, adopted the Inter-American Convention on the Law Applicable to International Contracts (hereafter : ICLAIC). The 1980 Rome Convention on the Law Applicable to Contractual Obligations and the 1986 Hague Convention on the Law Applicable to International Sale of Goods served as a model. The ICLAIC expressly provides freedom for the parties to choose the law which is to govern their contractual relationship. The parties are permitted to modify their choice of law, in whole or in part, at any time. More essentially, some authors have argued that the ICLAIC clearly permits both the parties and the courts to select the *lex mercatoria* as the law which is applicable to international contracts. According to one of its drafters Article 7 (1) of the ICLAIC grants to the parties to a contract full autonomy to select any law they wish, be it the law of some State or nation or a non-positive law, such as the UNIDROIT Principles of International

---

[346] Oser, *op. cit.*, footnote 6, 137-138.
[347] Consisting of 32 Member States.

Commercial Contracts, which are specifically designed to govern transnational contracts and are therefore praised for their superior quality [348]. Legal opinion is divided [349]. Other scholars argue that it is more plausible to exclude their choice, since Article 7 only refers — like traditional choice of law rules — to "law". Article 9 ICLAIC sheds some light in this darkness. This provision determines that non-State norms may be applied in the absence of a choice by the parties. The second paragraph of Article 9, which lists the factors which a court should look at in determining the legal system which has the closest relationship with the contract, determines that if the parties have not selected the applicable law, or if this selection proves to be ineffective, the contract shall be governed by the general principles of international commercial law accepted by international organizations. The conflict of law rule proposed by the United States delegation — but rejected by the Conference — went yet a step further *in favorem principii*. In the absence of a reference to the applicable law by the parties, the United States proposal suggested making the contract directly subject to the general principles of international commercial law as commonly accepted by international organizations [350]. In support of this solution it has been argued that the parties to an international agreement have no reason to complain, should they have failed to stipulate the applicable law, if their dispute is decided according to a law of superior quality, which is specifically designed to govern transnational contracts. It would therefore seem "far more sensible to apply a neutral

---

[348] Juenger, *op. cit.*, footnote 289, 234. See also Struycken, *op. cit.*, footnote 1, 394.

[349] Michaelis, *op. cit.*, footnote 293, No. 59, with further references.

[350] Boele-Woelki, *op. cit.*, footnote 14, 673-675.

transnational law, rather than the home-state law of either party" [351].

166. Rejecting the idea that, under Article 7, parties would not have the possibility to designate non-State law, on the one hand, and allowing the courts to apply general principles of contract law, on the other, leads to discrepancies since the whole debate about whether conflict of law rules should designate non-State norms as applicable law has so far focused primarily on the freedom of the parties to agree on this kind of law. This would turn the world upside down : party autonomy would be restricted to the choice of national substantive law whereas adjudicators would be free to apply non-national law. It is doubtful that the drafters of the ICLAIC had this inconsistency in mind.

167. Despite its progressive approach — it has been submitted that in comparison to the Rome Convention on the Law Applicable to Contracts of 1980 the American states had managed to produce a superior conflict of laws system [352] — the ICLAIC has only been ratified by Mexico and Venezuela [353]. In particular the United States, whose delegation had proposed such innovative solutions, has not taken any action [354] and

---

[351] See F. K. Juenger, "The Inter-American Convention on the Law Applicable to International Contracts : Some Highlights and Comparisons", 42 *American Journal of Comparative Law* (1994) 383-391 (391).

[352] See Juenger, *op. cit.*, footnote 351, and M. J. Bonell, *An International Restatement of Contract Law — the UNIDROIT Principles of International Commercial Contracts* (1994) 122-123.

[353] According to Article 28 the ICLAIC became effective on 15 December 1996.

[354] According to S. A. Malloy, "The Inter-American Convention on the Law Applicable to International Contracts : Another Piece of the Puzzle of the Law Applicable to International Contracts", *Fordham International Law Journal* (1995) 662-735, the United States should not

the American report on "Contracts Subject to Non-State Norms", submitted to the 2006 Conference of the International Academy of Comparative Law, did not even mention the ICLAIC at all [355].

How the Convention is applied in both contracting States, this author was not able to verify [356].

168. Finally, it should be reported that the draft of the Inter-American Convention on the Law Applicable to International Consumer Contracts and Transactions, which will be adopted in 2010, explicitly states that the choice of non-national law is not possible [357]. Consumer interests might be better protected if only national law is to be applied. Moreover, rules of non-national law for B2C contracts in the form of Principles are only available within the European setting.

3.1.2. *The indistinct approach of the Rome I Regulation*

169. Since 2003 the conversion of the 1980 Rome Convention on the Law Applicable to Contractual Obligations into a Regulation has been on the legisla-

---

adopt it since ICLAIC will inject a greater degree of uncertainty and unpredictability into international contracts.

[355] Symeonides, *op. cit.*, footnote 287, 209-231.

[356] See further on the restrictive approach towards party autonomy in Latin-America : Michaelis, *op. cit.*, footnote 293, No. 60, and M. M. Albornoz, "Choice of Law in International Contracts in Latin American Legal Systems", *NYU and Journal of Private International Conference on Private International Law*, April 17-18, 2009.

[357] See Articles 4, 5, 6 and 12 of the Convention which stipulates which State law can be chosen. Article 3 of the Draft Additional Protocol on the Application of the Convention (II) states : "Applicable Law to the Contract : In all cases, the parties may select only one applicable law to the contract, which must be the law of a State."

tive agenda of the European institutions [358]. The first
Proposal for this Regulation (hereinafter : *Proposal*) [359]
published in 2005 was critically received. In 2007 it
was replaced by a new Proposal in the form of a Compromise (hereinafter : *Compromise*) [360] which finally
led to the adoption, on 17 June 2008, of the Regulation
of the European Parliament and of the Council on the
law applicable to contractual obligations (Rome I) [361].
The Regulation applies to contracts concluded after
17 December 2009. The absence of the possibility to
choose supranational or a-national rules of law in the
1980 Rome Convention as the law governing the contract was criticized by some scholars [362]. An important
change to the text of the Convention was provided in

---

[358] K. Boele-Woelki and V. Lazic, "Where Do We
Stand on the Rome I Regulation ?", in K. Boele-Woelki
and F. Grosheide (eds.), *The Future of European Contract
Law* (2007) 19-41.

[359] Proposal for a Regulation of the European Parliament and the Council on the law applicable to contractual
obligations (Rome I), presented by the Commission,
Brussels, 15 December 2005, COM (2005) 650 final. See
extensively on this Proposal, the Comments on the
European Commission's Proposal for a Regulation of the
European Parliament and the Council on the Law Appli-
cable to Contractual Obligations by the Working Group on
Rome I within the Max Planck Institute for Comparative
and International Private Law (hereinafter : Comments),
*Rabels Zeitschrift für ausländisches und internationales
Privatrecht* (2007) 225-344.

[360] Proposal for a Regulation of the European
Parliament and the Council on the law applicable to contractual obligations (Rome I), Compromise package by
the Presidency, Brussels, 13 April 2007, 8022/07 ADD 1
REV 1 ; text available at http://register.consilium.europa.eu/
pdf/en/07/st08/st08022-ad01re01.en07.pdf.

[361] (EC) No. 593/2008, *Official Journal of the European Union* 2008, L 177/6.

[362] Juenger, *op. cit.*, footnote 351, 381-393, and Boele-
Woelki, *op. cit.*, footnote 14, 652-678.

Article 3 (2) of the *Proposal*, according to which the parties were permitted to choose a non-national law [363]. The wording used was supposed to indicate that the parties were authorized to choose the UNIDROIT Principles or Principles of European Contract Law [364], as well as "possible future optional Community instruments" [365] which would supersede any mandatory provisions which would be applicable otherwise. However, a reference to the *lex mercatoria* was excluded as it was considered to be insufficiently precise. A choice for "private codifications not adequately recognized by the international community" was excluded as well [366].

170. The same provision, Article 3 (2) of the *Proposal,* also dealt with those issues not expressly regulated by such Principles as are chosen by the parties. Thereby an approach similar to the one applied in Article 7 (2) of the CISG was proposed. It would have provided that such a question was to be governed by the general principles underlying the Principles themselves or in accordance with the law which would be

---

[363] Article 3 (2), first sentence, of the *Proposal* reads as follows : "The parties may also choose as the applicable law the principles and rules of the substantive law of contract recognised internationally or in the Community." The choice of non-national law was particularly endorsed by the MPI working group, *op. cit.*, footnote 359, 243.

[364] This is the answer to the hypothetical question posed by this author in 1998 : "What would the conflicts rule of the EC Contracts Convention have looked like if the drafters had known of the Principles ?" See Boele-Woelki, *op. cit.*, footnote 14, 203-240.

[365] Explanatory Memorandum for the Proposal for a Regulation of the European Parliament and the Council on the law applicable to contractual obligations (hereinafter : Explanatory Memorandum), COM (2005) 650 final, 5. Such an exclusion of the *lex mercatoria* was supported by the MPI working group, *op. cit.*, footnote 359, 243.

[366] Explanatory Memorandum, COM (2005) 650 final, 5.

applicable under the Regulation in the absence of the parties' choice.

Although the possibility of applying a non-national law was met with approval by some legal scholars [367], and also by the European Economic and Social Committee [368], it has been omitted [369], first from the text of the *Compromise* and later from the final text of Article 3 of the Rome I Regulation [370].

---

[367] See P. A. Nielsen and O. Lando, "The Rome I Proposal", 3 *Journal of Private International Law* (2007) 29-51 (32). See in particular D. Martiny, "Europäisches Internationales Vertragsrecht in Erwartung der Rom I-Verordnung", *Zeitschrift für Europäisches Privatrecht* (2008) 79-108 (88, with further references in note 61).

[368] Opinion of the European Economic and Social Committee on the Proposal for a Regulation of the European Parliament and of the Council on the law applicable to contractual obligations (Rome I), 13 September 2006, COM (2005) 650 final — 2005/0261 (COD), 4-5, stating that it "would for the first time allow parties to use European standard contracts, which to a large extent, would be genuinely harmonised and would represent a significant step towards completion of the Internal Market".

[369] P. Lagarde, "Remarques sur la proposition de règlement de la Commission européenne sur la loi applicable aux obligations contractuelles (Rome I)", 95 *Revue critique de droit international privé* (2006) 331-349 (336), S. Dutson, "A Dangerous Proposal — the European Commission's Attempt to Amend the Law Applicable to Contractual Obligations", *Journal of Business Law* (2006) 608-618 (609) and H. Heiss, "Party-Autonomy : The Fundamental Principle in European PIL of Contracts", in F. Ferrari and S. Leible (eds.), *Rome I Regulation, the Law Applicable to Contractual Obligations in Europe* (2009) 1-16. Applauded also by Leible, *op. cit.*, footnote 216, 69 : "It seems that the time was not ripe for the bold extension of party autonomy that was envisaged in the proposal."

[370] Regretted by Kessedjian, *op. cit.*, footnote 7, 115-116, who favours the *materiellrechtliche Verweisung* but only for B2B contracts. In her opinion, the deletion of this provision may send the wrong signal to the parties and

171. Yet, the Preamble to the Rome I Regulation in recital (13) states that "[t]his Regulation does not preclude parties from incorporating by reference into their contract a non-State body of law or an international Convention". In addition, recital (14) states that

> "[s]hould the Community adopt, in an appropriate legal instrument, rules of substantive contract law, including standard terms and conditions, such instrument may provide that the parties may choose to apply those rules".

This latter wording undoubtedly refers to the prospective future European substantive law instrument (see Chapter VII, Section 5) which poses other questions in terms of application than harmonizing substantive law instruments. Is it indispensable to determine in the Rome I Regulation the selectability of this potential uniform law ? One might argue that recital 14 is superfluous since the European substantive law instrument should itself regulate its scope of application [371]. This depends, however, on the decision to be taken as to the instrument's applicability. Strictly speaking, an opt-out regime does not generally need choice of law rules to determine its applicability, and this is only so if the scope of application is widened with the help of conflict of law rules [372]. If an optional instrument were to be enacted, Article 3 of the Rome I Regulation should

---

could represent a retrograde step in the evolution of the law of contract around the world as many contract law bodies are developing, most of them on a private basis, rules which are very useful for international markets. See also Calvo A.-L. Caravaca, "El Reglamento Roma I sobre la ley aplicable a las obligaciones contractuales : cuestiones escogidas", *Cuadernos de Derecho Transnacional* (2009) 52-133 (57-81).

[371] Mankowski, *op. cit.*, footnote 195, 391-433.

[372] Like Article 1, Section 1 under *(b)* CISG.

be amended [373] and an amended provision should mention explicitly the possibility to opt into the European substantive law rules [374] since they will then be put on an equal footing with national substantive law. Methodologically, the Rome I Regulation is the right place to acknowledge this effect.

172. The wording of recital 13 of the Rome I Regulation has given rise to different interpretations as to its meaning and reach [375]. Does it indicate a smouldering lack of consensus about what to do generally

---

[373] But see P. Lagarde and A. Tenenbaum, "De la Convention de Rome au règlement Rome I", *Revue critique de droit international privé* (2008) 727-780 (736-737) :

"Assurément, ce que le règlement Rome I n'a pas voulu permettre, un autre règlement pourrait l'autoriser. Cela dit, rien n'empêchera évidemment les parties désireuses de choisir un droit non étatique de le faire, en assortissant ce choix d'une clause d'arbitrage."

[374] In contrast S. Leible and M. Lehmann, "Die Verordnung über das auf vertragliche Schuldverhältnisse anzuwendende Recht ('Rom I')", *Recht der Internationalen Wirtschaft* (2008) 528-544 (533-534), and Mankowski, *op. cit.*, footnote 195, 401, who suggests to include such a provision in the optional instrument. According to Heiss, *op. cit.*, footnote 369, 14, such a rule should be modelled as follows : "This Regulation shall apply when the parties, notwithstanding any limitations of choice of law rules under private international law, have agreed that their contract shall be governed by it." In his view such a rule would explicitly free the choice of the optional Instrument form any restrictions imposed by private international law.

[375] Ironically Mankowski, *op. cit.*, footnote 195, 399-402 :

"Wenn nach einer langen und intensiven Diskussion in einem Punkt nicht mehr als ein Satz Erwägungsgründe heraus kommt, dann hat es dieser Satz verdient, ernst genommen und Wort für Wort, Silbe für Silbe, Nuance für Nuance analysiert zu werden."

with international instruments ? It will come as no surprise that here the path of traditionalists and liberalists separates [376]. First, the wording that the "Regulation does not preclude" a choice for a non-national law does not form part of the text of the Regulation in Article 3. It implies that no uniform view of policy was able to be achieved in that respect among the EU Member States.

173. It is up to the courts of each Member State to decide how the reference to, or incorporation of, non-State law into a contract is to be interpreted and to do so the Member States' own conflict of law rules are to be consulted [377]. It is true that there are unlikely to be other conflict of law rules applicable to contractual obligations in the Member States, considering the uniform application of the Regulation as expressed in Article 2. Since, however, the Rome I Regulation has failed to address clearly the issue of the choice of (1) an international Convention and (2) the Contract Principles, the application of certain principles of private international law accepted in a particular Member State, in order to allow rules of such a Convention or such Principles to apply, is not to be excluded [378]. As a result one might consider the Rome I Regulation to be inapplicable to the extent that an international Convention, containing substantive law rules or the Contract

---

[376] A. Metzger, *Extra legem, intra ius : Allgemeine Rechtsgrundsätze im Europäischen Privatrecht* (2009) 254-263.

[377] See also R. Plender and M. Wilderspin, *The European Private International Law of Obligations* (2009) 138 No. 6-013.

[378] The same is true with respect to court decisions, in particular those delivered by the highest judicial instances. Even though they are not considered to be precedents, these decisions usually present persuasive authorities, even in civil law jurisdictions.

Principles, has been chosen by the parties. It would follow, therefore, that the forum would have to apply its internal rules of private international law, both for the purpose of determining whether rules of non-national contract law might be applicable and for that of ascertaining whether such a law would be applicable in the particular case [379]. A Member State, which would have to decide on the effects of a choice of, reference to, or incorporation of non-State rules, would, as a consequence, at least take into account the interpretation of the Rome I Regulation's predecessor concerning this issue [380], prevailing in that Member State, in the absence of any clear guidelines provided by the European legislator [381]. Furthermore, jointly based upon the consent explicit in recital 13 of the Preamble, a Member State's law might develop from its traditional approach (the mandatory rules of the otherwise applicable law remain applicable) to the more liberal approach ; the chosen non-State law is the *lex contractus* to the exclusion of mandatory rules of the objectively applicable law.

174. Subsequently, the question whether an international Convention or the Contract Principles [382], can be "the applicable law" must be answered separately for

---

[379] Raised by Plender and Wilderspin, *op. cit.*, footnote 377, 138, No. 6-014.

[380] Admittedly, the 1980 Convention remained silent on this point. Kessedjian, *op. cit.*, footnote 7, 114.

[381] Kessedjian, *op. cit.*, footnote 7, 114, who refers to a decision by the French Cour de cassation of 22 October 1991 which decided that non-State law is law and may be applicable to a contract ; *Revue de l'arbitrage* (1992), 457, commented upon by P. Lagarde, *Journal du droit international (Clunet)* (1992) 177, commented upon by B. Goldman.

[382] Kessedjian, *op. cit.*, footnote 7, 116, questions whether rules which have been developed by a trade association such as the International Federation of Consulting Engineers should not also be accepted.

each legal system. In respect of a choice by the parties to apply an international Convention, such as the CISG, the following situation may arise. Suppose that, in a contract for the sale of goods concluded between a German buyer and an English seller, the parties purport to choose the CISG as the law applicable. It has been submitted that it is possible that this would be interpreted as a choice of German law, including the CISG, since, on the one hand, Germany is a contracting party whereas the United Kingdom is not and, on the other hand, in the absence of such an explicit reference, the terms of the CISG would not be incorporated into the contract [383]. Why the choice of the CISG should only lead via a detour, through the national system of a contracting State, to its applicability, whereas in this case direct application thereof as the *lex contractus* would respond to the parties' intentions, is not convincing. Moreover, business people wherever they are situated — in a contracting or non-contracting State of the CISG — should have the freedom to choose the Convention regime since it is proper sales law, dealing with the rights and duties of the seller and buyer, passing of risk, the definition of the term "non-conformity" in a sales law context, and so forth. Since the Contract Principles were drafted having the CISG in mind their use in the interpretation and gap-filling of the Convention is beginning to be seen in practice [384]. Hence conflict of law rules could — and should — enable the designation of a body of uniform law as governing law [385].

---

[383] Plender and Wilderspin, *op. cit.*, footnote 377, 138, No. 6-013.

[384] P. Perales Viscasillas, "The Role of the UNIDROIT Principles and the PECL in the Interpretation and Gap-filling of CISG", in A. Janssen and O. Meyer, O. (eds.), *CISG Methodology* (2009) 287-317.

[385] Struycken, *op. cit.*, footnote 1, 385, with examples of case-law taken from the international carriage of goods.

175. Were courts of the Member States to be faced with a choice by the parties of the Contract Principles as the applicable law, the following answers might be provided. Most likely an investigation into the practices of the courts of the Member States would reveal that the choice of non-State law has, generally, been rejected so far [386]; moreover, that the great majority of legal scholars [387], despite some claims to the contrary [388], support this restrictive interpretation [389]. The meticulous study by Ralf Michaels, which he has undertaken with respect to the use of the UNIDROIT Principles for International Commercial Contracts, covers a large number of legal systems situated in Europe, North America, Latin America and Asia. His conclusion is that, at the global level, almost all State legal orders reject the application of the UNIDROIT

---

[386] See in particular the decision of the English Court of Appeal, 3 April 2007, *Halpern* v. *Halpern*, England and Wales Court of Appeals (EWCA) Civ 291 (the implicit choice of Jewish law was not accepted). See Plender and Wilderspin, *op. cit.*, footnote 377, 138, No. 6-015, and M. Heidemann, "*Halpern* v. *Halpern* : Zur Anwendbarkeit nicht-staatlichen Rechts und 'Rom I' in England", *Zeitschrift für europäisches Privatrecht* (2008) 618-632. Diedrich, *op. cit.*, footnote 334, 383.

[387] Blase, *op. cit.*, footnote 317, 221-234, with further references.

[388] Metzger, *op. cit.*, footnote 376, 541 :

"Geht man . . . davon aus, dass sich die lex mercatoria einschließlich der UNDROIT-Principles zu einer geltenden transnationalen Rechtsordnung entwickelt hat, so steht ihrer Wahl als Vertragsstatut in Verfahren vor staatlichen Gerichten prima facie nichts entgegen."

See in particular page 541, note 332, with references to legal scholars from various jurisdictions which support the selectability of the Contract Principles as the law governing a contract.

[389] Michaelis, *op. cit.*, footnote 293, No. 50, with extensive references.

Principles as law "by confining the status of 'applicable law' to state law, whether as selected law within the scope of party autonomy or as objectively applicable law in the absence of a choice." [390]

176. In this respect it might be interesting to explore one of the European jurisdictions a little further : that of the Netherlands [391], which clearly constitutes an exception in the debate. In this jurisdiction, one might investigate, are the Contract Principles considered to be eligible to replace the otherwise applicable law, including its mandatory provisions ? Some authors have expressed the view that Article 3 of the Rome Convention was to be interpreted so as to enable the inclusion of a choice of a non-State body of law, such as the Contract Principles or international Conventions [392]. Others have rejected such an extensive interpretation of this provision [393]. Yet, when applying the Convention, decisions of the courts in the Netherlands illustrate that the parties are permitted to agree on the application of an international Convention containing the uniform substantive rules. In other words, a reference by the parties to a contract to a Convention containing uniform rules has been accepted by the courts in the Netherlands as a valid determination of the *lex contractus*. Such a choice may be made validly

---

[390] Michaelis, *op. cit.*, footnote 293, No. 49, and Michaels, *op. cit.*, footnote 6, 870-872.

[391] D. Busch, "The Principles of European Contract Law before the Supreme Court of the Netherlands — On the Influence of the PECL in Dutch Legal Practice", *Zeitschrift für Europäisches Privatrecht* (2008) 549-562.

[392] Boele-Woelki, *op. cit.*, footnote 14, and R. Goode, "Contract and Commercial Law : The Logic and Limits of Harmonisation", *Ius Commune Lectures on European Private Law*, No. 3 (2003) 16.

[393] M. V. Polak, "Principles en IPR : geen broodnodig en pasklaar alternatief 'recht' ", No. 6225 *WPNR* (1996) 391-392.

if a particular Convention permits this, or at least does not preclude its application on the basis of choice by the parties [394]. Thus, the Dutch Supreme Court [395] has held that a choice of the Convention on the Contract for the International Carriage of Goods by Road (CMR) [396] as the *lex contractus* had been validly made even though that Convention was not otherwise applicable [397]. Obviously, the Rome Convention and its reference to a "law" have not been a hindrance to the parties in choosing an a-national body of law [398]. The relevant part of the Preamble to the Rome I Regulation implies that such an interpretation was in accordance with, or at least was not contrary to, the spirit and the underlying purpose of the Convention [399]. If international Conventions regarding uniform substantive law containing mandatory rules are considered suitable to be incorporated in contracts through selection in choice of law clauses, there are strong arguments in favour of

---

[394] L. Strikwerda, *Inleiding tot het Nederlandse Internationaal Privaatrecht* (2008) 177.

[395] Dutch Supreme Court 26 May 1989, Nederlandse Jurisprudentie (1992) 105 ; see also Dutch Supreme Court 5 January 2001, Nederlandse Jurisprudentie (2001) 391.

[396] Convention on the Contract for the International Carriage of Goods by Road (CMR), Geneva, 19 May 1956.

[397] Similarly, the District Court of Rotterdam 21 November 1996, Nederlands Internationaal Privaatrecht (1997) 223 held that the parties had validly made a choice for the CISG as the *lex contractus* even though the dispute was outside the Convention's formal scope of application..

[398] P. Bernardini, "International Arbitration and A-National Rules of Law", *ICC International Court of Arbitration Bulletin* 2 (2004) 58-69 (64, note 23), stating, *inter alia*, that the international Conventions, such as the 1980 Rome Convention, "provide for criteria identifying State law" and that accordingly "a-national rules may not be recognised by State courts as having the effects of a choice of law within the meaning of the conflict of law rules".

[399] Boele-Woelki, *op. cit.*, footnote 14.

a similar qualification of the Contract Principles since there are only minimal differences between the one and the other [400]. Once the choice of uniform substantive law as "the applicable law" were accepted, the next small step to be taken would consist of tolerating the choice for highly authoritative rules, such as the Contract Principles [401], since they are presented in the form of a code, comprising articles which, like the American Restatements, are supplemented with comments explaining their operation, and their legal quality is regularly emphasized [402].

177. In general, a better approach would have been had an express provision on the possibility of choosing a non-national law, as expressed in the 2005 Proposal, remained in the final text of Article 3 of the Rome I Regulation. The possibility for the parties to choose a non-national law as the *lex contractus* would have been ensured clearly in all States of the European Union. Such express regulation would have been in line with the approach which the vast majority of EU Member States maintain with respect to the freedom to choose a non-State body of law in arbitration [403]. In general,

---

[400] Fountoulakis, *op. cit.*, footnote 247, 304.

[401] De Ly, *op. cit.*, footnote 321, 143, and Diedrich, *op. cit.*, footnote 334, 385 : "bereits heute stehen mit den UNIDROIT Principles und den PECL umfassende, erwachsen gewordene Regelungen als alternatives Vertragsstatut zur Verfügung".

[402] Fountoulakis, *op. cit.*, footnote 247, 324.

[403] See, e.g., Article 1051 of the German Code of Civil Procedure, according to which the arbitrators shall decide the dispute "in accordance with . . . *rules of law*" chosen by the parties (emphasis added). Similarly, Article 834 of the Italian Code of Civil Procedure refers to the "rules" agreed upon by the parties. See also Article 34 of the Spanish Arbitration Act, Article 31 of the Finnish Arbitration Act, Article 1700 of the Belgian Code judiciaire, Article 1054 (2) of the Dutch Arbitration Act.

there are no obvious reasons to justify such a different treatment in determining the law applicable to commercial transactions between the courts and the arbitrators in the European Union [404]. A clear provision in Article 3 of the Rome I Regulation [405] would have avoided the risk of inconsistent interpretation between the text of the Regulation and the wording in recital (13) of the preamble.

178. As a result, however, a disparity among the Member States remains on this issue : a choice of a non-national law is considered a valid determination of the *lex contractus* in those legal systems where such a choice has been permitted. The Member States where such a choice has not been recognized will be under no obligation to alter their practice either, considering the absence of an express provision in that respect in the text of the Regulation. Thus, these Member States may continue to qualify the choice for a non-State body of law, such as the Contract Principles, as a *materiell-rechtliche Verweisung*. Accordingly, such Principles are part of the contract terms, but a *kollisionsrechtliche Verweisung* cannot effectively be made.

3.1.3. *The silence of the Rome II Regulation*

179. Party autonomy in non-contractual obligations can be seen as the little brother [406] of party autonomy in contractual relationships [407]. What is permitted in contracts is possible, to an almost similar extent, in delicts,

---

[404] In contrast Mankowski, *op. cit.*, footnote 195, 407-409.

[405] The term "State" could have been easily added to the term "law".

[406] Mankowski, *op. cit.*, footnote 195, 429.

[407] E. Lein, "The New Rome I/Rome II/Brussels I Synergy", *Yearbook of Private International Law* (2008) 177-198 (181-182).

torts and unjust enrichment as far as the will of the parties is concerned. Unlike the Rome I Regulation, the Rome II Regulation on the law applicable to non-contractual obligations of 11 July 2007 [408] does not state in its Preamble that the Regulation does not preclude parties from incorporating, by reference in their choice of law clause, a non-State body of law or an international Convention. Also a reference to the freedom of the parties to choose rules of substantive law in a future Community legal instrument containing such rules, is lacking [409]. During the drafting process the possible applicability of a law other than a national law of delict or tort was never discussed. Other issues were of more importance, such as whether the parties were to be able to agree to submit non-contractual obligations to the law of their choice and whether they might enter into such an agreement after the event giving rise to the damage had occurred [410]. Finally, both questions were answered in the affirmative and included in the Rome II Regulation. It is striking to note, however, that the discussion on the application of non-national law in the field of contract law, which started with the publication

---

[408] (EC) No. 864/2007, *Official Journal of the European Union* 2007/L 199/40. Article 32 determines that the regulation shall apply from 11 January 2009. Opinions differ as to whether Member State courts are under a duty to apply the Regulation not only to all events giving rise to damage, which occurs after the same day, but to all events which occur or have occurred since 20 August 2007. See J. Glöckner, "Keine klare Sache : Der zeitliche Anwendungsbereich der Rom II-Verordnung", *Praxis des internationa-len Privat- und Verfahrensrechts* (2009) 121-124, and A. Bücken, "Intertemporaler Anwendungsbereich der Rom II-VO", *Praxis des internationalen Privat- und Verfahrensrechts* (2009) 125-128.

[409] (EC) No. 593/2008, *Official Journal of the European Union* 2008, L 177/6.

[410] Mankowski, *op. cit.*, footnote 195, 428.

of the Contract Principles in 1994, was not mentioned
at all by specialists of delict and tort in international
law [411]. Hence, the Rome II Regulation, which is a year
older than its sibling, the Rome I Regulation, is silent
about the application of non-State norms. It was only
after the adoption of the Rome II Regulation that this
issue was mentioned incidentally in connection with
the Principles of European Tort Law [412] and, more
prominently, in respect of the optional European substantive law instrument [413]. Meanwhile, by contrast, at
several conferences which were aimed at presenting
the Rome I and Rome II regimes, attention was paid to
the selectability of laws other than national law [414].

180. In particular it has been advocated, in respect
of the Principles of European Tort Law, that the parties
should be allowed to choose non-State rules to govern
their liability in delict and tort even though these lack,

---

[411] Non-State law is not mentioned at all by Th. De
Boer, "Party Autonomy and Its Limitations in the Rome II
Regulation", *Yearbook of Private International Law*
(2007) 19-29, and "The Purpose of Uniform Choice-of-
Law Rules : The Rome II Regulation", *Netherlands
International Law Review* (2009) 295-332.

[412] Th. Kadner Graziano, "Das auf außervertragliche
Schuldverhältnisse anwendbare Recht nach Inkrafttreten
der Rom II-Verordnung", *Rabels Zeitschrift für ausländisches und internationales Privatrecht* (2009) 1-77 (9-11) ;
Th. Kadner Graziano, "Le nouveau droit international
privé communautaire en matière de responsabilité extracontractuelle", *Revue critique de droit international privé*
(2008) 445-511 (455) ; Th. Kadner Graziano, "Freedom to
Choose the Applicable Law in Tort — Articles 14 and 4
(3) of the Rome II Regulation", in B. William and J. Ahern
(eds.), *The Rome II Regulation on the Law Applicable to
Non-Contractual Obligations : A New Tort Litigation
Regime* (2009) 113-132 (118-119).

[413] Leible, *op. cit.*, footnote 208, 261.

[414] Verona Conference on the Rome I Regulation, 19-
20 March 2009, Vienna, 10 June 2009, Rechtswahl —
Grenzen und Chancen.

in particular, gap-filling devices. It seems possible that in situations where the parties have equal bargaining power and they do not reach an agreement on the application of the law of one of the parties, they might well agree on the application of the Principles of European Tort Law for any potential extra-contractual liability [415]. This choice should be permitted in so far as the national law, which falls to be applied according to the conflict of law rules, does not contain mandatory rules concerning the problem which it is intended to solve by application of the Principles or, in other words, ". . ., soweit das jeweils massgebliche staatliche Recht dispositiv ist" [416]. If, as might follow, the parties may not be allowed to displace any mandatory provisions of the national law of delict or tort which would fall to be applied in the situation to be resolved, their choice of the Principles of European Tort Law can only be categorized as a *materiellrechtliche Verweisung*. Due, in particular, to the lack of a gap-filling mechanism, it has not yet been proposed that a choice for the application of the Principles of European Tort Law should enable mandatory rules of the otherwise applicable law to be set aside although, according to certain views which have been expressed, the Principles "are perfectly adapted to the needs of transnational actors" [417]. A European Tort Litigation Regime is not yet considered to be selectable as the "applicable law".

---

[415] It is interesting to note, for instance, that Mankowski, *op. cit.*, footnote 195, 428, does not mention the Principles of European Tort Law at all ("Mangels ins Auge springenden Objekts für eine Wahl . . .") when discussing the problem as to whether parties in a non-contractual relationship should be allowed to choose a law other than national substantive law.

[416] Kadner Graziano, *op. cit.*, footnote 412, 9-11.

[417] *Ibid.*, 119.

3.1.4. Future European regulations in cross-border family matters

181. Choice by the parties of non-State law in cross-border family relations has not yet been debated at any great length. However, the choice for an optional *Matrimonium Europaeum*[418] has been proposed[419]. If such a set of rules for cross-border family relations were ever to be adopted by the European legislator it would have binding force. It has been proposed that such a uniform European family law should regulate its own scope of application and that it should only be applicable subject to the choice of the parties (opt in)[420].

182. Unlike in the field of liability arising in delict and tort, it has not yet been proposed in respect of family relations — at least to this author's knowledge — to allow the incorporation of rules which harmonize substantive law instruments (*materiellrechtliche Verweisung*) into agreements which the parties may conclude. The next step, which would be to allow the choice of non-national family rules, such as the CEFL Principles, which would govern, for example, property relations between spouses or maintenance obligations after divorce to the exclusion of the mandatory rules of a national family law (*kollisionsrechtliche Verweisung*), has not yet been ventured either. This

---

[418] This option has been discussed in the previous Chapter VII, Section 6.2.

[419] TMC Asser Instituut/Département de droit international UCL, Etude sur les régimes matrimoniaux des couples maries et sur le patrimoine des couples non maries dans le droit international privé et le droit interne des états membres de l'Union Européenne effectuée à la demande de la Commission Européenne Direction générale Justice et Affaires intérieures Unité A3 Coopération judiciaire en matière civile, JAI/A3/2001/03, 181.

[420] Dethloff, *op. cit.*, footnote 305, 255.

may change, however, if, in areas where spouses and parents are allowed and encouraged to conclude agreements, more choices for a law other than national law are made available. However, it should be borne in mind that as far as the CEFL Principles are concerned, not all sets are equally suitable for a cross-border relationship. They might be ineffective in solving specific problems since they have been initially designed as comparative information tools providing guidance as to how more convergence of family law systems in Europe can be achieved. Unlike the Divorce and Maintenance between Former Spouses Principles only the Parental Responsibilities Principles are more detailed and drafted, almost like a statute. Furthermore, it should be taken into account that, according to many family law systems, the autonomy of the parties is extremely limited due to State interests and the protection of the weaker party. For instance, in no European legal system to date are spouses entitled to agree on the application of their own divorce rules. This predominantly mandatory character of family law has also been taken into account in drafting the European Principles.

183. The next set of Principles of the CEFL, which is expected to be finalized in 2011, will address property relations between spouses [421]. Most of the Member States allow spouses to choose the law which is to be applicable to the matrimonial property regime. Pre- and post-marital contracts are permitted [422]. It is to be

---

[421] K. Boele-Woelki, B. Braat and I. Curry-Sumner (eds.), *European Family Law in Action*, Vol. IV, *Property Relations between Spouses*, European Family Law Series No. 24 (2009).

[422] See for a recent change in English law the judgment of the Court of Appeal of 2 July 2009 (*Radmacher* v. *Granatino*, England and Wales Court of Appeal (UK) Civ. 649), where it has been decided that the spouses should be bound by the terms of a German marriage contract.

expected that the CEFL will draft a European matrimonial property regime [423]. Would it not be an attractive proposition to include such a regime — if it were to be beneficial to both parties — in an ante-nuptial agreement? At least such incorporation should be classified as a *materiellrechtliche Verweisung*. Whether the choice of a CEFL European Property Regime would be recognized as a *kollisionsrechtliche Verweisung* is, again, a decision to be taken by the respective choice of law rules.

184. Where do we currently stand on the unification of conflict of law rules in family relations in Europe [424]? Is it likely that any future private international law Regulations will pay any attention to the possible application of a law other than national substantive family law?

3.1.4.1. Divorce

185. For more than 10 years the Member States of the European Union have been in the process of unifying their rules on cross-border divorce law [425] and it

---

[423] It might even be possible that this set of principles will "offer" its application in cross-border cases. See also the *Accord entre la République fédérale d'Allemagne et la République française instituant un régime matrimonial optionnel de la participation aux acquêts* which was signed on 4 February 2010.

[424] M. Jänterä-Jareborg, "Family Law in the European Judicial Space — Concerns Regarding Nation-State's Autonomy and Legal Coherence", in E. J. Hollo (ed.), *Kansallinen oikeus ja liittovaltioistuva Eurooppa/National Law and Europeanisation* (2009) 29-61.

[425] See A. Borrás, "From Brussels II to Brussels II *bis* and Further", in K. Boele-Woelki and C. González Beilfuss (eds.), *Brussels II* bis : *Its Impact and Application in the Member States*, European Family Law Series No. 14 (2007) 3-22.

was expected that unified conflict of law rules concerning matrimonial matters and parental responsibilities for international relationships would have been adopted during 2008. But the attempts have failed so far and the conflict of law rules in cross-border family matters continue to differ considerably [426]. They are united in diversity.

186. It all started in 1993 with the preparation of a Convention — the so-called Brussels II Convention — which contained rules on jurisdiction and the enforcement of judgments in matrimonial matters [427]. This Convention, which was adopted in May 1998, never entered into force. Instead — due to the entry into force of the Amsterdam Treaty in May 1999 [428] which paved the way for European legislative measures to be taken in cross-border situations — the Convention was transformed into a Regulation. On 1 March 2001 the Brussels II Regulation [429] entered into force for the then 15 Member States (except Denmark) [430] and from

---

[426] Conflict of law rules differ, from the regular application of the *lex fori* to the application of the national law of the spouses, the law of their habitual residence or the law with the "closest connection". These discrepancies may seem to be in dissonance with the fact that within the European Union there has been a free movement of divorce decisions since 2001, which provides that divorces obtained in one Member State are recognized in all other Member States.

[427] Brussels II Convention (28 May 1998) OJ 1998, C 221/1.

[428] Amsterdam Treaty (2 October 1997) OJ 1997, C 340/1.

[429] Council Regulation (EC) No. 1347/2000 of 29 May 2000 on jurisdiction and the recognition and enforcement of judgments in matrimonial matters and in matters of parental responsibility for children of both spouses, *Official Journal of the European Union*, L 160/19.

[430] In accordance with Articles 1 and 2 of the Protocol on the Position of Denmark annexed to the TEU Union

1 May 2004 onwards it also became effective — as part of the *acquis communitaire* — in the 10 European countries which acceded to the European Union on that date. Shortly afterwards, on 1 March 2005, Brussels II was replaced by the Brussels II *bis* Regulation [431]. The scope of application in respect of issues of parental responsibility was widened whereas matters regarding divorce essentially remained untouched [432]. In the same year, in 2005, it was announced that the Brussels II *bis* Regulation would be amended. This proposal, which was presented in 2006 [433], was aimed at complementing the jurisdiction and recognition rules with conflict of law rules on the law applicable to divorce.

187. The proposal to unify divorce rules for cross-border situations in Europe contained two significant elements : firstly, spouses would have been permitted jointly to select the competent court and, secondly, conflict of law rules which determine the law to be applied in cross-border divorce cases would have

---

and the TFEU, Denmark does not participate in the adoption of this regulation and is therefore neither bound by it nor subject to its application.

[431] Council Regulation (EC) No. 2201/2003 of 27 November 2003 concerning Jurisdiction and the Recognition and Enforcement in Matrimonial Matters and the Matters of Parental Responsibility, Repealing Regulation (EC) No. 1347/2000, *Official Journal of the European Union*, L 338.

[432] No differences as regards their substantive content exist between the Brussels II and the Brussels II *bis* versions of the jurisdiction rules concerning divorce, only the numbering of the articles changed. The issues addressed in Articles 2 to 8 in Brussels II moved to Articles 3-7 in Brussels II *bis*.

[433] Proposal for a Council Regulation Amending Regulation (EC) No. 2201/2003 as Regards Jurisdiction and Introducing Rules concerning Applicable Law in Matrimonial Matters, Brussels, 17 July 2006 COM (2006) 399 final, 2006/0135 (CNS).

become part of Community law [434]. Whereas, generally, the adoption of the choice of forum was generally welcomed, the conflict of law rules were highly disputed. The discussions were passionate and extensive. Little can be added to this debate [435]. The proposal to allow spouses to agree on the law which was to be applicable to divorce, however, were met by some concerns but not as great as those around the "default" rule and not such as to lead *per se* to non-adoption of the instrument. The law which could have been chosen was, however, restricted ; it must have had a connection with the parties, such as with their habitual residence or nationality, or the place where the marriage had taken place. Also parties would have been able to select the law of the forum. Given, in particular, the requirement for a reasonable relationship between the law designated by the parties and their personal situation, no reference whatsoever was made to non-national law. It was simply not a matter for discussion.

188. Conversely, the conflict of law rule which would have been applied in the absence of a choice of law by the parties caused the gulf between the Member

---

[434] See, for a comparison between the proposed European and the American approach, L. Silberman, "Rethinking Rules of Conflict of Laws in Marriage and Divorce in the United States : What Can We Learn from Europe ?", 82 *Tulane Law Review* (2008) 1999-2020.

[435] See, for all the arguments which have emerged, Th. De Boer, "The Second Revision of the Brussels II Regulation : Jurisdiction and Applicable Law", in K. Boele-Woelki and T. Sverdrup (eds.), *European Challenges in Contemporary Family Law*, European Family Law Series No. 19, (2008) 321-341. See further M. Jänterä-Jareborg, "Jurisdiction and Applicable Law in Cross-Border Divorce Cases in Europe", in J. Basedow, H. Baum and Y. Nishitani (eds.), *Japanese and European Private International Law in Comparative Perspective* (2008) 317-343.

States. It was proposed that where the spouses had not made a choice of the applicable law, the law of the State *(a)* where the spouses had their common habitual residence, or failing that *(b)* where the spouses had their last common habitual residence, in so far as one of them still resided there, or failing that *(c)* of which both spouses were nationals [436], or failing that *(d)* where the application was lodged, would have been applicable. The intended universality of this multi-stage conflict of law rule could have led to the application of a foreign law, not only the divorce law of another Member State but also the law of other jurisdictions. Some of these jurisdictions where, for instance, religion (such as Islam) plays a central role, might disrespect the principle of the spouses' equality. For this and several other reasons some Member States consider the application of foreign divorce law to be impossible. Instead they favoured the application of the *lex fori* as the general rule.

189. As a result, for the first time during the EC's legislative activities in cross-border matters, unanimity in adopting (an amendment of) a Regulation could not be reached. At the end of July 2008 several Member States [437] requested that a start be made with the — so-called — enhanced co-operation procedure [438] which was introduced under the Treaty of Amsterdam of 1997 as amended by the Treaty of Nice in 2001 [439]. Astonish-

---

[436] In the case of the United Kingdom and Ireland : where both spouses had their "domicile".

[437] Austria, France, Greece, Hungary, Italy, Luxembourg, Romania, Slovenia and Spain.

[438] K. Boele-Woelki, "To Be or Not to Be : Enhanced Cooperation in International Divorce Law within the European Union", *Victoria Wellington University Law Review* (2008) 779-792.

[439] In view of the enlargement of the European Union to 27 Member States.

ingly, the private international law rules for divorce would be, therefore, the first test case for the use of this only remaining option, which may well lead to a divided, two-speed European Union. At this stage it is uncertain how the partial unification of conflict of law rules in divorce will further develop. In any case, it is likely that the freedom of the spouses to choose the applicable divorce law will be upheld, albeit in a restricted sense, since this proposal received the support of a large majority of the Member States [440].

3.1.4.2. Maintenance obligations

190. The new European Regulation on jurisdiction, applicable law, recognition and enforcement of decisions and co-operation in matters relating to maintenance obligations of 18 December 2008 [441] refers in its provision on the determination of the applicable law (Art. 15) to the Hague Protocol of 23 November 2007 on the law applicable to maintenance obligations. This is a Protocol to the Hague Convention on the International Recovery of Child Support and other Forms of Family Maintenance, also concluded on 23 November 2007, and it is intended that the Member States should become bound by the Convention and, at least most of them, also by the Protocol. As yet, signature by the European Union of these instruments has not taken place. It is however envisaged that in the near future the European Union will accede to the Convention and

---

[440] See A. Fiorini, "Rome III — Choice of Law in Divorce : Is the Europeanization of Family Law Going Too Far ?", *International Journal of Law, Policy and the Family* (2000) 178-195.

[441] (EC) No. 4/2009, *Official Journal of the European Union* of 10 January 2009 L 7/1. According to Article 76 the Regulation became effective on 30 January 2009 but will only apply from 18 June 2011 onwards.

also to the Protocol, since it took part actively in the negotiations on both instruments [442]. Under Article 7 of the Hague Protocol the maintenance creditor and debtor may choose the law of the forum whereas under Article 8 they may designate the applicable maintenance law at any time and even before a dispute arises.

191. The Explanatory Report to the Hague Protocol considers two aspects to be of particular importance. In the first place,

> "the main advantage of the choice of applicable law is to secure a measure of stability and foreseeability : if the parties have made such a choice, the law designated remains applicable despite any changes in their personal situations, and regardless of the authority seised in the event of a dispute. In particular, a change of the maintenance creditor's habitual residence will not entail a change of the applicable law".

Secondly,

> "the choice of applicable law is particularly useful in the relationship between the spouses when they conclude, before or during the marriage, an agreement relating to maintenance obligations and/or ownership of their respective property. Thanks to this choice, the law applicable to the maintenance obligation is set in advance, which avoids any questioning of the agreement later." [443]

---

[442] Letter of the European Commission sent to the Hague Conference on Private International Law on 14 October 2008 concerning the accession by the European Community to Conventions of the Hague Conference on Private International Law, 15226/08, JUSTCIV 235.

[443] A. Bonomi, Preliminary Draft Protocol on the Law Applicable to Maintenance Obligations, Explanatory Report, Preliminary Document No. 33 of August 2007 for the attention of the Twenty-First Session of November 2007, 17.

192. The parties' choice is subject to a number of limitations. They may choose the law of (any) State of which either party is a national or of the habitual residence of either party at the time of the designation. It clearly follows from the wording *the law of the State* that national substantive law is meant. Conversely, this is not the case in respect of the following two possibilities providing for accessory connections : the parties may choose *the law* which has been applied to their property regime, their divorce or legal separation. This possibility is aimed at allowing the spouses to make the law applicable to the maintenance obligations on the one hand, and that governing the matrimonial property regime and/or the divorce or legal separation, on the other, coincide [444].

193. If the choice of a European matrimonial property regime drafted by the Commission on European Family Law — as indicated above — were to be accepted, under the conflict of law rules, as a choice for the "applicable law", this law might also govern the maintenance obligation if the creditor and debtor were to so agree, provided that the parties also refer to the CEFL Principles on Maintenance between Former Spouses. Most likely, the drafters of the Hague Protocol only had in mind national law as the law governing a maintenance obligation ; it is likely, therefore, that such an extensive interpretation would be rejected. However, theoretically, this option exists and, were either a European uniform family law to be adopted as an optional instrument, for example, or the reference to or incorporation of the Family Law Principles into family agreements be made possible, the conflict of law rules of the 2007 Hague Protocol should at least allow such an extensive interpretation.

---

[444] Bonomi, *op. cit.*, footnote 443, 17-18, and Bonomi, *op. cit.*, footnote 150, 354-355.

3.1.4.3. *Property relations between spouses*

194. Currently a European Regulation on conflict of laws in matters concerning matrimonial property regimes, including the question of jurisdiction and mutual recognition, is being prepared [445]. To that end a Green Paper was published in July 2006 [446]. The Green Paper launched a wide-ranging consultation exercise on the legal questions which arise in an international context as regards matrimonial property regimes in order to detect whether there is an apparent need for the adoption of Community legislative rules. The Green Paper was based upon an extensive comparative study on the rules governing conflicts of jurisdiction and laws on matrimonial property regimes and the implications for property issues when unmarried couples separate in the then 15 Member States. This study [447], which also made a comparison of domestic matrimonial property systems, proposed "l'instauration d'un régime matrimonial européen 'subsidiaire'. Celui-ci, de nature Conventionnelle, serait commun à tous les États membres et pourrait, dans chacun d'eux, être librement adopté par les époux, lors de la conclusion de leur mariage, à l'instar de tout autre régime matrimonial Conventionnel". Thus a subsidiary European matrimonial property regime should be made available in all Member States. This idea is not new.

---

[445] C. M. V. Clarkson, "Matrimonial Property on Divorce : All Change in Europe", *Journal of Private International Law* (2008) 421-442 (442). According to the author's view, there are valid reasons for the United Kingdom to give serious consideration to opting in to the proposed instrument.

[446] See Green Paper on Conflicts of Laws in Matters concerning Matrimonial Property Regimes, Including the Question of Jurisdiction and Mutual Recognition of 17 July 2006 ; COM (2006) 400 final.

[447] TMC Asser Instituut, *op. cit.*, footnote 419, 181.

195. Already in 1995 [448] and, later, 2001 [449] it had been proposed to draft a Treaty presenting a Uniform Law regarding an optional international marital contract. The idea was that, at the moment of entering into a marriage, the spouses should be allowed to choose this regime like any other normal regime. The Green Paper issued by the European Commission, however, does not deal with this specific notion. This is to be regretted since it would have been interesting to know how a European matrimonial property regime would have been received in the Member States. Surprisingly however, in 2009, the European Commission requested an impact assessment on community instruments on the rights of property arising out of matrimonial property regimes and property of unmarried couples [450], which mainly focuses on the possibility of drafting an optional uniform European matrimonial property regime [451]. A draft of such a regime has lately been submitted by a group of European notaries [452]. In addi-

---

[448] A. Agell, "The Division of Property upon Divorce from a European Perspective", in *Liber amicorum Marie-Thérèse Meulders-Klein : Droit comparé des personnes et de la famille* (1998) 1-20 (18-20).

[449] A. Verbeke, "Perspectives for an International Marital Contract", *Maastricht Journal of European and Comparative Law* (2001) 189-200.

[450] Task specifications for the assignment were issued by Direction E : Justice.

[451] The contractor is asked to : (1) assess the feasibility of such a uniform European optional regime ; (2) analyse the added value, advantages and problems of such European optional regime and its certificate ; (3) assess what could be the impact of such measures for citizens, stakeholders and Member States, including obstacles and advantages ; (4) assess the main difficulties of this proposal ; and (5) assess — if possible — whether there could be a relevant impact on activity of stakeholders and on taxation.

[452] F. Salerno Cardillo (rapporteur), Propositions pour un contrat de mariage "Européen".

tion, we have to await both the aforementioned *Matrimonium Europeum* and the CEFL Principles on Property Relations between Spouses to know whether they will be considered to be eligible as the chosen *lex matrimonio propietad*. In view of these developments, it might be that the Regulation will address the issue of selecting a European matrimonial property regime. As regards the possibility for the spouses to designate the national law applicable to the marital relationship, there will be no major problems. Spouses will be permitted, either before or during the marriage, to choose the law applicable since it facilitates the organization of their relations towards third parties and between themselves. Yet the choice will be subject to several limitations : a close connection between the spouses and the chosen law will be required and, to that end, objective connecting factors such as the habitual residence or the nationality of one of the spouses at the time at which the choice is made will most likely be used [453]. The Proposal is expected in 2010.

3.1.4.4. Succession

196. Family law mainly governs all legal relationships linked to marriage and partnerships, parentage and the civil status of persons. As a rule, the law of succession is classified as a matter distinct from family law on account of the fact that it mainly aims at defining the rules for passing on the inheritance and for regulating the transfer of the inheritance itself. However, both fields of law are akin to each other. On

---

[453] On 5 February 2008, the European Commission published a summary of the 40 replies which it had received from Governments, academia and associations. See http://ec.europa.eu/civiljustice/news/docs/summary_answers_com_2006_400_en.pdf.

14 October 2009, the Proposal for a Regulation on jurisdiction, applicable law, recognition and enforcement of decisions and authentic instruments in matters of succession and the creation of a European Certificate of Succession was issued [454]. It constitutes another building block in the codification of European private international law [455]. As far as the proposed conflict of law rules are concerned the traditional approach has been chosen. According to the general rule laid down in Article 16 the law applicable to the succession as a whole shall be that of the State in which the deceased had his or her habitual residence at the time of his or her death. In a disposition of property upon death — the Proposal does neither contain a definition of this term nor does it refer to the term "will" — a person may choose, as the law to govern the succession as a whole, the law of the State whose nationality he or she possesses (Article 17 of the Proposal). As a result, only State law, which is able to be localized through the use of the connecting factors habitual residence and nationality, may govern a cross-border succession relationship. This was expected since there has been no discussion to apply any other law because neither unifying nor harmonizing substantive law instruments in the field of succession law have ever been adopted by any international organization or academic commission [456].

---

[454] COM (2009)154 final.

[455] A. Dutta, "Succession and Wills in the Conflict of Laws on the Eve of the Europeanisation", *Rabels Zeitschrift für ausländisches und internationales Privatrecht* (2009) 547-606.

[456] Zimmermann, *op. cit.*, footnote 82, 503-510, 512, however rightly considers the perception highly questionable that the law of succession is widely held to be shaped by national culture and not to lend itself to comparative discourse. In line with this conclusion it is to be expected

3.2. *The traditional approach is still dominating : choice of non-national law cannot supersede mandatory rules of the otherwise applicable law*

197. The exploration of the various conflict of law instruments reveals that only the ICLAIC explicitly refers to non-State law as the *lex contractus*, however opinions differ as to whether the wording of the respective conflict of law rules in fact justifies this interpretation. In respect of the Rome I and the Rome II Regulations the general view is that a choice of the Contract or Tort Principles should only be considered as contract terms since the mandatory rules of the otherwise applicable law cannot be superseded. The classical limits on choice of law, by eliminating the State legislative monopoly and by permitting the choice of a law other than a national law [457], still pertain. Recognizing such a choice as a *kollisionsrechtliche Verweisung* would be going one step too far though an attempt has been made to argue against this restrictive approach. Furthermore, it has been submitted that the choice of a Convention containing uniform substantive law is a choice for a "law" which has the same authoritative quality as any domestic national law.

198. In family law the idea of applying a non-State body of law instead of national law has been proposed but has not yet gained any substantial support. Given the mandatory character of family law in many areas

---

that once also Principles of European Succession Law will be drafted. See also R. Foqué and A. Verbeke, "Conclusions. Towards an Open and Flexible Imperative Inheritance Law", in Ch. Castelein, R. Foqué and A. Verbeke (eds.), *Imperative Inheritance Law in a Late-Modern Society, Five Perspectives*, European Family Law Series No. 26 (2009) 203-221.

[457] Lein, *op. cit.*, footnote 407, 181.

this is not surprising. But, even in areas where parties may conclude a contract, opportunities to explore new possibilities have been dismissed by the European Commission. The coming into existence of an optional unified European family law system might enhance the debate. Once this stage is reached the discussion about the interrelationship between the European uniform substantive law instruments in the law of obligations and conflict of laws will become of equal importance.

4. Application of Non-National Substantive Law in Case of Arbitration

199. In arbitration the vast majority of States have a very different approach regarding the freedom of the parties to choose the applicable law [458]. In general, the possibility for the parties to influence various aspects of arbitration by their agreement is inherent in international commercial arbitration law and practice. The same is true with respect to the choice of the applicable substantive law. The UNCITRAL Model Law on International Commercial Arbitration of 1985, on which almost all modern arbitration laws are based [459], allows the parties to subject their contract to the "rules of law" which they wish [460]. This freedom is incorporated into arbitration statutes as well as in various arbitration rules worldwide. The parties are generally given a full opportunity to choose any system of law, any set

---

[458] V. Lazic, "The Impact of Uniform Law on the National Law in the Netherlands : Limits and Possibilities — Commercial Arbitration", Vol. 13.2, *Electronic Journal of Comparative Law* (2009) http ://www.ejcl.org/132/article132-3.pdf.

[459] P. Binder, *International Commercial Arbitration and Conciliation in UNCITRAL Model Law Jurisdictions*, 2009.

[460] Article 28, Section 1, sentence 1.

of rules or principles, including non-national law [461].
This right of the parties is virtually undisputed in contemporary arbitration law and practice [462]. More significantly, many statutes, as well as arbitration rules [463],
do not require arbitrators to apply the conflict of law
method in determining the applicable substantive law
in the absence of the parties' choice [464], but they may
use the so-called *voie directe*. It is widely recognized
that arbitrators may apply "rules of law" which they
consider appropriate [465], including the Contract Principles, which have been considered frequently as general
rules of contract law or as part of the *lex mercatoria*.

---

[461] The annotated UNCITRAL Explanatory Note by
the UNCITRAL Secretariat on the Model Law on International Commercial Arbitration, http://www.uncitral.org/
uncitral/en/uncitral_texts/arbitration/1985Model_arbitration.
html., states that

"by referring to the choice of 'rules of law' instead of
'law', the Model Law gives the parties a wider range of
options as regards the designation of the law applicable
to the substance of the dispute in that they may, for
example, agree on rules of law that have been elaborated by an international forum but have not been incorporated into any national legal system".

[462] See, for example, Article 1051 of the German Code
of Civil Procedure, according to which the arbitrators
shall decide the dispute "in accordance with . . . *rules
of law*" chosen by the parties (emphasis added). Similarly, Article 834 of the Italian Code of Civil Procedure
refers to the "rules" agreed upon by the parties. See also,
Article 34 of the Spanish Arbitration Act, Article 31 of the
Finnish Arbitration Act, Article 1700 of the Belgian Code
judiciaire.

[463] See, for example, Article 1054 of the Netherlands
Code of Civil Procedure ; Article 1496 of the French Code
of Civil Procedure. A similar approach has been followed
in rules of arbitral institutions worldwide. See, for
example, Article 17 ICC Rules ; Article 23.3 LCIA Rules.

[464] Metzger, *op. cit.*, footnote 376, 534-541.

[465] Fountoulakis, *op. cit.*, footnote 247, 325.

Moreover in the context of arbitration, it has been reported, that the Contract Principles can be chosen as the applicable law [466]. Choice by the parties' of a non-national law is not frequent but it is also not unusual. Besides, the regularity — or not — with which such a choice is made and such a law is applied is not, in itself, a convincing argument [467]. What is important is that disputes have been decided according to transnational law to the exclusion of national substantive law.

200. Consequently, commercial parties are allowed to refer, in arbitration, to the UNIDROIT or European Contract Principles when choosing the law to govern their commercial transaction. This constitutes a good reason for the parties to prefer their disputes to be resolved by arbitration rather than by national courts. Even though there is a favourable enforcement regime for court decisions and authentic instruments in the European Union under the Brussels I Regulation on jurisdiction and the recognition and enforcement of judgments in civil and commercial matters, which regime is comparable to that in the 1958 New York Convention relating to the enforcement of foreign arbitral awards, the parties' freedom to choose a non-State body of law will, in all likelihood, not exclude the

---

[466] Critically commented upon by Mankowski, *op. cit.*, footnote 195, 407 :

"In der Schiedspraxis mag sich die Wahl der Principles . . . schon heute immerhin ein Stück weit etabliert haben. Im Gesamtspektrum ist dies aber nur ein kleiner Ausschnitt. Dieser Ausschnitt mag prominent dokumentiert sein, weil gerade diese Schiedssprüche mit überproportionaler Häufigkeit publiziert werden, da ihre Urheber ein eigenes Interesse an Publizität haben."

[467] Oser, *op. cit.*, footnote 6, 155 : "The relative recent date of their publication needs to be borne in mind and, following from that, the backlog in judicial or arbitral decisions dealing with them."

application of the mandatory rules of the otherwise applicable law if the dispute is to be decided by a court, not only within the European Union but worldwide. In international business, parties should have the security of knowing the possible consequences and effects of their choice of law clause in a certain and predictable way.

201. The question arises as to whether the perceived discrepancy as between litigation and arbitration concerning the determination of the law which is applicable to commercial transactions, actually matters [468]. Are there convincing arguments which justify the distinction between the liberal approach towards non-national law in international commercial arbitration and the restrictive attitude in court litigation under the Rome I Regulation [469] ? Obviously, views vary. Some want to preserve the disparity between the one and the other due to the differences regarding, respectively, procedure, party autonomy, costs and the enforcement of a decision or award [470]. Others argue that such significant differences should not be maintained [471]. In the case of court litigation, judges should also apply such commercial "codifications" as the *lex contractus* since the Contract Principles are designed specifically for international transactions. In turn, they

---

[468] F. Rigaux, "Examen de quelques questions laissées ouvertes par la Convention de Rome sur la loi applicable aux obligations contractuelles", *Cahiers de droit européen* (1988), 306-321 (318).

[469] De Ly, *op. cit.*, footnote 321, 144.

[470] Mankowski, *op. cit.*, footnote 195, 407-409.

[471] W.-H. Roth, "Zur Wählbarkeit nichtstaatlichen Rechts", in H.-P. Mansel, Th. Pfeiffer, H. Kronke, Ch. Kohler and R. Hausmann (eds.), *Festschrift Erik Jayme* (2004) 757-772. P. Béraudo, "Faut-il avoir peur du contrat sans loi ?", in *Le droit international privé : esprit et méthodes, Mélanges en l'honneur de Paul Lagarde* (2005) 93-112 (98).

can be characterized as achieving re-regulation at a higher level than the national State level[472], the corollary to this being that the obligatory *Zwischenschaltung* of conflict of law rules, which generally only permit State law to govern cross-border relationships, makes litigation less attractive. Hence, the restrictive, traditional point of view risks driving parties out of domestic courts and into international commercial arbitration which may be too expensive in relation to smaller claims and for small and medium-sized enterprises[473]. The weighing of the (dis-)advantages in respect of the choice between litigation and arbitration should be left to the parties and should not decided by a paternalistic legislator[474].

202. As far as the courts in the Union Member States are concerned the opportunity has been missed to capture the "arbitration approach". It is understandable that the European legislator was reluctant to go so far as to provide the opportunity for national judges to apply non-national law in the absence of the parties' choice. Yet, it would have been more appropriate to incorporate fully the principle of party autonomy and provide the business community in Europe with the same degree of freedom as they have in arbitration when choosing the applicable substantive law. Hence, the recent submission that the choice of non-State law should at least be possible between parties to a commercial contract (B2B contracts) should be supported. This is particularly so bearing in mind that, from a practical point of view, in some cases it may be easier to determine the contents of, for example, the UNIDROIT Principles than the contents of "foreign" law.

---

[472] De Ly, *op. cit.*, footnote 321, 145.
[473] De Ly, *op. cit.*, footnote 321, 144.
[474] Metzger, *op. cit.*, footnote 376, 542.

5. *Application of Non-national Substantive Law in Case of Mediation in Family Matters*

203. Corresponding to international arbitration in commercial matters is international mediation, or alternative dispute resolution, in family matters. In almost all European legal systems mediation is recognized as a valuable notion and a beneficial practice. A common core of opinion exists, and there is increasing awareness, as to the fact that the most efficient and successful way to achieve and guarantee a common understanding is for the parties to have gone through the process of seeking, negotiating and drafting an agreement on their own terms. Whilst the Council of Europe is highly active in this field [475], a new tool to promote international family mediation within the European Union has been provided by the European Directive on certain aspects of mediation in civil and commercial matters which was adopted on 21 May 2008 [476]. Member States are obliged to have transposed the Directive into their national law before 21 May 2011. The Directive applies to processes whereby two or more parties to a cross-border dispute attempt by themselves, on a voluntary basis, to reach an amicable agreement on the settlement of their dispute with the assistance of a mediator.

204. According to Article 1 (2) the Directive is to apply, in cross-border disputes [477], to civil and commer-

---

[475] European Commission for the Efficiency of Justice, Guidelines for a better implementation of the existing recommendation concerning family mediation and mediation in civil matters, 7 December 2007, CEPEJ (2007)14.

[476] 2008/52/EC, *Official Journal of the European Community* L 136/3.

[477] Nothing prevents Member States from applying the provisions based on the Directive also to internal mediation processes.

cial matters except as regards rights and obligations which are not at the parties' disposal under the relevant applicable law. This is the only time that reference is made to the law to be applied. If the parties are not free to decide about their rights and obligations, which is particularly frequent in family law and employment law [478], the Directive is not applicable. Mediation conducted by a judge, who is not responsible for any judicial proceedings concerning the dispute in question, is included whereas attempts made, by the court or the judge seised, to settle a dispute in the course of judicial proceedings concerning the dispute in question are excluded from the scope of application [479]. According to Article 2, for a dispute to be characterized as "cross-border" requires that, as at the date on which the parties agree to use mediation after the dispute has arisen, at least one of the parties is domiciled or habitually resident in a Member State other than that of any other party ; mediation may be ordered by the court ; an obligation to use mediation may arise under national law or when a court invites the parties to use mediation.

205. Like international arbitrators, international mediators have no forum. However, unlike arbitration no award is rendered in mediation. A successful mediation is finalized in the form of an agreement to which, in the optimum situation, both parties have contributed equally. The question arises as to which rules and laws are to be applied in cross-border cases, such as disputes about contact with children, relocation of children or child abduction ? International mediation is becoming increasingly important in particular in these kinds of child-related disputes [480]. New ways are being

---

[478] Recital 10 of the Mediation Directive.

[479] Article 3 *(a)*.

[480] See for instance the successful work of the Reunite International Child Abduction Centre, www.reunite.org.

developed to help separating couples in seeking to resolve their dispute outside court.

206. If successful, cross-border mediation results in an agreement between parties who, by definition, are located in different countries. If they are at liberty to dispose of their rights and duties in relation to, say, a child according to the law of the habitual residence of that child, which is the commonly applied rule, it seems logical that they should be able, also, to choose the applicable law governing their — resulting — parental agreement. The Mediation Directive is silent on this point [481]. It lacks any applicable law provision and nothing on the issue was suggested during the drafting of the Directive, far less prescribed in the final text. Bearing in mind that the ontological background to mediation lies in the law of voluntary obligations the law applicable to such obligations should be considered as being relevant. This means that only the rules of the Rome I Regulation can determine this issue within the ambit of activity anticipated by the Mediation Directive. Hence, in every case, on entering into a mediation process, it is advisable for the parties to include an applicable law clause in the mediation agreement. This becomes even more important when one of the parties finally requests the enforcement of such an agreement, which, according to Article 6 of the Mediation Directive, is to be made possible in all Member States. The content of an agreement resulting from mediation shall be enforceable unless, in the case in question, either the content of that agreement is *con-*

---

[481] Under Article 46 of Brussels II *bis* — see also recital (22) — an agreement which is enforceable as an authentic instrument in one Member State would be enforceable elsewhere in the European Union on the same basis as a court decision ; it is for consideration in how far agreements involving parental responsibility will be so enforceable.

trary to the law of the Member State where the request is made or the law of that Member State does not provide for its enforceability.

207. All in all it is unclear how far party autonomy reaches in the case of mediation in respect of the applicable law. Seemingly the parties' will is not unlimited since at the enforcement stage the content of the mediation agreement is scrutinized. If it is considered to be contrary to the law of the Member State where enforcement is sought the request will be dismissed. For the future it remains to be seen whether, for instance, a parental agreement resulting from mediation in which the parties determine the terms of their future relationship as parents in respect of their child will not be enforced because reference is made to non-national rules, such as the CEFL Principles regarding Parental Responsibilities.

6. Limited Freedom to Determine the Applicable Law

208. It has been demonstrated that, where conflict of law rules are to be applied by domestic courts, these rules generally do not permit the designation of a law other than national law. If the parties have not agreed on a choice of law clause this is always the case when the court has to determine the applicable law. In addition, the freedom of the parties to determine that their private relationship should be governed by a law other than a national substantive law is, all in all, fairly limited. Whether we should maintain this restricted approach of conflict of law rules will be questioned in the final chapter.

CHAPTER IX

FINAL OBSERVATIONS : DENATIONALIZATION
OF PRIVATE LAW

209. What does the foregoing analysis of the interaction between unifying and harmonizing substantive
law and conflict of laws reveal ? In this final chapter,
firstly the function of conflict of law rules is addressed
in order to explain why the application of non-State
law encounters difficulties when it comes to its application in international cases ; secondly, it is questioned
whether there are convincing arguments for making a
distinction between State legislation and private law-
making. What kind of law is better attuned to regulate
international relationships ? Additionally, the question
arises whether it should be taken for granted that private law is only acceptable if adopted as democratically legitimate — say parliamentary — law. Next, as
far as co-operation between unifying and harmonizing
substantive law instruments on the one side and conflict of law rules on the other is concerned, it is questionable how (inter)dependently the one can achieve its
aims and objectives without the support of the other.
Differentiations are apparent. The state of the art in the
application of a law other than national law in cross-
border relationships is described almost at the end of
these final observations. Finally, a visionary picture is
sketched (a door is opened to another world).

1. The Sufferings of Conflict of Law Rules

210. One characteristic of (continental) European
conflict of law systems is that their rules tend to function according to geographical terms. The cross-border

relationship is to be locatable within the territory of one State, whereas such a relationship is, by definition, connected to more than one State. Also when parties have not determined the applicable law, only national substantive law is designated by conflict of law rules. Their main role is to connect the international relationship with a State law and to determine that that law is applicable. The international legal relationship in question is pushed or drawn to one single jurisdiction ; it is nationalized. The conflict of law rules select national systems of law instead of rules. This is the traditional approach in (continental) Europe — the judiciary is strictly obliged to apply State law — which has been applied for more than 200 years, though this does not obtain in the United States of America. Rules of unifying and harmonizing substantive law cannot be located resulting in the main problem which has been discussed in the various fields in the previous chapters. So far conflict of law rules have only national law to offer [482]. It is evident that they have not been adapted to allow a law other than a national law to govern a cross-border relationship. Sayings like "private international lawis the cause of a problem, for which it regards itself a solution" [483] probably provide a succinct analysis but do not take us any further. Instead, and in particular in view of the increasing body of unifying and harmonizing substantive law, we need a new perspective. This vision was already expressed more than 30 years ago by the great comparatist and tireless champion of the *lex mercatoria* Clive M. Schmitthoff :

"Private international law, and especially the

---

[482] D. Schmidtchen, "Lex Mercatoria und die Evolution des Rechts", in C. Ott and H. B. Schäfer, *Vereinheitlichung und Diversität des Zivilrechts in transnationalen Wirtschaftsräumen* (2002) 1-31 (9).

[483] Schmidtchen, *op. cit.*, footnote 481,11.

search for the applicable law, is an artificial man-made obstacle to international trade. . . . No matter how important private international law still is and will remain in the future, we must rethink our attitude to it." [484]

What should the new approach look like ? The crucial question is what kind of law is acceptable to conflict of law rules. Should this law be restricted to national law or should it be extended to de-localized law ?

2. *Private Law-making and Its Legitimation*

211. In their chapter on uniform private law, comparative law and private international law, the authors of a well-known German handbook on private international law [485] dedicate one chapter to the — as they call it — *Unechtes (nichtstaatliches) Einheitsrecht und "Lex Mercatoria"*. The first part of this title can be translated either as "false" or "artificial" or "not genuine" (non-State) uniform law which clearly constitutes a *contradictio in terminis* since the meanings of the words so combined are in conflict with one another. Non-State law can be uniform law, uniform law is also State law, false uniform law does not exist and neither does the combination false and non-State law make any sense.

212. In this same chapter the authors state that "the final word always rests with the state ; whatever it fails to authorise has no prospect of recognition — especially within a democratic state" [486]. The democratic

---

[484] C. M. Schmitthoff, "Die künftigen Aufgaben der Rechtsvergleichung", *Juristenzeitung* (1978) 495-499 (497).

[485] Ch. Von Bar and P. Mankowski, *Internationales Privatrecht*, Band I, *Allgemeine Lehren* (2003) 75-88.

[486] Von Bar and Mankowski, *op. cit.*, footnote 484, 81.

legitimacy of State law should, however, be put into perspective [487]. It has been observed rightly that more than half of the world's population still lives in non-liberal or semi-liberal States where private law can hardly be seen as having democratic legitimacy whereas even in the so-called liberal States the bulk of private law is often democratically legitimized only in a formal manner [488]. Within the European Union there exists a decisive legitimacy deficit for the individual Member States in respect of today's private laws since they possess practically no leeway in the process of implementing EC Directives [489]. Moreover, the adoption of Regulations even excludes any participation of national parliaments [490]. Therefore the democracy argument should not be over-emphasized.

213. What is more important is the quality of the law-making [491]. In this respect the harmonizing substantive law instruments, in particular, are conceived as the expression of universally valid legal principles, which constitute the common core of different national systems of private law [492]. The private harmonization projects are developed without a political mandate for

---

[487] Michaels, *op. cit.*, footnote 6, 887, and Oser, *op. cit.*, footnote 6, 76-91.

[488] See Calliess, *op. cit.*, footnote 22, 477, with further references.

[489] Calliess, *op. cit.*, footnote 22, 478.

[490] Except in family law with cross-border implications where they do have a blocking role, see Article 81.3 TFEU.

[491] Oser, *op. cit.*, footnote 6, 11-13.

[492] R. Michaels, *op. cit.*, footnote 6, 872 : "Sie [die UNIDROIT Principles, KBW] sind eine Kodifikation, keine Rechtsordnung ; sie sind 'rules of law', nicht 'law' ", whereas Kessedjian, *op. cit.*, footnote 7, 325 states : "The UNIDROIT Principles are really not principles but rules, some fairly detailed, which cover most of the issues encountered in the life of an international contract."

legislation [493]. The members of the academic organizations do not represent their national systems. Instead they distance themselves from their own legal background because within the European or global setting these latter perspectives should, ultimately, prevail. Each of these projects, and its associated extensive intellectual labour, has required many years of deliberation, sound judgment and technical skills. The drafters detected differences and similarities and diverging and converging tendencies. They built on the one and coped with the other. In doing so they drafted transnational rules which are based on comparative research. In this context it has been submitted that such scientific activity at the comparative level is the province of scholars rather than civil servants, however knowledgable and dedicated the latter may be [494]. For each field of law it falls to be decided by the stakeholders involved whether the respective Principles produced by the various private organizations are indeed an improvement, as far as cross-border relationships are concerned, in comparison with national law. This has been confirmed frequently, in respect of the Contract Principles, by business lawyers, judges and arbitrators alike. A true choice of the Contract Principles as the law to be applied, with conflict of laws effects before State courts, should be favoured, since the Principles provide a self-contained, coherent and balanced system of rules of law, that is a consistent framework of common values which lay open "the relative worth and importance of competing legislative grounds", thus allowing a court to develop and refine the "law" [495].

---

[493] Calliess, *op. cit.*, footnote 22, 475.

[494] Goode, *op. cit.*, footnote 285, 32.

[495] In this sense Oser, *op. cit.*, footnote 6, 157-158. In particular in respect of the UNIDROIT Principles he states that they have been drafted with the mandate and approval of an internationally recognized organization.

Moreover, in the case of a sales contract, the Contract Principles constitute a perfect supplement for resolving those questions not addressed by the CISG because their legal solutions are on a par, internationally, with the CISG [496].

214. In respect of the applicability of the European Principles on Tort Law, as the law governing a non-contractual cross-border relationship, it is generally acknowledged that they "are perfectly adapted to the needs of transnational actors". Also the Family Law Principles have been tested empirically as to whether they are indeed acceptable and/or regarded as improving on existing national laws. The answer in respect of both sets — divorce and maintenance between former spouses and parental responsibilities is positive [497]. The subsequent question would be as to whether they are better attuned to regulate an international family relationship than a national family law. Since the drafters of the Family Law Principles have not so far envisaged this purpose, it is not yet on the agenda. However, the matter will gain more attention once a European matrimonial property regime has been proposed and/or established.

215. In conclusion : no doubt the notion of non-State law in the form of Principles is off limits to those who still believe in the idea that only a sovereign — and, by extension, a "sovereign" parliament — can make law [498], but the drafting thereof is being widely undertaken and it is considered to be a promising alternative.

3. Co-operation : Does the One Need the Other ?

216. The question whether unifying and harmonizing substantive law instruments need conflict of laws

---

[496] Fountoulakis, *op. cit.*, footnote 247, 326.
[497] Örücü and Mair, *op. cit.*, footnote 300.
[498] Juenger, *op. cit.*, footnote 289, 230.

and *vice versa* can be subdivided into four combinations :

1. Unifying substantive law and conflict of laws.
2. Conflict of laws and unifying substantive law.
3. Harmonizing substantive law and conflict of laws.
4. Conflict of laws and harmonizing substantive law.

Since the first subject of each combination indicates the perspective which will be taken, combinations 1 and 3 are dissimilar to combinations 2 and 4 even though the same subjects are interacting.

3.1. Unifying substantive law and conflict of laws

217. Generally, unifying substantive law instruments prescribe their own scope of application. They refer to objective circumstances such as the places of business of the parties in contracting States. If this requirement is fulfilled the uniform rules are to be applied automatically. Conflict of law rules are not to be consulted, since uniform law takes precedence over the conflict of law rules. The latter only come into play when uniform substantive law does not command its own application. The picture looks different, however, if the scope of application is enlarged through the use of conflict of law rules which lead to the application of the law of a State which is a party to the unifying substantive law instrument. This is the CISG technique. Which conflict of law rules are then to be applied ? The CISG, for instance, only makes reference to "the rules of private international law" without any further indication. Generally, these are, in the case of a domestic court, the rules of the forum which has been seised whereas in the case of international arbitration, arbitrators may choose which conflict of law rules, if any, they want to apply. Admittedly, reference to conflict of law rules is an additional measure to widen the scope

of application of uniform law but this is not strictly necessary. On the other hand, the more countries become bound by a multilateral Convention which contains uniform law the less reference to conflict of law rules is needed and theoretically this fall-back may even become obsolete if all countries in the world were to apply the same uniform law in cross-border relationships. However, this may only happen in utopia.

3.2. *Conflict of laws and unifying substantive law*

218. Depending on whether the unifying substantive law instrument uses the opt-out or opt-in method the answer as to whether conflict of law rules need uniform law differs. If contracting parties validly opt out of the application of uniform law their declaration is to be considered as a negative choice of the applicable law. Uniform law is excluded from its application in their particular relationship. The next step is then provided by conflict of law rules. Which national law is then to be applied ? Usually, and this is recommendable in terms of clarity, parties combine the exclusion of uniform law with a clear choice of law clause which designates the applicable national law. Should the parties fail to stipulate the applicable law the objective conflict of law rules should provide the answer. The conflict of law mechanism of Article 1 (1) *(b)* of the CISG demonstrates particularly that the control in deciding which substantive law is applicable is taken away from the conflict of law rules. The final decision — as to whether either the CISG rules or national sales law are applicable — is taken by the contracting States. They consider the designation of a national contract law as a reference to the Convention rules unless they have made the reservation not to apply the intermediary function/task of conflict of law rules.

219. Conflict of law rules are, however, needed

when parties make a choice for the application of the uniform substantive law even though their relationship appears not to fall within the geographical scope of application of that law. If an English seller and a Portuguese buyer agree that their sales contract should be governed by the CISG, should this choice only be recognized as a *materiellrechtliche Verweisung* because the United Kingdom and Portugal are not contracting States to the CISG ? In this author's view there is no difference between such a choice of the applicable law and the effect of the applicable law rules in a Spanish-German sales contract which is automatically governed by the CISG rules when the parties did not choose any national law or when they have made a choice in favour of the law of a State party to the CISG.

220. If the application of a unifying substantive law instrument merely depends on the agreement of the parties, conflict of law rules should also allow the choice of uniform law. To date, as far as this author has been able to verify, no conflict of laws rule exists which determines explicitly that parties may choose uniform law as the law governing their relationship. It goes without saying that in those areas where party autonomy is permitted uniform law may be considered as having been incorporated into the contract terms. A *materiellrechtliche Verweisung* is always possible. More important, however, is that, were the parties to express a choice in favour of an optional instrument, such as that which is being considered currently for the European Union, such a choice would require to be recognized as a *kollisionsrechtliche Verweisung*. Otherwise the existence of an optional instrument to be applied in cross-border situations would not make any sense. This effect should be determined explicitly by the relevant conflict of law system. If the optional substantive law instrument alone were to regulate that the parties could determine its application, it would be

uncertain whether this would be allowed by the conflict of law rules of the forum. Within the European setting, since only one legislator is in charge, it should be relatively uncomplicated to legislate correspondingly : quintessentially, the right hand should know what the left hand is doing.

221. A different question is whether the chosen uniform law should always be part of the legal system whose conflict of law rules are consulted. Is approval by a national legislator a *conditio sine qua non* for a State court to recognize the Convention containing uniform law as the exclusively governing law ? Should it make any difference whether the Convention has been ratified by the forum State ? Or may the extensive preparation which goes into the making of such a Convention impart sufficient authority to that legal instrument for such recognition to be acceptable and justified ? Those who argue that only State law can be the exclusive guarantor of a balanced social and economic order might require that uniform law embodied in international Conventions should always be approved by national parliaments whose formal law-making competence is beyond doubt. Others might rely on the required standing and authority of the organization or institution under whose auspices the Convention was prepared. This should be sufficient to meet the expectations of the parties themselves since it provides sufficient assurance that their choice does not extend the concept of party-autonomy. The latter view is taken by this author. The ordinary limits, particularly overriding mandatory rules, which are always reserved to the State, regardless of what kind of law is applicable, should suffice to safeguard the interests of the forum State [499].

---

[499] Convincingly proposed by Oser, *op. cit.*, footnote 6, 118-120.

3.3. *Harmonizing substantive law and conflict of laws*

222. It has been demonstrated in the previous chapters that harmonizing substantive law instruments have a different position from unifying substantive law instruments as is made apparent when it comes to examining and debating their applicability in cross-border relationships. In contrast to unifying substantive law instruments, which are intended to become uniform law, harmonizing substantive law instruments, like Restatements, Principles or Model Laws initially have a different objective. Some of these instruments were never intended to be applied in cross-border relationships. The American Restatements and the Model Laws of international organizations, for instance, are mainly addressed to national legislators and judges by providing solutions based on comparative research which might be enacted or be applied in a particular case, if the national law does not offer a (satisfactory) solution. If these rules are not convincing *ratione imperii*, but *imperio rationis,* nevertheless their goal has been achieved in so far as differences between national systems become less pronounced. In contrast, some of the Principles which have been discussed not only aim to achieve approximation of national laws but also "offer" their application in cross-border situations. They prescribe their scope of application as if they were a binding instrument, which is actually impossible.

223. Two aspects are to be taken into account. First, a positive response is required from the application of conflict of law rules in order for the Principles to be applied in cross-border situations. Whether, within the European context, the conflict of law rules in the field of contractual and non-contractual obligations allow a *kollisionsrechtliche Rechtswahl* is debatable. It has

been reported that during the drafting of the Rome I Regulation the initial positive approach in the draft text was later removed and became instead a vague statement in the recital clauses which may well lead to different interpretations. In the field of family relations the discussion is still in its infancy ; however, the emergence of a European matrimonial property regime will also challenge those interpreting and monitoring the effects of conflict of law systems to consider their attitude to it.

224. If the conflict of law rules play the most important role as regards the possibility of applying harmonizing substantive law rules, it is — and this is the second aspect — not necessary that, for instance, the Contract Principles determine that the parties may agree that their contract is to be governed by them, by "general principles of law", the *lex mercatoria* or the like, or when the parties have not chosen any system or rules of law to govern their contract. If the application of the conflict of law system does not lead to a positive response, nothing happens. As a result, the Principles need conflict of law rules which will enable their application, irrespective of whether or not they "offer" that. One might wonder why the drafters of the Contract Principles prescribed the circumstances under which they consider the application of the Principles to be appropriate given that they are familiar with the interdependence of the Principles with conflict of law rules. The answer is apparent. Only by challenging the effects of conflict of law rules in this way could the discussion about the applicability of the Principles have started.

Moreover, disputes arising out of international business transactions are often settled through arbitration. In this area the prescription of the applicability of the Principles is not hindered by the effects of conflict of law rules.

3.4. Conflict of laws and harmonizing substantive law

225. Whereas Principles, in particular, need conflict of law rules if their application in cross-border situations is to be considered, conflict of law rules are not dependent on Principles or any other harmonizing substantive law instrument. Generally, a national law can always be designated by applying such rules. However, the question arises whether such a national law provides, in all circumstances, the best solution for the cross-border relationship. This observation touches the raison d'être of our conflict of law system since, generally, conflict of law rules are not concerned about the content of the rules to be applied unless fundamental rights and values are infringed. They determine — blindly — the applicable national law even though this is designed to apply to situations internal to the particular legal system. The international element of the legal relationship in question is not taken into account by either.

226. Another policy argument might be of considerable importance and that is the aim of enhancing party autonomy. Why should parties be restricted in their choice of the applicable law ? If they are in agreement why should they not have the possibility of selecting non-State law, such as the Contract Principles, to the exclusion of the otherwise applicable law since the Principles also provide for a gap-filling mechanism and, more important, contain mandatory rules ? Rules which are designed to be applied in transnational or trans-State situations can actually increase the scope of the choices available to the parties and this argument applies equally to Restatements and Conventions as well as to non-binding rules, such as the Contract Principles. In addition, non-binding rules increase the choice of laws available to the parties when they choose to resolve disputes through arbi-

tration rather than through the domestic courts of a particular forum [500], and, furthermore, the suitability of the Principles for application in cross-border business transactions has already been proved through their having been tested in arbitration.

4. Limited Acceptance of Non-national Law as the Lex Causae

227. In our world of the increasing interdependence of individuals, societies, economies and legal systems it is striking to note that the role which national systems play in cross-border relationships is still almost unaffected. The designation of one of the national laws with which a private legal relationship is to be connected takes place through the application of conflict of law rules.

The process of globalization, which is predominantly a matter of private initiative, expanding markets, growing mobility and the instant sharing of information [501], has not changed this situation. Generally, national laws differ from each other and the conflict of law approach thrives on these differences. The rules on applicable law determine which of the national systems in question shall govern the relationship. In the absence of a globally adopted uniform substantive law this approach is still considered, generally, to be the best solution, even though it is a makeshift or second-best solution. The traditional conflict of law systems, at least in Europe, sustain the position and function of national law whereas in important fields of law, whereby international transactions, for instance, are regulated, an increasing body of unifying and harmonizing substantive law has been created and adopted, a

---

[500] See Linarelli, *op. cit.*, footnote 240, 1407.
[501] Van Loon, *op. cit.*, footnote 149, 33.

great deal of which has been designed specifically for application to cross-border relationships.

228. The possibility of applying a law other than national law is at its most advanced and accepted in international arbitration. Arbitrators are free to determine the rules to be applied. They are not bound by any choice of law rules, whereas courts must adhere to and apply their conflict of law rules. These rules are rather restrictive being intended, primarily, to designate a national substantive law as the law governing the cross-border relationship.

229. Since bodies of laws other than State law have become available the role and function of conflict of law rules have been questioned. Might these laws govern the relationship, as the *lex causae,* to the exclusion of otherwise applicable national substantive laws ? The answer depends on the content of the choice of law rules and, in particular, how they are formulated. If these rules were to determine, expressly, that non-State law could be chosen by the parties as the applicable law, the result would be evident. Non-State law and

Table 10. The Application of a Law Other
than National Law : the State of the Art

Choice of a law other than national law	Contracts	Delicts/torts	Family relations
Litigation	disputed	disputed	not yet
Arbitration/ mediation	yes	yes	not clear

Absence of any choice	Contracts	Delicts/torts	Family relations
Litigation	no	no	no
Arbitration/ mediation	yes	yes	not clear

State law would then be placed on an equal footing as far as the *lex causae* is concerned. However, a very large majority of the conflict of law rules, which courts have to consult and apply, do not contain, any express reference to the application of rules of non-State law. If no explicit reference to *State law* is made, does this allow an extensive reading which includes non-State law as the law governing the relationship ? It has been demonstrated above that, in this respect, the views of legal practitioners and the opinions of legal scholars differ. The answers are either yes or no. Moreover, the kind of legal relationship in question is considered to be relevant. In those areas where party autonomy plays a significant role (contracts) the idea of applying non-State law has received more support than in areas (family relationships) where party autonomy is merely admitted in some specific fields. This is another crucial aspect to consider. It justifies making differentiations.

The reference to non-State law is at least recognized as a *materiellrechtliche Verweisung*. In the field of contracts and delict and torts this is generally accepted. As regards family agreements a law other than national family law is, so far, not yet available. The European Principles regarding the Property Relations between Spouses, which are currently being prepared, might change and challenge this situation.

5. *There Is a World Beyond National Law*

230. It has been demonstrated that there is a world beyond national law [502]. This other world consists of unifying and harmonizing substantive law based on comparative research. So far this world has been largely disregarded, rejected or ignored since national substantive law retains a dominant role when the issue,

---

[502] Schwenzer and Hachem, *op. cit.*, footnote 124, 478.

which falls to be determined through the application of rules of conflict of law, is decided. It is true that conflict of law rules fulfil a function as long as the rules on substantive law are not identical [503]. However, private law is denationalizing. Within the European Union this process is more advanced than in other parts of the world. In particular the law of obligations is overwhelmingly influenced by European law-making in the form of Directives, an example of top-down development within which the adoption of more instruments, which are aimed at unifying substantive law, can be also included. The bottom-up approach is exemplified by the harmonizing substantive law instruments drafted and adopted by predominantly private groups and institutions. Many of these instruments are specifically designed for application in cross-border relationships. The different ways as to how this goal can be achieved have been indicated. This goal is hindered by conflict of law rules. Only if these were to admit the application of a law other than national law as the *lex causae* would the door to the other world be unlocked, as far as domestic courts are concerned. This, subsequent, step would require new conflict of law rules whose application would allow this option.

6. *Towards a New Approach in Conflict of Laws as Regards Contracts*

231. Who will undertake this next step ? One "institution" of which one could think which might well have been able to this — the European legislator — recently missed a golden opportunity to do so and,

---

[503] Jänterä-Jareborg, *op. cit.*, footnote 269, 367 : "At present we are far from any global or even regional unity in civil law. This makes choice of law rules a necessity for cross-border relations."

thus, to depart from the traditional approach. The evaluation of the two Rome applicable law Regulations is scheduled for 2011, in respect of that on non-contractual obligations, and 2013 as regards that on contractual obligations. If the respective evaluations were to be accompanied by proposals to adapt the Regulations according to the view taken by this author, and expressed in these pages, a more liberal approach might be able to be followed. Why should the initial proposal to allow parties to choose non-national law not be renegotiated ? As far as the United States of America is concerned one could think of the Restatement 3rd on Conflict of Law [504], however it will take years to finish such a project and, admittedly, it has not even started yet. The actual need for this project is even debated.

232. Finally, we can think of the most prominent international organization in private international law : the Hague Conference on Private International Law. In 2006, the Permanent Bureau of the Conference undertook a feasibility study into the development of an instrument on the choice of law in international contracts. Two comparative studies were carried out : one described and analysed the existing rules generally applied in litigation by domestic courts and the other focused on the context of international arbitration. The recent report by the Permanent Bureau on the work to be carried out and the suggested work programme for the development of a future instrument was only published in March 2009 [505]. The development of a non-

---

[504] See Chapter VII, Section 6.

[505] Feasibility Study on the Choice of Law in International Contracts : Report on Work Carried Out and Suggested Work Programme for the Development of a Future Instrument, Note prepared by the Permanent Bureau, Prel. Doc. No. 7, March 2009.

binding instrument is envisaged, its principal aim being to establish a global model for conflict of law rules which are applicable to contracts [506]. As a corollary, the Conference's mission has been enlarged. Not only the unification but, also, the harmonization of private international law has been put on the agenda of the conference.

This change of objectives — to draft a non-binding instrument, probably a Model Law — can be seen to be derived, almost certainly, from the fact that, whilst, within the European Union, the Rome I Regulation has become effective, albeit only recently, in many other countries in the world the freedom of contracting parties to determine the *lex contractus* is not yet even accepted. From a strategic point of view, it has been envisaged that the instrument would be able to be used later as a source of inspiration for future binding instruments, whether at the national, regional or international level.

233. As far as concerns the issue which we have been discussing in this lecture the following aspect is of great importance. The report by the Permanent Bureau substantiates the need to clarify whether it is permissible for parties to choose not only national laws but also transnational or non-national rules or principles to govern a dispute. It is stated that this — the choice of non-State law — has for a long time played an important role in arbitration but is also of growing importance in court proceedings.

---

[506] See also the Resolution on the Autonomy of the Parties in International Contracts between Private Persons or Entities, www.idi-iil.org/idiE/resolutionsE/1991_bal_ 02_en.PDF, adopted in 1991 by the Institute of International Law (established in 1873). Article 2, Section 1, of this Resolution determines : "The parties shall be free to choose the law applicable to their contract. They may agree on the application of the law of any State."

"It must nevertheless be recognised that where the freedom of choice of law appears progressively to be won in international commercial relations, the big challenge will be to identify the extent and possible limitations of this freedom. In this regard, important questions will nevertheless have to be examined during the development of the instrument such as the suitability of admitting the parties' ability to choose a set of non-State rules, such as the UNIDROIT Principles, or the admission of the implicit choice of law. To settle these questions, the future Working Group shall have to take into consideration both the rules applied by State courts and specific international arbitration rules."

234. In respect of the form of the future instrument several arguments in favour of a non-binding instrument are put forward. It has been argued for instance that :

"an instrument of this type could be developed initially without the restrictions and compromises that are inherent to treaty negotiation. The instrument would progressively evolve outside a Conventional setting, thanks to the objectivity and scientific quality of the experts involved together with the solutions retained."

This is a remarkable argument since, so far in its history ; the Hague Conference has adopted, predominantly, binding instruments. Furthermore, it is stated

"that the absence of any obligatory force of the future instrument would avoid all risk of conflict of norms. For example, there would be no direct interference with the Rome I Regulation, or with the specific Hague Conventions on the Law Applicable to Agency, to Contracts for International Sales, or to Securities held with an Intermediary."

Indeed a conflict of conflict of law rules could not arise since, for the time being at any rate, the "Hague International Contract Rules" would not become binding law.

235. Finally it is expected that the principal aim of such a future instrument would be for it to become a constant source of inspiration for the progressive development of uniform rules in the field of the law applicable to international contracts. It would then be up to national and regional legislatures to decide whether they wished to adopt these rules. It has been argued that, in respect of recital 13 of the Rome I Regulation, for instance, it is up the courts of each individual Member State to determine whether or not they will recognize a choice of non-national law as the law governing a contract. In this respect rules drafted by an international organization might well turn out to be highly necessary and supportive.

It is beyond doubt that the future drafting of a global Model Law of choice of law in international contracts by the Hague Conference on Private International Law would provide an excellent opportunity to enhance party autonomy. In so doing non-national law might come to be recognized as the law governing an international contract. In this respect the application of non-national law as the *lex contractus* might progress beyond its, at present, embryonic stage.

BIBLIOGRAPHY

Agell, A., "The Division of Property upon Divorce from a European Perspective", in *Liber Amicorum Marie-Thérèse Meulders-Klein : droit comparé des personnes et de la famille* (1998) 1-20.

Albert, J., *Compensation of Victims of Cross-Border Road Traffic Accidents in the EU : Comparison of National Practices, Analysis of Problems and Evaluation of Options for Improving the Position of Cross-border Victims* (2008) (http://ec.europa.eu/civiljustice/news/docs/study_compensation_road_victims_en.pdf).

Albornoz, M. M., "Choice of Law in International Contracts in Latin American Legal Systems", *NYU and Journal of Private International Conference on Private International Law*, April 17-18 2009.

Antokolskaia, M., "Family Law and National Culture, Arguing against the Cultural Contraints Argument", *Utrecht Law Review* (2008) 25-34.

TMC Asser Instituut/Département de droit international UCL, *Etude sur les régimes matrimoniaux des couples mariés et sur le patrimoine des couples non mariés dans le droit international privé et le droit interne des Etats membres de l'Union européenne effectuée à la demande de la Commission européenne, Direction générale Justice et Affaires intérieures, Unité A3, Coopération judiciaire en matière civile*, JAI/A3/2001/03.

Bach, I., "Neuere Rechtsprechung zum UN-Kaufrecht", *Praxis des internationalen Privat- und Verfahrensrechts* (2009) 299-306.

Bachmann, G., "Die Societas Europaea und das europäische Privatrecht", *Zeitschrift für Europäisches Privatrecht* (2008) 32-58.

Bailey, J. E., "Facing the Truth : Seeing the Convention on Contracts for the International Sale of Goods as an Obstacle to a Uniform Law of International Sales", *Cornell International Law Journal* (1999) 273-317.

Von Bar, Ch., "A Common Frame of Reference for European Private Law — Academic Efforts and Political Realities", *Electronic Journal of Comparative Law* (2008) 1-10.

Von Bar, Ch. and P. Mankowski, *Internationales Privatrecht, Band I, Allgemeine Lehren* (2003) 75-88.

Von Bar, Ch., H. Beale, E. Clive and Schulte-Nölke, "Introduction", in *Principles, Definitions and Model Rules of European Private Law, Draft Common Frame of Reference (DCFR)* (2008) 1-38.

Basedow, J., "Worldwide Harmonisation of Private Law and Regional Economic Integration — General report", *Uniform Law Review* (2003) 31-52.

Béraudo, P., "Faut-il avoir peur du contrat sans loi ?", in *Le droit international privé : esprit et méthodes, Mélanges en l'honneur de Paul Lagarde* (2005) 93-112.

Van den Bergh, R., and L. Visscher, "The Principles of European Tort Law : The Right Path to Harmonization ?", *European Review of Private Law* (2006) 511-543.

Bernardini, P., "International Arbitration and A-National Rules of Law", 15 *ICC International Court of Arbitration Bulletin* (2004) 58-69.

Binder, P., *International Commercial Arbitration and Conciliation in UNCITRAL Model Law Jurisdictions*, 2009.

Blackie, J., "The Torts Provisions of the Study Group on a Euroepan Code", in M. Bussani, *European Tort Law* (2007) 55-80.

Blase, F., "A Uniform European Law of Contracts — Why and How", 8 *Columbia Journal of European Law* (2002) 487-491.

—, *Die Grundregeln des Europäischen Vertragsrechts als Recht grenzüberschreitender Verträge* (2001).

Blomstrand, S., "Nordic Co-operation on Legislation in the Field of Private Law", *Scandinavian Studies in Law* (2000) 59-77.

Boele-Woelki, K., "Geünificeerd materieel recht gaat vóór een conflictenrechtelijke toets", in S. C. J. J. Kortmann, J. M. M. Maeijer, A. J. M. Nuytink and S. Perrick (eds.), *Op Recht, Liber Amicorum A. V. M. Struycken* (1996) 11-18.

—, "Principles and Private International Law — The UNIDROIT Principles of International Commercial Contracts and the Principles of European Contract Law : How to Apply Them to International Contracts", *Uniform Law Review* (1996) 652-678.

—, "Unification and Harmonization of Private International Law in Europe", in J. Basedow, I. Meier, A. K. Schnyder, T. Einhorn and D. Girsberger, *Private Law in the International Arena, from National Conflict Rules Towards Harmonization and Unification, Liber Amicorum Kurt Siehr* (2000) 61-77.

—, "Terms of Co-Existence : The UN Sales Convention and the UNIDROIT Principles of International Commercial Contracts", in P. Volken and P. Srcevic (eds.), *CISG Revisited, Dubrovnik Lectures 1998* (2001) 203-240.

— (ed.), *Perspectives for the Unification and Harmonisation of Family Law in Europe*, European Family Law Series No. 4 (2003).

—, "The Principles of European Family Law : Its Aims and Prospects", 1 *Utrecht Law Review* (2005) 160-168.

—, "The Working Method of the Commission on European Family Law", in K. Boele-Woelki (ed.), *Common Core and Better Law in European Family Law*, European Family Law Series No. 10 (2005) 14-38.

—, "Building on Convergence and Coping with Divergence in the CEFL Principles of European Family Law", in M. Antokolskaia (ed.), *Convergence and Divergence of Family Law in Europe*, European Family Law Series No. 18 (2007) 253-269.

—, "The CEFL Principles Regarding Parental Responsibilities : Predominance of the Common Core", in K. Boele-Woelki and T. Sverdrup (eds.), *European Challenges in Contemporary Family Law*, European Family Law Series No. 19 (2008) 63-91.

—, "To Be or Not to Be : Enhanced Cooperation in International Divorce Law within the European Union", *Victoria Wellington University Law Review* (2008) 779-792.

—, "What Comparative Family Law Should Entail", 4/2 *Utrecht Law Review* (2008) 1-24 ; also published in K. Boele-Woelki (ed.), *Debates in Family Law around the Globe at the Dawn of the 21st Century*, European Family Law Series No. 23 (2009) 3-35.

—, "Umzug von Kindern aus den Niederlanden in die Schweiz : die niederländische Perspektive", *Praxis des Familienrechts* (2009) 381-396.

Boele-Woelki, K., and D. van Iterson, "The Dutch Private International Law Codification : Principles, Objectives and Opportunities", Contribution to the International Academy of Comparative Law, Washington, D.C., July 25 to August 1, 2010.

Boele-Woelki, K., and R. Van Ooik, "The Communautarization of Private International Law", *Yearbook of Private International Law* (2002) 1-36.

Boele-Woelki, K., F. Ferrand, C. González Beilfuss, M. Jänterä-Jareborg, N. Lowe, D. Martiny, and W. Pintens, *Principles of European Family Law Regarding Divorce and Maintenance between Former Spouses*, European Family Law Series No. 7 (2004).

Boele-Woelki, K., F. Ferrand, C. Gonzàlez Beilfuss, M. Jänterä-Jareborg, N. Lowe, D. Martiny and W. Pintens, *Principles of European Family Law Regarding Parental Responsibilities*, European Family Law Series No. 16 (2007) 193-198.

Boele-Woelki, K., and V. Lazic, "Where Do We Stand on the Rome I Regulation ?", in K. Boele-Woelki and F. Grosheide (eds.), *The Future of European Contract Law* (2007) 19-41.

Boele-Woelki, K., B. Braat and I. Curry-Sumner (eds.), *European Family Law in Action*, Vol. IV, *Property Relations between Spouses*, European Family Law Series No. 24 (2009).

De Boer, Th., "Party Autonomy and Its Limitations in the Rome II Regulation", *Yearbook of Private International Law* (2007) 19-29.

—, "The Second Revision of the Brussels II Regulation : Jurisdiction and Applicable Law", in K. Boele-Woelki and T. Sverdrup (eds.), *European Challenges in Contemporary Family Law*, European Family Law Series No. 19 (2008) 321-341.

—, "The Purpose of Uniform Choice-of-Law Rules : The Rome II Regulation", *Netherlands International Law Review* (2009) 295-332.

Bogdan, M., "The Rome I Regulation on the Law Applicable to Contractual Obligations and the Choice of Law by the Parties", *Nederlands Internationaal Privaatrecht* (2009) 407-410 (407-408).

Bonell, M. J., *An International Restatement of Contract Law — The UNIDROIT Principles of International Commercial Contracts* (1994).

—, "The CISG, European Contract Law and the Development of a World Contract Law", *American Journal of Comparative Law* (2008) 1-28.

—, "Towards a Legislative Codification of the UNIDROIT Principles ?", *Uniform Law Review/Revue de droit uniforme* (2007) 233-245.

Bonomi, A., *Preliminary Draft Protocol on the Law Applicable to Maintenance Obligations, Explanatory Report*, Preliminary Document No. 33 of August 2007 for the attention of the Twenty-First Session of November 2007, 17.

—, "The Hague Protocol on the Law Applicable to Maintenance Obligations", *Yearbook of Private International Law* (2008) 333-357

Van Boom, W., *Harmonizing Tort Law : A Comparative Tort Law and Economic Analysis*, Rotterdam Institute of Private Law Working Paper Series (2008), 1-16 (http://papers.ssrn.com/sol3/papers.cfm ?abstract_id=1156739).

De Booys, T. Q., E. J. A. De Volder and D. Raic, *Bestaat er behoefte aan een gemeenschappelijk referentiekader voor Europees contractenrecht*, Hague Institute for the Internationalisation of Law (HiiL) (2009) (www.justitie.nl).

Borrás, A., "From Brussels II to Brussels II *bis* and Further", in K. Boele-Woelki and C. González Beilfuss (eds.), *Brussels II bis : Its Impact and Application in the Member States*, European Family Law Series No. 14 (2007) 3-22.

Bücken, A., "Intertemporaler Anwendungsbereich der Rom II-VO", *Praxis des internationalen Privat- und Verfahrensrechts* (2009) 125-128.

Busch, D., "The Principles of European Contract Law before the Supreme Court of the Netherlands — On the Influence of the PECL in Dutch Legal Practice", *Zeitschrift für Europäisches Privatrecht* (2008) 549-562.

Butler, P., *The Doctrines of Parol Evidence Rule and Consideration — A Deterrence to the Common Law Lawyer ?*, Collation of Papers at UNCITRAL-SIAC Conference 22-23 September 2005, Singapore International Arbitration Centre.

Calliess, G.-P., "The Making of Transnational Contract Law", *Indiana Journal of Global Legal Studies* (2007) 469-483.

Calvo Caravaca, A.-L., "El Reglamento Roma I sobre la ley aplicable a las obligaciones contractuales : cuestiones escogidas", *Cuadernos de Derecho Transnacional* (2009) 52-133.

Castellani, L. G., "International Trade Law Reform in Africa", *Yearbook of Private International Law* (2008) 547-563.

Clarkson, C. M. V., "Matrimonial Property on Divorce : All Change in Europe", *Journal of Private International Law* (2008) 421-442.

Cranston, R., "Theorizing Transnational Commercial Law", *Texas International Law Journal* (2007) 597-617.

Cuniberti, G., "Is the CISG Benefiting Anybody", *Vanderbilt Journal of Transnational Law* (2006) 1511-1550.

Date-Bah, S. K., "The Preliminary Draft OHADA Uniform Act on Contract Law as Seen by a Common Law Lawyer", *Uniform Law Review* (2008) 217-222.

David, R., "The Methods of Unification", *American Journal of Comparative Law* (1968) 13-27.

De Ly, F., "Choice of Law Clauses, Unidroit Principles of International Commercial Contracts and Article 3 Rome Convention : The Lex Mercatoria before Domestic Courts or Arbitration Privilege ?", in F. Lefebvre (eds.), *Etudes offertes à Barthélemy Mercadal* (2002) 133-145.

Dethloff, N., "Die Europäische Ehe", *Zeitschrift für das Standesamtswesen* (2006) 253-260.

—, "Arguments for the Unification and Harmonisation of Family Law in Europe", in K. Boele-Woelki (ed.), *Perspectives for the Unification and Harmonisation of Family Law in Europe*, European Family Law Series No. 4 (2002) 37-64.

Diedrich, F., "Rechtswahlfreiheit und Vertragsstatut — eine Zwischenbilanz angesichts der Rome I-Verordnung", *Recht der internationalen Wirtschaft* (2009) 378-385.

Duncan, W., "The Hague Convention of 23 November 2007 on the International Recovery of Child Support and Other Forms of Family Maintenance, Comments on its Objectives and some of its Special Features", *Yearbook of Private International Law* (2008) 313-331.

Dutheil de la Rochère, J., "The Lisbon Compromise : A Synthesis between Community Method and Union Acquis", *Fordham International Law Journal* (2008) 1143-1160.

Dutson, S., "A Dangerous Proposal — the European Commission's Attempt to Amend the Law Applicable to Contractual Obligations", *Journal of Business Law* (2006) 608-618.

Dutta, A., "Succession and Wills in the Conflict of Laws on the Eve of the Europeanisation", *Rabels Zeitschrift für internationales und ausländisches Privatrecht* (2009) 547-606.

Ellman, I. M., *Inventing Family Law*, University of California (1999) 855-886.

Erauw, J., "Brief Description of the Draft Belgian Code on Private International Law", *Yearbook of Private International Law* (2002) 145-161.

The European Group on Tort Law (ed.), *Principles of European Tort Law : Text and Commentary* (2005).

Ferrari, F., "Homeward Trend : What, Why and Why Not", in A. Janssen and O. Meyer (eds.), *CISG Methodology* (2009) 171-206.

—, (ed.), *The CISG and Its Impact on National Legal Legislation* (2008).

Fiorini, A., "Rome III — Choice of Law in Divorce : Is the Europeanization of Family Law Going Too Far ?", *International Journal of Law, Policy and the Family* (2000) 178-195.

Foqué, R., and A. Verbeke, "Conclusions. Towards an Open and Flexible Imperative Inheritance Law", in Ch. Castelein, R. Foqué and A. Verbeke (eds.), *Imperative Inheritance Law in a Late-Modern Society, Five Perspectives*, European Family Law Series No. 26 (2009) 203-221.

Fountoulakis, C., "The Parties' Choice of 'Neutral Law' in International Sales Contracts", *European Journal of Law Reform* (2006) 303-329.

Frattini, F., "European Area of Civil Justice — Has the Community Reached the Limits ?", *Zeitschrift für Europäisches Privatrecht* (2006) 225-235.

Fretwell Wilson, R., "The Harmonization of Family Law in the United States", in K. Boele-Woelki and T. Sverdrup (eds.), *European Challenges in Contemporary Family Law* (2008) 27-49.

Gannagé, L., "Le contrat sans loi en droit international privé", in K. Boele-Woelki and S. Van Erp (eds.), *General Reports of the XVIIth Congress of the International Academy of Comparative Law — Rapports généraux, XVII Congrès international du droit comparé* (2007) 275-308 ; also published in *Electronic Journal of Comparative Law* (2007) (www.ejcl.org/113/abs113-10.html).

Gillette, C. P., and R. E. Scott, "The Political Economy of International Sales Law", *International Review of Law and Economics* (2005) 446-486.

Glöckner, J., "Keine klare Sache : Der zeitliche Anwendungsbereich der Rom II-Verordnung", *Praxis des internationalen Privat- und Verfahrensrechts* (2009) 121-124.

Goode, R., "The Harmonization of Dispositive Contract and Commercial Law — Should the European Community Be Involved ?", in E.-A. Kieninger, *Denationalisierung des Privatrechts ?* (2005) 19-32.

—, "Contract and Commercial Law : The Logic and Limits of Harmonisation", *Ius Commune Lectures on European Private Law*, No. 3 (2003).

De Groot, G.-R., "Op weg naar een Europees personen- en familierecht ?", *Ars Aequi* (1995) 29-33.

De Groot, G.-R., and J.-J. Kuipers, "The New Provisions on Private International Law in the Treaty of Lisbon", *Maastricht Journal of International and Comparative Law* (2008) 113-118.

Grundmann, S., "La structure du DCFR : quelle forme pour un droit européen des contrats ?", *Revue de droit international et de droit comparé* (2009) 423-453.

Grundmann, S., and M. Schauer (eds.), *The Architecture of European Codes and Contract Law* (2006) 3-30.

Hagge, N., *Das einheitliche Kaufrecht der OHADA* (2004).

Hartkamp, A., "Principles of Contract Law", in A. Hartkamp *et al.* (eds.), *Towards a European Civil Code* (2004) 125-143.

Harris, J., "Understanding the English Response to the Europeanisation of Private International Law", *Journal of Private International Law* (2008) 347-395.

Hazard, G. C., *The American Law Institute : What It Is and What It Does* (w3.uniroma1.it/idc/centro/publications/14 hazard.pdf).

Heidemann, M., *Methodology of Uniform Contract Law, The UNIDROIT Principles in International Legal Doctrine and Practice*, Springer (2007).

Heidemann, M., "Halpern v. Halpern : Zur Anwendbarkeit nicht-staatlichen Rechts und 'Rom I' in England", *Zeitschrift für europäisches Privatrecht* (2008) 618-632.

Heiss, H., "Party-Autonomy : The Fundamental Principle in European PIL of Contracts", in F. Ferrari and S. Leible (eds.), *Rome I Regulation, the Law Applicable to Contractual Obligations in Europe* (2009) 1-16.

Helfer, L. R., and G. B. Dinwoodie, "Designing Non-national Systems : The Case of the Uniform Domain Name Dispute Resolution Policy", *Stanford/Yale Junior Faculty Forum* (2001) 141-273.

Hesselink, M., "European Contract Law : A Matter of Consumer Protection, Citizenship, or Justice ?", *European Review of Private Law* (2007) 323-348.

Hesselink, M. W., J. W. Rutgers and T. De Booys, *The Legal Basis for an Optional Instrument on European Contract Law*, Centre for the Study of European Contract Law Working Paper Series (2007) No. 04.

Hondius, E., "Towards a European Ius Commune : The Current Situation in Other Fields of Private Law", in K. Boele-Woelki (ed.), *Perspectives for the Unification and Harmonisation of Family Law in Europe*, European Family Law Series No. 4, (2003) 118-139.

Hondius, E., "CISG and a European Civil Code, Some Reflexions", *Rabels Zeitschrift für ausländisches und internationales Privatrecht* (2007) 99-114.

Jansen, N., "Negotiorum gestio und Benevolent Intervention in Another's Affairs : Principles of European Law ?", *Zeitschrift für Europäisches Privatrecht* (2007) 958-991.
—, "The State of the Art of European Tort Law", in M. Bussani, *European Tort Law* (2007) 15-45.
Jänterä-Jareborg, M., "Unification of International Family Law in Europe — A Critical Perspective", in K. Boele-Woelki (ed.), *Perspectives for the Unification and Harmonisation of Family Law in Europe* (2003) 194-216.
—, "Foreign Law in National Courts, A Comparative Perspective", *Recueil des cours*, Vol. 304 (2004), 185-385.
—, "Jurisdiction and Applicable Law in Cross-Border Divorce Cases in Europe", in J. Basedow, H. Baum and Y. Nishitani (eds.), *Japanese and European Private International Law in Comparative Perspective* (2008) 317-343.
—, "Family Law in the European Judicial Space — Concerns Regarding Nation-State's Autonomy and Legal Coherence", in E. J. Hollo (ed.), *Kansallinen oikeus ja liittovaltioistuva Eurooppa/National Law and Europeanisation* (2009) 29-61.
Jordanka, Z., and V. Stanceva-Minceva, "Gesetzbuch über das Internationale Privatrecht der Republik Bulgarien", *Rabels Zeitschrift für ausländisches und internationales Privatrecht* (2007) 398-456.
Juenger, F. K., "The Inter-American Convention on the Law Applicable to International Contracts : Some Highlights and Comparisons", *American Journal of Comparative Law* (1994) 383-391.
—, "The UNIDROIT Principles of Commercial Contracts and Inter-American Contract Choice of Law", *Contratación international, Comentarios a los Principios sobre los Contratos Comerciales Internationales del Unidroit*, Unversidad Nacional Autónoma de México — Unversidad Panamericana (1998) 229-236.
Kadner Graziano, Th., "Le nouveau droit international privé communautaire en matière de responsabilité extracontractuelle", *Revue critique de droit international privé* (2008) 445-511.
Kadner Graziano, Th., "Das auf außervertragliche Schuldverhältnisse anwendbare Recht nach Inkrafttreten der Rom II-Verordnung", *Rabels Zeitschrift für ausländisches und internationales Privatrecht* (2009) 1-77.
—, "Freedom to Choose the Applicable Law in Tort — Articles 14 and 4 (3) of the Rome II Regulation", in

B. William and J. Ahern (eds.), *The Rome II Regulation on the Law Applicable to Non-Contractual Obligations : A New Tort Litigation Regime* (2009) 113-132.

Kampf, A., "UN-Kaufrecht und Kollisionsrecht", *Recht der internationalen Wirtschaft* (2009) 297-301.

Kenny, M., "The 2003 Action Plan on European Contract Law : Is the Commission Running Wild ?", *European Law Review* (2003) 538-550.

Kessedjian, C., "Codification du droit commercial international et droit international privé", *Recueil des cours*, Vol. 300 (2002), 79-293.

—, "Party Autonomy and Characteristic Performance in the Rome Convention and the Rome I Proposal", in J. Basedow, H. Baum and Y. Nishitani (eds.), *Japanese and European Private International Law in Comparative Perspective* (2008) 105-125.

—, "Uniformity v. Diversity in Law in a Global World — The Example of Commercial and Procedural Law", *Hellenic Review of International Law* (2008) 319-333.

Koch, B. A., "The 'European Group on Tort Law' and Its 'Principles of European Tort Law' ", *American Journal of Comparative Law* (2005) 189-205.

Koziol, H., "Die 'Principles of European Tort Law' der 'European Group on Tort Law' ", *Zeitschrift für europäisches Privatrecht* (2004) 234-259.

Kronke, H., "A Bridge out of the Fortress : UNIDROIT's Work on Global Modernisation of Commercial Law and Its Relevance for Europe", *Zeitschrift für Europäisches Privatrecht* (2008) 1-5.

Lagarde, P., "Remarques sur la proposition de règlement de la Commission européenne sur la loi applicable aux obligations contractuelles (Rome I)", *Revue critique de droit international privé* (2006) 331-349.

Lagarde, P., and A. Tenenbaum, "De la Convention de Rome au règlement Rome I", *Revue critique de droit international privé* (2008) 727-780.

Lando, O., "CISG and its Followers : A Proposal to Adopt Some International Principles of Contract Law", *American Journal of Comparative Law* (2005) 379-401.

—, "Principles of European Contract Law and UNIDROIT Principles : Moving from Harmonisation to Unification ?", *Uniform Law Review/Revue de droit uniforme* (2003) 123-133.

Lando, O., and H. Beale (eds.), *Principles of European Contract Law Parts I and II* (1999).

Lando, O., E. Clive, A. Prüm and R. Zimmermann (eds.), *Principles of European Contract Law Part III* (2003).

Lazic, V., "The Impact of Uniform Law on the National Law in the Netherlands : Limits and Possibilities — Commercial Arbitration", *Electronic Journal of Comparative Law* (2009) (http ://www.ejcl.org/132/article132-3.pdf).

Leible, S., "Choice of the Applicable Law", in E. Cashin Ritaine and A. Bonomi (eds.), *Le nouveau règlement européen "Rome I" relatif à la loi applicable aux obligations contractuelles* (2008) 61-75.

—, "Rechtswahl im IPR der ausservertraglichen Schuldverhätnisse nach der Rom II-Verordnung", *Recht der Internationalen Wirtschaft* (2008) 257-264.

—, "Was tun mit dem Gemeinsamen Referenzrahmen für das Europäische Vertragsrecht ? — Plädoyer für ein optimales Instrument", *Betriebs Berater* (2008) 1469-1475.

Leible, S., and M. Lehmann, "Die Verordnung über das auf vertragliche Schuldverhältnisse anzuwendende Recht ('Rom I')", *Recht der Internationalen Wirtschaft* (2008) 528-544.

Leible, S., and M. Müller, "Der 'blue button' für den Internetshop, Ein optionales Instrument für den E-Commerce ?", *Kommunikation und Recht* (2009) 7-14.

Lein, E., "The New Rome I/Rome II/Brussels I Synergy", *Yearbook of Private International Law* (2008) 177-198

Linarelli, J., "The Economics of Uniform Law and Uniform Lawmaking", *Wayne Law Review* (2003) 1387- 1447

Lødrup, P., "The Reharmonisation of Nordic Family Law", in T. Boele-Woelki and T. Sverdrup (eds.), *European Challenges in Contemporary Family Law*, European Family Law Series No. 23 (2008) 17-26.

Van Loon, H., "Unification of Private International Law in a Multi-forum Context", in E.-M. Kieninger (ed.), *Denationaliserung des Privatrechts ?* (2005) 33-52.

Van Loon, H., and A. Schulz, "The European Community and the Hague Conference on Private International Law", in B. Martenczuk and S. Van Thiel (eds.) *Justice, Liberty, Security : New Challenges for EU External Relations* (2008) 257-299.

López Rodríguez, A. M., *Lex Mercatoria and Harmonization of Contract Law in the EU* (2003).

Loquin, E., "Les règles matérielles internationales", *Recueil des cours*, Vol. 322 (2006) 9-241.

Lund-Andersen, I., "Approximation of Nordic Family Law within the Framework of Nordic Cooperation", in

M. Antokolskaia (ed.), *Convergence and Divergence of Family Law in Europe*, European Family Law Series No. 18, (2007) 51-61.

Magnus, U., "Europäisches Vertragsrecht und materielles Einheitsrecht — künftige Symbiose oder störende Konkurrenz", in H.-P. Mansel, Th. Pfeiffer, H. Kronke, Ch. Kohler and R. Hausmann (eds.), *Festschrift für Erik Jayme*, Vol. 2 (2004) 1307-1321.

Malintoppi, A., "Les rapports entre droit uniforme et droit international privé", *Recueil des cours*, Vol. 116 (1965) 1-87.

Malloy, S. A., "The Inter-American Convention on the Law Applicable to International Contracts : Another Piece of the Puzzle of the Law Applicable to International Contracts", *Fordham International Law Journal* (1995) 662-735.

Mancuso, S., *Trends on the Harmonization of Contract Law in Africa*, Annual Survey of International & Comparative Law, Golden Gate University School of Law (2007) 157-178.

Mankowski, P., "CFR und Rechtswahl", in M. Schmidt-Kessel (ed.), *Der Gemeinsame Referenzrahmen, Entstehung, Inhalte, Anwendung* (2009) 391-433.

Martiny, D., "Europäisches Internationales Vertragsrecht in Erwartung der Rom I-Verordnung", *Zeitschrift für Europäisches Privatrecht* (2008) 79-108.

Mattei U., "Hard Code Now !", 2 *Global Juris Frontiers* (2002), (www.bepress.com/gj/frontiers/vol2/iss1/art1).

Max Planck Institute for Comparative and International Private Law, "Comments on the European Commission's Proposal for a Regulation of the European Parliament and the Council on the Law Applicable to Contractual Obligations by the Working Group on Rome I", *Rabels Zeitschrift für ausländisches und internationales Privatrecht* (2007) 225-344.

McAuley, S., "Achieving the Harmonization of Transnational Civil Procedure : Will the ALI/UNIDROIT Principles Succeed ?", *American Review of International Arbitration* (2004) 231-252.

Metzger, A., *Extra legem, intra ius : Allgemeine Rechtsgrundsätze im Europäischen Privatrecht* (2009).

Meulders-Klein, M.-T., "Towards a European Civil Code on Family Laws ? Ends and Means", in K. Boele-Woelki (ed.), *Perspectives for the Unification and Harmonisation of Family Law in Europe*, European Family Law Series No. 4 (2003) 105-117.

Meyer, J., "UN-Kaufrecht in der deutschen Anwaltspraxis", *Rabels Zeitschrift für ausländisches und internationales Privatrecht* (2005) 457-486.

Michaels, R., "The Re-State-ment of Non-State Law : The State, Choice of Law, and the Challenge from Global Pluralism", 51 *Wayne Law Review* (2005) 1209-1259.

Michaels, R., in S. Vogenauer and J. Kleinheisterkamp (eds.), *Commentary on the UNIDROIT Principles of International Commercial Contracts* (2009).

Michaels, R., "Umdenken für die UNIDROIT-Prinzipien, Vom Rechtswahlstatut zum Allgemeinen Teil des transnationalen Vertragsrechts", *Rabels Zeitschrift für internationales und ausländisches Privatrecht* (2009) 866-888.

Micklitz, H. W., and N. Reich, "Cronica de una muerte anunciada : the Commission Proposal for a Directive of Consumer Rights", *Common Market Law Review* (2009) 471-519.

Mistelis, L., "CISG and Arbitration", in A. Janssen and O. Meyer (eds.), *CISG Methodology* (2009) 375-395.

Mourre, A., "Application of the Vienna International Sales Convention", *International Court of Arbitration Bulletin* (2006) 43-50.

Mo Zhang, "Party Autonomy and Beyond : An International Perspective of Contractual Choice of Law", *Emory International Law Review* (2006) 511-561.

Nielsen, P. A., and O. Lando, "The Rome I Proposal", *Journal of Private International Law* (2007) 29-51.

Örücü, E., "A Family Law for Europe : Necessary, Feasible, Desirable ?", in K. Boele-Woelki (ed.), *Perspectives for the Unification and Harmonisation of Family Law in Europe*, European Family Law Series No. 4 (2003) 551-572.

Örücü, E., and J. Mair (eds.), *Juxtaposing Legal Systems and the Principles of European Family Law on Divorce and Maintenance*, European Family Law Series No. 17 (2007).

Örücü, E., and J. Mair (eds.), *Juxtaposing Legal Systems and the Principles of European Family Law on Parental Responsibilities*, European Family Law Series No. 26 (2009).

Oser, D., *The Unidroit Principles of International Commercial Contracts : A Governing Law ?* (2008).

Pamboukis, C. P., "Droit international privé holistique : droit uniforme et droit international privé", *Recueil des cours*, Vol. 330 (2007).

Perales Viscasillas, P., "The Role of the UNIDROIT

Principles and the PECL in the Interpretation and Gap-filling of CISG", in A. Janssen and O. Meyer (eds.), *CISG Methodology* (2009) 287-317.

Pfeiffer, Th., "The ALI/UNIDROIT Project : Are Principles Sufficient, Without the Rules ?", *Uniform Law Review* (2001) 1015-1033.

Philippopoulos, G. V., "Awareness of the CISG among American Attorneys", *Uniform Commercial Code Law Journal* (2008) 357-371.

Plender, R., and M. Wilderspin, *The European Private International Law of Obligations* (2009).

Pintens, W., "Europeanisation of Family Law", in K. Boele-Woelki (ed.), *Perspectives for the Unification and Harmonisation of Family Law in Europe* (2003) 3-33.

—, "Materielles Familienrecht in Europa — Rechtseinheit oder — vielfalt ?", in R. Freitag, S. Leible, H. Sippel and U. Wanitzek (eds.), *Internationales Familienrecht für das 21. Jahrhundert* (2006) 137-150.

Polak, M. V., "Principles en IPR : geen broodnodig en pasklaar alternatief 'recht' ", No. 6225 *WPNR* (1996) 391-392.

Reimann, M., "The CISG in the United States : Why It Has Been Neglected and Why Europeans Should Care", *Rabels Zeitschrift für ausländisches und internationales Privatrecht* (2007) 115-129.

Remien, O., "On the Trend towards Recodification and Reorientation in Private and Business Law", *Electronic Journal of Comparative Law* (2008).

—, "Zweck, Inhalt, Anwendungsbereich und Rechtswirkung des Gemeinsamen Referenzrahmens : Eine erste Analyse des Standpunktes des Justizministerrates vom 18.4.2008", *Gemeinschaftsprivatrecht* (2008) 124-128.

Rigaux, F., "Examen de quelques questions laissées ouvertes par la Convention de Rome sur la loi applicable aux obligations contractuelles", *Cahiers de droit européen* (1988) 306-321.

Rösler, H., "Europeanisation of Private Law through Directives — Determining Factors and Modalities of Implementation", *European Journal of Law Reform* (2009) 305-322.

Roth, W.-H., "Zur Wählbarkeit nichtstaatlichen Rechts", in H.-P. Mansel, Th. Pfeiffer, H. Kronke, Ch. Kohler and R. Hausmann (eds.), *Festschrift Erik Jayme* (2004) 757-772.

Rühl, G., "Konvergenzen im Internationalen Vertragsrecht ?, Zu jüngeren Entwicklungen im US-amerikanischen und europäischen Kollisionsrecht", *Zeitschrift für Rechtsvergleichung* (2006) 175-182.

Schlechtriem, P., *Einheitliches Kaufrecht — wissenschaftliches Modell oder praxisnahe Regelung ?* (1978).

Schlechtriem, P., and I. Schwenzer (eds.), *Kommentar zum einheitlichen Kaufrecht* (2008).

Schmidtchen, D., "Lex Mercatoria und die Evolution des Rechts", in C. Ott and H. B. Schäfer, *Vereinheitlichung und Diversität des Zivilrechts in transnationalen Wirtschaftsräumen* (2002) 1-31.

Schmitthoff, C. M., "Die künftigen Aufgaben der Rechtsvergleichung", *Juristenzeitung* (1978) 495-499.

Schroeter, U. G., "Schaffung und Akzeptanz einheitlichen Privatrechts in Europa", *Lehren aus der Anwendung des UN-Kaufrechts für ein Europäisches Vertragsrecht*, Internationale Juristenvereinigung Osnabrück, Jahresheft 2007 (2008) 35-58.

Schulte-Nölke, H., C. Twigg-Flesner and M. Ebers, EC Consumer Law Compendium — The Consumer Acquis and its Transposition in the Member States (2008).

—, "Arbeiten an einem europäischen Vertragsrecht — Fakten und populäre Irrtümer", *Neue Juristische Wochenschrift* (2009) 2161-2167.

Schultz, T., "Some Critical Comments on the Juridicity of *Lex Mercatoria*", *Yearbook of Private International Law* (2008) 667-710.

Schwenzer, I., "The Application of the CISG in Light of National Law", *NYU and Journal of Private International Conference on Private International Law*, 17-18 April 2009.

Schwenzer, I., and P. Hachem, "The CISG — Successes and Pitfalls", *American Journal of Comparative Law* (2009) 457-478.

Sheaffer, Ch., "The Failure of the United Nations Conventions on Contracts for the International Sales of Goods and a Proposal for a New Uniform Global Code in International Sales Law", 15 *Cardozo Journal of International and Comparative Law* (2007) 461-495.

Silberman, L., "Rethinking Rules of Conflict of Laws in Marriage and Divorce in the United States : What Can We Learn from Europe ?", *Tulane Law Review* (2008) 1999-2020.

Smits, J. M., *The Need of a European Contract Law* (2005) 155-179.

—, "Europese integratie in het vermogensrecht : een pleidooi voor keuzevrijheid, Preadvies Nederlandse Juristen-Vereniging 2006", in 136 *Handelingen Nederlandse Juristen-Vereniging* (2006) 57-104.

—, "Europees Burgerlijk Wetboek mag enkel een optionele code zijn", 82 *Nederlands Juristenblad* (2007) 2487-2488.

—, "Full Harmonization of Consumer Law ? A Critique of the Draft Directive on Consumer Rights", *Tidskrift utgiven av Juridiska föreningen i Finland* (2009) 573-581.

Steenhoff, G. J. W., *Avec patience et courage, A History of the Foundation of the Hague Conference on Private International Law*, Dutch Ministry of Justice (1993).

Strikwerda, L., *Inleiding tot het Nederlandse Internationaal Privaatrecht* (2008).

Struycken, A. V. M., "Co-ordination and Co-operation in Respectful Disagreement, General Course on Private International Law", *Recueil des cours*, Vol. 311 (2004).

Study Group on a European Civil Code/Research Group on EC Private Law (Acquis Group), *Principles, Definitions and Model Rules of European Private Law* (2009).

Symeonides, S., "A Third Restatement for Choice of Law, Why Not ?", *Bi-Annual Conference the Journal of Private International Law*, New York, 17-18 April 2009.

Symeonides, S. C., "Contracts Subject to Non-State Norms", *American Journal of Comparative Law* (2006) 209-231.

Tell, O., *Choosing as Applicable Law the Principles and Rules of the Substantive Law of Contract Recognised Internationally or in the Community*, Bari Conference 23-24 March 2009 (The New European Contract Law : From the Rome Convention to the "Rome I" Regulation).

Tenreiro, M., *et al.*, "Unification of Private International Law in Family Law Matters within the European Union", in K. Boele-Woelki (ed.), *Perspectives for the Unification and Harmonisation of Family Law in Europe*, European Family Law Series No. 4 (2003) 185-193.

Tetley, W., "Uniformity of International Private Maritime Law — The Pros, Cons and Alternatives to International Conventions — How to Adopt an International Convention", *Tulane Maritime Law Journal* (2000) 775-856.

Veillard, I., "Le caractère général et commercial des Principes d'UNIDROIT relatifs aux contrats du commerce international [The General and Commercial Character of the UNIDROIT Principles of International Commercial Contracts]", *Revue de droit des affaires internationales/International Business Law Journal* (2007) 479-492.

Verbeke, A., "Perspectives for an International Marital Contract", *Maastricht Journal of European and Comparative Law* (2001) 189-200.

Voigt, S., "Are International Merchants Stupid ? — Their Choice of Law Sheds Doubt on the Legal Origin Theory", *Journal of Empirical Legal Studies* (2008) 1-20.

Voser, N., and Ch. Boog, "Die Wahl des Schweizer Rechts — was man wissen sollte", *Recht der internationalen Wirtschaft* (2009) 126-139.

Wagner, G., "The Project of Harmonizing European Tort Law", *Common Market Law Review* (2005), 1269-1312.

Wagner, R., "Die Haager Konferenz für Internationales Privatrecht zehn Jahre nach der Vergemeinschaftung der Gesetzgebungskompetenz in der justiziellen Zusammenarbeit in Zivilsachen", *Rabels Zeitschrift für internationales und ausländisches Privatrecht* (2009) 215-240.

Wallis, D., "Is It a Code ?", *Zeitschrift für Europäisches Privatrecht* (2006) 513-514.

Wardle, L. D., and L. C. Nolan, "United States of America (latest update 1998)", in W. Pintens (ed.), *International Encyclopedia of Laws*, Vol. 4, *Family and Succession Law*, No. 11, 37.

Wethmar-Lemmer, M., "When Could a South African Court Be Expected to Apply the CISG ?", Paper delivered on 2008-01-21 at the Society of Teachers of Law of Southern Africa and the Southern African Society of Legal Historians Conference held at the University of Pretoria from 2008-01-21 to 2008-01-24.

Zaman, D. F. M. M., C. A. Schwarz, M. L. Lennarts, H. De Kluiver and A. F. M. Dorresteijn (eds.), *The European Private Company (SPE)* (2009).

Zeller, B., *CISG and the Unification of International Trade Law* (2007).

Zimmermann, R., "The Present State of European Private Law", *American Journal of Comparative Law* (2009) 479-512.

Zoll, F., *Rome I Regulation and Common Frame of Reference, Verona Conference 19-20 March 2009 (The Rome I Regulation)*.

ABOUT THE AUTHOR

Biographical Note

Katharina Boele-Woelki, born at Baden-Baden (Germany), on 13 June 1956.

Professor of Private International Law, Comparative Law and Family Law at Utrecht University, Netherlands, and Extraordinary Professor at the University of the Western Cape, South Africa.

Since 2001 has been chair of the Commission on European Family Law which was established upon her initiative. President of the Dutch Association of Family Law, member of the board of the Dutch Association of Comparative Law, of the Netherlands Society of International Law and member of several editorial boards of Dutch and European law journals. Also a member of various associations, such as the Deutsche Gesellschaft für Völkerrecht as well as the Wissenschaftliche Vereinigung für Familienrecht.

Since 2003 has been one of the editors of the European Family Law Series. In 2007 established the Utrecht Centre for European Research into Family Law (UCERF).

Titular member of the International Academy of Comparative Law.

Has organized prestigious international conferences, delivered numerous guest lectures at various universities around the world and has acted as a reporter, speaker, expert and panel member in many international conferences.

Principal Publications

Books/Editorships

Die Effektivitätsprüfung der Staatsangehörigkeit im niederländischen internationalen Familienrecht, Juristische Fakultät der Freien Universität Berlin, Kluwer Law and Taxation Publishers/Alfred Metzner Verlag, 1983.

Comparability and Evaluation, Liber amicorum D. Kokkini-Iatridou, Martinus Nijhoff Publishers, 1994 (in co-operation with F. W. Grosheide, E. H. Hondius and G. J. W. Steenhoff).

Europees privaatrecht, Opstellen over internationale transacties en intellectuele eigendom, Molengrafica, 1995, 1996, 1997, 1998, 1999/2000 (in co-operation with F. W. Grosheide).

Internet : "Which Court Decides, Which Law Applies ?", Kluwer Law International, 1998 (in co-operation with C. Kessedjian).

(On)geoorloofdheid van het draagmoederschap in rechtsvergelijkend perspectief, Ius commune europeanum, Intersentia, 1999 (in co-operation with A. E. Oderkerk).

Volwassen maar onzelfstandig, Meerderjarigenbescherming in Europees en internationaal privaatrechtelijk perspectief, Ius commune europeanum, Intersentia, Antwerp, 1999 (in co-operation with P. M. M. Mostermans).

Huwelijksvermogensrecht in rechtsvergelijkend perspectief, Ars Notariatus CIII, Kluwer, Deventer, 2000 (in co-operation with B. Braat, A. E. Oderkerk and G. J. W. Steenhoff).

Algehele gemeenschap van goederen : Afschaffen ! ?, Ars Notariatus CVII, Kluwer, Deventer, 2001.

Legal Recognition of Same-Sex Couples in Europe, European Family Law Series No. 1, Intersentia, 2003 (in co-operation with A. Fuchs).

European Family Law in Action, Vol. I : *Grounds for Divorce*, European Family Law Series No. 2, Intersentia, 2003 (in co-operation with B. Braat and I. Sumner).

European Family Law in Action, Vol. 2 : *Maintenance between Former Spouses*, European Family Law Series No. 3, Intersentia, 2003 (in co-operation with B. Braat and I. Sumner).

Het plezier van de rechtsvergelijking, Opstellen over unificatie en harmonisatie van het recht in Europa aangeboden aan prof. mr. E.H. Hondius, Nederlandse Vereniging voor Rechtsvergelijking No. 63, 2003 (in co-operation with C. H. Brants and G. J. W. Steenhoff).

Perspectives for the Unification and Harmonisation of Family Law in Europe, European Family Law Series No. 4, Intersentia, 2003.

European Family Law in Action, Vol. III : *Parental Responsibilities*, European Family Law Series No. 9, Intersentia, 2005 (in co-operation with B. Braat and I. Curry-Sumner).

Principles of European Family Law Regarding Divorce and Maintenance between Former Spouses, European Family Law Series No. 7, Intersentia, 2004 (in co-operation with F. Ferrand, C. González Beilfuss, M. Jänterä-Jareborg, N. Lowe, D. Martiny, W. Pintens).

Common Core and Better Law in European Family Law, European Family Law Series No. 10, Intersentia, 2005.

Brussels II bis : *Its Impact and Application in the Member States*, European Family Law Series No. 14, Intersentia, 2007 (in co-operation with C. Gonzàlez Beilfuss).

General Reports to the 17th World Congress of Comparative Law, Eleven Publishing 2007 (in co-operation with S. van Erp).

The Future of European Contract Laws, Kluwer Law International, 2007 (in co-operation with F. W. Grosheide).

Principles of European Family Law Regarding Parental Responsibilities, European Family Law Series No. 16 (in co-operation with F. Ferrand, C. González Beilfuss, M. Jänterä-Jareborg, N. Lowe, D. Martiny and D. Pintens).

European Challenges in Contemporary Family Law, European Family Law Series No. 19, Intersentia, Antwerp, 2008 (in co-operation with T. Sverdrup).

Debates in Family Law around the Globe at the Dawn of the 21st Century, European Family Law Series No. 23, Intersentia, Antwerp, 2009.

European Family Law in Action, Vol. IV : *Property Relations between Spouses*, European Family Law Series No. 24, Intersentia, Antwerp, 2009 (in co-operation with B. Braat and I. Curry-Sumner).

Academic Publications

"The Exception Clauses in Private International Law — Netherlands (National Report IACL 1994 in Athens", in D. Kokkini-Iatridou (ed.), *Les clauses d'exception en matière de conflits de lois et de conflits de juridictions* (1994), pp. 235-271.

"Die Rechtsnatur des Finanzierungsleasingvertrages im deutschen und schweizerischen Recht im Lichte der Neuregelung des Verbraucher- (Konsum-) kreditrechts", Molengrafica, 1994, pp. 119-162.

"Principles and Private International Law, The UNIDROIT Principles of International Commercial Contracts and the Principles of European Contract Law : How to Apply Them in International Contracts", *ULR*, 1996, pp. 652-678.

"Geünificeerd materieel recht gaat vóór een conflictenrechtelijke toets", in *Op Recht, liber amicorum A. V. M. Struycken*, Tjeenk Willink, Zwolle, 1996, pp. 11-18.

"The Road towards a European Family Law", *EJCL*, 1997, http://ejcl.kub.nl.

"UNIDROIT and European Contract Principles : Some Private

International Law Reflections", in B. von Hoffmann (ed.), *European Conflict of Laws, Ars Aequi Libri*, 1998, pp. 67-85.

"The Limitation of Rights and Actions in the International Sale of Goods", *Uniform Law Review*, 1999-3, pp. 621-650.

"Die Stellung von Menschen mit homosexueller Veranlagung im niederländischen Recht", in J. Basedow, K. J. Hopt, H. Kötz and P. Dopffel (eds.), *Die Rechtsstellung gleichgeschlechtlicher Lebensgemeinschaften*, Mohr Siebeck, Tübingen, 2000, pp. 51-112 (in co-operation with W. M. Schrama).

"Tien jaar internationaal namenrecht in Nederland", *Tijdschrift voor familie- en jeugdrecht*, 2000, pp. 133-141.

"Internet und IPR : Wo geht jemand ins Netz ?", in *Völkerrecht und Internationales Privatrecht in einem sich globalisierenden internationalen System — Auswirkungen der Entstaatlichung transnationaler Rechtsbeziehungen*, Deutsche Gesellschaft für Völkerrecht, C. F. Müller Verlag, Heidelberg, 2000, pp. 307-352.

"Unification and Harmonisation of Private International Law in Europe", in J. Basedow *et al.* (eds.), *Private Law in the International Arena*, T.M.C. Asser Press, The Hague, 2000, pp. 61-77.

"Private International Law Aspects of Registered Partnerships and Other Forms of Non-marital Cohabitation in Europe", *Lousiana Law Review*, 2000, pp. 1053-1059.

"Terms of Co-Existence : The UN Sales Convention and the UNIDROIT Principles of International Commercial Contracts", in P. Volken and Sarcevic, *CISG Revisited*, Dubrovnik Lectures, 1998, Kluwer Law International, 2001, pp. 203-240.

"Brüssel II : Die Verordnung über die Zuständigkeit und die Anerkennung von Entscheidungen in Ehesachen", *Zeitschrift für Rechtsvergleichung, IPR und Europarecht (ZRvgl)*, 2001, pp. 121-130.

"Divorce in Europe : Unification of Private International Law and Harmonisation of Substantive Law", in P. Vlas *et al.*, *Met recht gekregen*, *Liber amicorum Ingrid Joppe*, Kluwer, Deventer, 2002, pp. 17-28.

"Comparative Research-based Drafting of Principles of European Family Law", in M. G. Faure, J. M. Smits and H. Schneider (eds.), *Towards a European Ius Commune in Legal Education and Research* (Ius Commune Europaeum, 40, Intersentia, 2002, pp. 171-189).

"Dutch Family Law in the 21st Century : Trend Setting and Straggling Behind at the Same Time", in *Dutch Reports for the XVIIth Conference of Comparative Law*, Intersentia, 2002, pp. 53-74 (in co-operation with M. V. Antokolskaia).

"Dutch Report on Grounds for Divorce and Maintenance between Former Spouses", Commission on European Family Law, 2002 (in co-operation with O. Cheredny-chenko and L. Coenraad), http ://www.law.uu.nl/priv/cefl.

"De ingrijpende communautarisering van het internationale pri-vaatrecht", *SEW*, 2002, pp. 396-409 (in co-operation with R. van Ooik).

"The Communautarization of Private International Law", *Year-book of Private International Law*, Vol. 4 (2002), Kluwer Law International and Swiss Institute of Comparative Law, 2003, pp. 1-36 (in co-operation with R. van Ooik).

"B(l)oeiend vergelijkend familierecht : De Commission on Eu-ropean Family Law", in K. Boele-Woelki, C. H. Brants and G. J. W. Steenhoff (eds.), *Het plezier van de rechtsvergelijking, Opstellen over unificatie en harmonisatie van het recht in Eu-ropa aangeboden aan prof. mr. E.H. Hondius*, Nederlandse Vereniging voor Rechtsvergelijking No. 63, 2003, pp. 141-154.

"Het WODC-rapport 'De gekozen achternaam', Reactie vanuit een interdisciplinair perspectief", *Tijdschrift voor familie- en jeugdrecht*, 2003, pp. 36-43.

"Registered Partnership and Same-Sex Marriage in the Nether-lands", in K. Boele-Woelki and A. Fuchs, *Legal Recognition of Same-Sex Couples in Europe* (eds.), European Family Law Series No. 1, Intersentia, 2003, pp. 42-54.

"Scheidung und nachehelicher Unterhalt im niederländischen Recht", in S. Hofer, D. Henrich and D. Schwab, *Scheidung und nachehelicher Unterhalt im europäischen Vergleich*, Beiträge zum europäischen Familienrecht, Nr. 8, Gieseking Verlag, 2003, pp. 197-219.

"Naar een Europees Restatement voor familierecht", *FJR* 2004, pp. 249-256.

"Dutch Report on Parental Responsibilities, Commission on European Family Law", 2004 (in co-operation with W. Schrama and M. Vonk) (http://www.law.uu.nl/priv/cefl).

"Die nichteheliche Lebensgemeinschaft im niederländischen Recht", in Scherpe and Yassari (eds.), *Max-Planck Institut für internationales und ausländisches Privatrecht*, J. C. B. Mohr, Tübingen, 2005, pp. 307-374 (in co-operation with W. M. Schrama).

"The Working Method of the Commission on European Family Law", in K. Boele-Woelki (ed.), *Common Core and Better Law in European Family Law*, European Family Law Series No. 10, Intersentia, 2005, pp. 14-38 ; also published in M. Claudia Andrini (ed.), *Un nuovo diritto di famiglia europeo*, CEDAM, 2007, pp. 197-224.

"Il metodo di lavoro della Commissione sul diritto europeo de famiglia", in M. Claudia Andrini (ed.), *Un nuovo diritto di famiglia europeo*, CEDAM, 2007, pp. 225-254.

"Parental Responsibilities — CEFL's Initial Results", in K. Boele-Woelki (ed.), *Common Core and Better Law in European Family Law*, European Family Law Series No. 10, Intersentia, 2005, pp. 141-168.

"La famille et le droit international — introduction", *International Law FORUM de droit international*, 2005, pp. 146-152.

"The Principles of European Family Law : Its Aims and Prospects", *Utrecht Law Review* Vol. 1, Issue 2, December 2005, http ://www.utrechtlawreview.org.

"Comisión de Derecho de Familia Europeo : Formulando Principios en el ámbito de divorcio y alimentos entre cónyuges divorciados", in *Nous reptes del dret de família, Materials de les Tretzenes Jornades de Dret Català a Tossa*, Documenta Universitaria, 2005, pp. 39-60.

"Nieuw Europees IPR voor overeenkomsten, Van Verdrag naar Verordening", in M. de Cock Bunning, J. Brinkhof and E. H. Hondius (eds.), *Internationaal contracteren, feestbundel voor Willem Grosheide*, Boom Juridische uitgevers, The Hague, 2006, pp. 257-273.

"Die Prinzipien zum Europäischen Familienrecht betreffend Ehescheidung und nachehelicher Unterhalt", *Zeitschrift für Europäisches Privatrecht*, 2006, pp. 6-20 (in co-operation with D. Martiny).

"Europäisierung des Unterhaltsrechts : Vereinheitlichung des Kollisionsrechts und Angleichung des materiellen Rechts", *Familie, Partnerschaft und Recht*, 2006, 6th ed., pp. 232-237 (in co-operation with A. Mom).

"De erkenning van administratieve echtscheidingen in Europa", in M. Antokolskaia (ed.), *Herziening van het echtscheidingsrecht. Administratieve echtscheiding, mediation, voortgezet ouderschap, ack-reeks*, SWP, Amsterdam, 2006, pp. 218-247 (in co-operation with A. Mom).

"Exclusieve externe bevoegdheden van de EG inzake het Internationaal Privaatrecht, Gevolgen voor de toetreding van de Haagse Conferentie voor IPR", *NTER*, 2006, pp. 194-201 (in co-operation with R. van Ooik).

"The European Agenda : An Overview of the Current Situation in the Field of Private International Law and Substantive Law", *International Family Law*, 2006, pp. 149-154.

"Os princípos do direito da família europeu : os seus objectivos e as suas perspectivas, Lex Familiae", *Revista Portuguesa de Direito da Família*, 2006, No. 5, pp. 5-17.

"Nieuw Europees IPR voor overeenkomsten, Van Verdrag naar Verordening", in M. de Cock Bunning, J. Brinkhof and E. H. Hondius (eds.), *Internationaal contracteren, feestbundel voor Willem Grosheide*, Boom Juridische uitgevers, The Hague, 2006, pp. 257-273.

"Huwelijk of geregistreerd partnerschap ? Een evaluatie van de Wet openstelling huwelijk en de wet geregistreerd partnerschap", Ars Notariatus No. 134, Kluwer, Deventer, 2007 (in co-operation with I. Curry-Sumner, M. Jansen and W. Schrama).

"The Impact and Application of the Brussels II bis Regulation in the Member States : Comparative Synthesis", in K. Boele-Woelki and C. González Beilfuss (eds.), *Brussels II bis : Its Impact and Application in the Member States*, European Family Law Series No. 14, Intersentia, Antwerp, 2007, pp. 23-40 (in co-operation with C. Gonzàlez Beilfuss).

"Principles of European Family Law Regarding Parental Responsibilities", European Family Law Series No. 16, Intersentia, Antwerp, 2007 (in co-operation with F. Ferrand, C. González Beilfuss, M. Jänterä-Jareborg, N. Lowe, D. Martiny and W. Pintens).

"The CEFL and Its Principles of European Family Law Regarding Parental Responsibilities", *ERA-forum*, Springer Verlag, 2007, pp. 125-143 (in co-operation with D. Martiny).

"The Evaluation of Same-Sex Marriages and Registered Partnerships in the Netherlands", *Yearbook of Private International Law*, Vol. VIII, 2007, pp. 27-35 (in co-operation with I. Curry-Sumner, M. Jansen and W. Schrama).

"Building on Convergence and Coping with Divergence in the CEFL Principles on European Family Law", in M. Antokolskaia (ed.), *Convergence and Divergence in European Family Law*, European Family Law Series No. 18, Intersentia, Antwerp, 2007, pp. 253-269.

"Where Do We Stand on the Rome I Regulation ?", in K. Boele-Woelki and F. Grosheide (eds.), *The Future of European Contract Law*, Kluwer Law International, 2007, pp. 19-41 (in co-operation with V. Lazic).

"The CEFL Principles Regarding Parental Responsibilities : Predominance of the Common Core", in K. Boele-Woelki and T. Sverdrup (eds.), *European Challenges in Contemporary Family Law*, European Family Law Series No. 19, Intersentia, Antwerp, 2008, pp. 63-91.

"European Challenges in Contemporary Family Law : Some Final Observations", in K. Boele-Woelki and T. Sverdrup (eds.), *European Challenges in Contemporary Family Law*,

European Family Law Series No. 19, Intersentia, Antwerp, 2008, pp. 413-423.

"Op weg naar universele toepasselijkheid van de Verordening inzake echtscheiding en ouderlijke verantwoordelijkheid", *Tijdschrift voor familie- en jeugdrecht*, 2008, pp. 52-56.

"A Harmonização Do Direito da Família na Europa : Uma Comparação entre a Nova Lei Portuguesa do Divórcio com o Princípos da CEFL sobre Direito da Família Europeu", in *Grupo Parlementar do Partido Socialista, Nova Lei do Divórcio*, 2008, pp. 29-47.

"What Comparative Family Law Should Entail", *Utrecht Law Review*, 2008, Vol. 4, Issue 2, pp. 1-24 ; also published in K. Boele-Woelki (ed.), *Debates in Family Law around the Globe at the Dawn of the 21st Century*, European Family Law Series No. 23, Intersentia, Antwerp, 2009, pp. 3-35.

"Legal Recognition of Same-Sex Relationships within the European Union", 82 *Tulane Law Review*, 2008, pp. 1949-1981.

"Umzugsmütter, Umgangsväter und Kindeswohlinteressen", in Vytautas Mizaras (ed.), *Private Law : Past, Present and Future, Liber Amicorum for Valentinas Mikelenas*, Vilnius Justitia, 2008, pp. 47-57.

"To Be, Or Not to Be : Enhanced Cooperation in International Divorce Law within the European Union", *Victoria University of Wellington Law Review*, 2008, Issue 4, pp. 779-792.

"Property Relations between Spouses : The Netherlands, Dutch Report for the Commission on European Family Law", 2008, www.ceflonline.net (in co-operation with F. Schonewille and W. Schrama).

"Research Questions in Family Law Derived from a Comparative Synthesis of General Developments and Trends", *Utrecht Law Review*, 2008, Vol. 4, Issue 2, pp. 279-289 (in co-operation with B. Braat, I. Curry-Sumner, C. Jeppesen de Boer, P. Lokin, M. Vonk, N. de Vries and W. Schrama) ; also published in K. Boele-Woelki (ed.), *Debates in Family Law around the Globe at the Dawn of the 21st Century*, European Family Law Series No. 23, Intersentia, Antwerp, 2009, pp. 399-414.

"Harmonisation of Family Law in Europe : A Comparison of the New Portuguese Divorce Law with the CEFL Principles of European Family Law", Lisbon, 25 September 2008.

"Zwischen Konvergenz und Divergenz : Die CEFL Prinzipien zum Europäischen Familienrecht", *Rabels Zeitschrift für internationales und ausländisches Privatrecht*, 2009, pp. 241-267.

"Umzug von Kindern aus den Niederlanden in die Schweiz : die niederländische Perspektive", *FamPra*, 2009, pp. 381-396.

"Die CEFL und die Prinzipien zum europäischen Familienrecht betreffend elterliche Verantwortung : mehr Übereinstimmungen als Unterschiede", *ZEuP* 2009, pp. 685-698 (in cooperation with D. Martiny).

"A Harmonização do Direito da Família na Europa : Uma Comparação entre a Nova Lei Portuguesa do Divóricio dom os Princípos da CEFL sobre Direito da Família Europeu", in *Grupo Parlamentar do Partido Socialista, Nova Lei do Divórcio*, 2009, pp. 29-47.

"New Questions in International Divorce Law within the European Union : Enhanced Cooperation", Merkourios, *Utrecht Journal for International and European Law*, 2009, pp. 4-13.

**PUBLICATIONS
OF THE HAGUE ACADEMY
OF INTERNATIONAL LAW**

COLLECTED COURSES

Since 1923 the top names in international law have taught at the Hague Academy of International Law. All the volumes of the *Collected Courses* which have been published since 1923 are available, as, since the very first volume, they are reprinted regularly in their original format. There is a complete and detailed catalogue. (See below.)

Since 2008, certain courses have been the subject of a pocketbook edition (see below).

In addition, the total collection now exists in electronic form. All works already published have been put "on line" and can be consulted under one of the proposed subscription methods, which offer a range of tariffs and possibilities.

WORKSHOPS

The Academy publishes the discussions from the Workshops which it organizes. The latest title of the Workshops already published is as follows : *Topicality of the 1907 Hague Conference, the Second Peace Conference* (2007).

CENTRE FOR STUDIES AND RESEARCH

The scientific works of the Centre for Studies and Research in International Law and International Relations of the Hague Academy of International Law, the subjects of which are chosen by the Curatorium of the Academy, have been published, since the Centre's 1985 session, in a publication in which the Directors of Studies report on the state of research of the Centre under their direction. The titles of the latest booklets published are as follows : *The Cultural Heritage of Mankind* (2005) ; *Terrorism and International Law* (2006) ; *Rules and Institutions of International Humanitarian Law Put to the Test of Recent Armed Conflicts* (2007). In addition, when the work of the Centre has been of particular interest and originality, the reports of the Directors of Studies together with the articles by the researchers form the subject of a collection published in the series The Law Books of the Academy. (See below.)

Requests for information, catalogues and orders for publications must be addressed to

MARTINUS NIJHOFF PUBLISHERS
P.O. Box 9000, 2300 PA Leiden — The Netherlands

(http://www.brill.nl)

INDEX BY VOLUME OF THE COURSES PUBLISHED THESE LAST YEARS

Muir Watt, H. : Aspects économiques du droit international privé (Réflexions sur l'impact de la globalisations économique sur les fondements des conflits de lois et de juridictions), 25-384.

(ISBN 978-90-04-14456-7)

Volume 308 (2004)

Rigo Sureda, A. : The Law Applicable to the Activities of International Development Banks, 9-252.

González Lapeyre, E. : Transport maritime et régime portuaire, 253-378.

(ISBN 978-90-04-14547-4)

Volume 309 (2004)

Karaquillo, J.-P. : Droit international du sport, 9-124.

Maresceau, M. : Bilateral Agreements Concluded by the European Community, 125-452.

(ISBN 978-90-04-14548-1)

Volume 310 (2004)

Kamto, M. : La volonté de l'Etat en droit international, 9-428.

(ISBN 978-90-04-14552-8)

Volume 311 (2004)

[A paraître/Forthcoming]

Volume 312 (2005)

Gaudemet-Tallon, H. : Le pluralisme en droit international privé : richesses et faiblesses (Le funambule et l'arc-en-ciel). Cours général, 9-488.

(ISBN 978-90-04-14554-2)

Volume 313 (2005)

Mani, V. S. : "Humanitarian" Intervention Today, 9-324.

David, E. : La Cour pénale internationale, 325-454.

(ISBN 978-90-04-14555-9)

Volume 314 (2005)

Draetta, U. : Internet et commerce électronique en droit international des affaires, 9-232.

Daillier, P. : Les opérations multinationales consécutives à des conflits armés en vue du rétablissement de la paix, 233-432.

(ISBN 978-90-04-14557-3)

Volume 315 (2005)

Dogauchi, M. : Four-Step Analysis of Private International Law, 9-140.

Mohamed Salah, M. M. : Loi d'autonomie et méthodes de protection de la partie faible en droit international privé, 141-264.

Radicati di Brozolo, L. G. : Arbitrage commercial international et lois de police. Considérations sur les conflits de juridictions dans le commerce international, 265-502.

(ISBN 978-90-04-14558-0)

Volume 316 (2005)

Cançado Trindade, A. A. : International Law for Humankind : Towards a New *Jus Gentium* (I). General Course on Public International Law, 9-440.

(ISBN 978-90-04-15375-2)

Volume 317 (2005)

Cançado Trindade, A. A. : International Law for Humankind : Towards a New *Jus Gentium* (II). General Course on Public International Law, 9-312.

Borrás, A. : Le droit international privé communautaire : réalités, problèmes et perspectives d'avenir, 313-536.

(ISBN 978-90-04-15376-9)

Volume 318 (2005)

Kinsch, P. : Droits de l'homme, droits fondamentaux et droit international privé, 9-332.

Bothe, M. : Environment, Development, Resources, 333-516.
(ISBN 978-90-04-15377-6)

Volume 319 (2006)

Hartley, T. C. : The Modern Approach to Private International Law. International Litigation and Transactions from a Common-Law Perspective. General Course on Private International Law, 9-324.

Crawford, J. : Multilateral Rights and Obligations in International Law, 325-482.

(ISBN 978-90-04-15378-3)

Volume 320 (2006)

Goldstein, G. : La cohabitation hors mariage en droit international privé, 9-390.

(ISBN 978-90-04-15379-0)

Volume 321 (2006)

Shaker, M. I. : The Evolving International Regime of Nuclear Non-Proliferation, 9-202
Klein, P. : Le droit international à l'épreuve du terrorisme, 203-484.　　　　　(ISBN 978-90-04-16100-0)

Volume 322 (2006)

Loquin, E. : Les règles matérielles internationales, 9-242.
Dinstein, Y. : The Interaction between Customary International Law and Treaties, 243-428.
　　　　　　　　　　　　(ISBN 978-90-04-16101-6)

Volume 323 (2006)

Fernández Arroyo, D. P. : Compétence exclusive et compétence exorbitante dans les relations privées internationales, 9-260.
Silberman, L. J.. : Co-operative Efforts in Private International Law on Behalf of Children : The Hague Children's Conventions, 261-478.　　　(ISBN 978-90-04-16102-3)

Volume 324 (2006)

Bedjaoui, M. : L'humanité en quête de paix et de développement (I). Cours général de droit international public, 9-530.
　　　　　　　　　　　　(ISBN 978-90-04-16103-0)

Volume 325 (2006)

Bedjaoui, M. : L'humanité en quête de paix et de développement (II). Cours général de droit international public, 9-542.
　　　　　　　　　　　　(ISBN 978-90-04-16104-7)

Volume 326 (2007)

Collins, L. : Revolution and Restitution : Foreign States in National Courts (Opening Lecture, Private International Law Session, 2007), 9-72.
Gotanda, J. Y. : Damages in Private International Law, 73-408.　　　　　　　　　(ISBN 978-90-04-16616-5)

Volume 327 (2007)

Mayer, P. : Le phénomène de la coordination des ordres juridiques étatiques en droit privé. Cours général de droit international privé (2003), 9-378.
　　　　　　　　　　　　(ISBN 978-90-04-16617-2)

Volume 328 (2007)

Garcimartín Alférez, F. J. : Cross-Border Listed Companies, 9-174.

Vrellis, S. : Conflit ou coordination de valeurs en droit international privé. A la recherche de la justice, 175-486.

(ISBN 978-90-04-16618-9)

Volume 329 (2007)

Pellet, A. : L'adaptation du droit international aux besoins changeants de la société internationale (conférence inaugurale, session de droit international public, 2007), 9-48.

Gaillard, E. : Aspects philosophiques du droit de l'arbitrage international, 49-216.

Schrijver, N. : The Evolution of Sustainable Development in International Law : Inception, Meaning and Status, 217-412.

(ISBN 978-90-04-16619-6)

Volume 330 (2007)

Pamboukis, Ch. P. : Droit international privé holistique : droit uniforme et droit international privé, 9-474.

(ISBN 978-90-04-16620-2)

Volume 331 (2007)

Pinto, M. : L'emploi de la force dans la jurisprudence des tribunaux internationaux, 9-160

Brown Weiss, E. : The Evolution of International Water Law, 161-404.   (ISBN 978-90-04-17288-3)

Volume 332 (2007)

Carlier, J.-Y. : Droit d'asile et des réfugiés. De la protection aux droits, 9-354.

Fatouros, A. A. : An International Legal Framework for Energy, 355-446.

(ISBN 978-90-04-17198-5)

Volume 333 (2008)

Müllerson, R. : Democracy Promotion : Institutions, International Law and Politics, 9-174.

Pisillo Mazzeschi, R. : Responsabilité de l'Etat pour violation des obligations positives relatives aux droits de l'homme, 174-506.   (ISBN 978-90-04-17284-5)

Volume 334 (2008)

Verhoeven, J. : Considérations sur ce qui est commun. Cours général de droit international public (2002), 9-434.

(ISBN 978-90-04-17289-0)

Volume 335 (2008)

Beaumont, P. R. : The Jurisprudence of the European Court of Human Rights and the European Court of Justice on the Hague Convention on International Child Abduction, 9-104.
Moura Vicente, D. : La propriété intellectuelle en droit international privé, 105-504.

(ISBN 978-90-04-17290-6)

Volume 336 (2008)

Decaux, E. : Les formes contemporaines de l'esclavage, 9-198.
McLachlan, C. : *Lis Pendens* in International Litigation, 199-554.

(ISBN 978-90-04-17291-3)

Volume 337 (2008)

Mahiou, A. : Le droit international ou la dialectique de la rigueur et de la flexibilité. Cours général de droit international public, 9-516. (ISBN 978-90-04-17292-0)

Volume 338 (2008)

[A paraître/Forthcoming]

Volume 339 (2008)

Sicilianos, L.-A. : Entre multilatéralisme et unilatéralisme : l'autorisation par le Conseil de sécurité de recourir à la force, 9-436.

(ISBN 978-90-04-17294-4)

Volume 340 (2009)

Beaumont, P. R. : Reflections on the Relevance of Public International Law to Private International Law Treaty Making (Opening Lecture, Private International Law Session, 2009), 9-62.
Carbone, S. M. : Conflits de lois en droit maritime, 63-270.
Boele-Woelki, K. : Unifying and Harmonizing Substantive Law and the Role of Conflict of Laws, 271-462.

(ISBN 978-90-04-17295-1)

Volume 341 (2009)

Bucher, A. : La dimension sociale du droit international privé. Cours général, 9-526.

(ISBN 978-90-04-18509-8)

Volume 342 (2009)

Musin, V. : The Influence of the International Sale of Goods Convention on Domestic Law Including Conflict of Laws (with Specific Reference to Russian Law), 9-76.

Onuma, Y. : A Transcivilizational Perspective on International Law (Questioning Prevalent Cognitive Frameworks in the Emerging Multi-Polar and Multi-Civilizational World of the Twenty-First Century), 77-418.

(ISBN 978-90-04-18510-4)

THE LAW BOOKS OF THE ACADEMY

(By chronological order of publication)

Dupuy, R.-J. (dir. publ./ed.) : Manuel sur les organisations internationales/A Handbook on International Organizations. (1988, 714 pages.)
(ISBN 978-90-247-3658-4)

Dupuy, R.-J., and D. Vignes (eds.) : A Handbook on the New Law of the Sea. (2 volumes)
Volume 1 : 1991, 900 pages. (ISBN 978-0-7923-0924-3)
Volume 2 : 1991, 882 pages. (ISBN 978-0-7923-1063-1)

Bardonnet, D. (dir. publ./ed.) : Le règlement pacifique des différends internationaux en Europe : perspectives d'avenir/The Peaceful Settlement of International Disputes in Europe : Future Prospects. (1992, 704 pages.) (Broché/PB.)
(ISBN 978-0-7923-1573-5)

Carreau, D., et/and M. N. Shaw (dir. publ./eds.) : La dette extérieure/The External Debt. (1995, 818 pages.)
(ISBN 978-90-411-0083-2)

Dupuy, R.-J. (dir. publ./ed.): Manuel sur les organisations internationales/A Handbook on International Organizations. (2ᵉ éd./2nd ed., 1998, 1008 pages.)
(ISBN 978-90-411-1119-7)

Eisemann, P. M., et/and M. Koskenniemi (dir. publ./eds.): La succession d'Etats : la codification à l'épreuve des faits/State Succession : Codification Tested against the Facts. (2000, 1058 pages.)
(ISBN 978-90-411-1392-4)

Caron, D. D., et/and Ch. Leben (dir. publ./eds.): Les aspects internationaux des catastrophes naturelles et industrielles/The International Aspects of Natural and Industrial Catastrophes. (2001, 912 pages.)
(ISBN 978-90-411-1485-3)

Bothe, M., et/and P. H. Sands (dir. publ./eds.) : La politique de l'environnement. De la réglementation aux instruments économiques/Environmental Policy. From Regulation to Economic Instruments. (2002, 958 pages.)
(ISBN 978-90-411-1604-8)

Forlati Picchio, L., et/and L.-A. Sicilianos (dir. publ./eds.) : Les sanctions économiques en droit international/Economic Sanctions in International Law. (2004, 912 pages.)
(ISBN 978-90-04-13701-1)

Boisson de Chazournes, L. et/and S. M. A. Salman (dir. publ./eds.) : Les ressources en eau et le droit international/Water Resources and International Law. (2005, 848 pages.)
(ISBN 978-90-04-13702-8)

Mahiou, A., et/and F. Snyder (dir. publ.) : La sécurité alimentaire/Food Security and Food Safety. (2006, 992 pages.)
(ISBN 978-90-04-14543-6)

Kahn, Ph., et/and T. W. Wälde (dir. publ./eds.) : Les aspects nouveaux du droit des investissements internationaux/New Aspects of International Investment Law. (2007, 1072 pages.)
(ISBN 978-90-04-15372-1)

Glennon, M. J., et/and S. Sur (dir. publ./eds.) : Terrorisme et droit international/Terrorism and International Law. (2008, 864 pages.)
(ISBN 978-90-04-16107-8)

Nafziger, J. A. R., et/and T. Scovazzi (dir. publ./eds.) : Le patrimoine culturel de l'humanité/The Cultural Heritage of Mankind. (2008, 1168 pages.)
(ISBN 978-90-04-16106-1)

Daudet, Y. (dir. publ./ed.) : Actualité de la Conférence de La Haye de 1907, Deuxième Conférence de la Paix/Topicality of the 1907 Hague Conference, the Second Peace Conference. (2008, 528 pages.) (Broché/PB.)
(ISBN 978-90-04-17422-1)

Forthcoming

Momtaz, D., et/and M. J. Matheson (dir. publ./eds.) : Les règles et institutions du droit international humanitaire à l'épreuve des conflits armés récents/Rules and Institutions of International Humanitarian Law Put to the Test of Recent Armed Conflicts. (2009)
(Relié/HB : ISBN 978-90-04-17283-8)
(Broché/PB : ISBN 978-90-04-18697-2)

POCKETBOOKS OF THE ACADEMY

(By chronological order of publication)

Gaillard, E. : Aspects philosophiques du droit de l'arbitrage international, 2008, 252 pages.
(ISBN 978-90-04-17148-0)

Schrijver, N. : The Evolution of Sustainable Development in International Law : Inception, Meaning and Status, 2008, 276 pages.
(ISBN 978-90-04-17407-8)

Moura Vicente, D. : La propriété intellectuelle en droit international privé, 2009, 516 pages.
(ISBN 978-90-04-17907-3)

Decaux, E. : Les formes contemporaines de l'esclavage, 2009, 264 pages.
(ISBN 978-90-04-17908-0)

McLachlan, C. : *Lis Pendens* in International Litigation, 2009, 492 pages.
(ISBN 978-90-04-17909-7)

Carbone, S. M. : Conflits de lois en droit maritime, 2010, 312 pages.
(ISBN 978-90-04-18688-0)

Boele-Woelki, K. : Unifying and Harmonizing Substantive Law and the Role of Conflict of Laws, 2010, 288 pages.
(ISBN 978-90-04-18683-5)

Onuma, Y. : A Transcivilizational Perspective in International Law, 2010.
(ISBN 978-90-04-18689-7)

[A paraître/Forthcoming]

Alvarez, J. : A New Public International Law Regime for Foreign Direct Investment, 2010.
(ISBN 978-90-04-18682-8)

Thürer, D. : International Humanitarian Law : Theory and Practice, 2010.
(ISBN 978-90-04-17910-3)

Printed in June 2010
by Triangle Bleu,
59600 Maubeuge (France)

Setting : R. Mirland,
59870 Warlaing (France)